NATURE
IN FOCUS

Subject: Female gerenuk (*Litocranius walleri*) with young
Location: Samburu Game Reserve, Kenya
Month: August
Time of day: Early morning
Lighting: Direct sun
Lens: 300 mm on Nikon
Film: Kodachrome 64

NATURE IN FOCUS

THE PHOTOGRAPHY OF
HEATHER ANGEL

PYRAMID

AUTHOR'S ACKNOWLEDGMENTS

I should like to thank everybody who so willingly gave their time to answer my queries in the preparation of this book. In particular Brian Coe (Curator of the National Centre of Photography), Hasselblad (UK) Ltd, Kodak Ltd, Leeds Camera Centre, the Nature Conservancy Council, Nikon UK Ltd, the Royal Society for the Protection of Birds, the Surrey Wildlife Trust and the World Wide Fund for Nature.

I am also indebted to the following organizations for donating or loaning photographic equipment: A. V. Distributors Ltd, Camera Care Systems Ltd, Jessops, Kennett Engineering Ltd, Keith Johnson + Pelling Ltd, Lastolite Ltd, Leeds Camera Centre, Nikon UK Ltd and Triggertec.

Several individuals and organizations aided my photography including: my son Giles Angel, Dr Bill Ballantine, Baja Expeditions, Graham Evelin, the Forestry Commission, Gardenia Magazine, the Great Britain China Centre, Alan Goodger, the Hawk Conservancy, Peter Hobson, the Hydestyle Wildlife Hospital, the London Wildlife Trust, Longleat Safari Park, Robin MacDonald of Iain MacDonald Safaris Ltd, Geoff Moon, Tony Morrison, Desmond Napier, Occidor Travel, the Royal Botanic Gardens at Kew, Safari Consultants, Ed Slater, Stratford-upon-Avon Butterfly Farm and Jungle Safari, Soames Summeryhays, Thames Television plc, Audrey Thomas, TV Man Union (Tokyo), Twickers World, Virgin Records, the Wildfowl Trust, Pat Wolseley and the Zambian Photographic Society. My husband Martin Angel and Brian Bower FRPS both assisted with photographing me working in the field. My grateful thanks to them all.

The black and white print of the Kearton brothers reproduced on p.6 is from The Royal Photographic Society's collection, and the print of the sparrowhawk is reproduced from *Pictures from Nature*, first published by Cassell and Company in 1905; the colour picture of the heron on p.133 originally appeared in the 1987 Kodak calendar and is reproduced by kind permission of Marketing Publications, Kodak Ltd.

Some aspects of the Introduction are based on part of my Presidential Address given in September 1985 to The Royal Photographic Society, originally published in the *Photographic Journal*, Volume 126 Number 9.

I should especially like to thank Colour Processing Laboratories for their efficient film processing service, and Penny Bantin for doing the lion's share of the word processing, with able assistance from both Rona Tiller and Susie Briars.

Finally, I am as always greatly indebted to my husband, Martin Angel, for carrying the cameras or tripod (on at least a few trips!) and for his constant help and encouragement.

PUBLISHERS' ACKNOWLEDGMENTS

Editor: **Tony Holdsworth**
Art Editor: **Lisa Tai**
Design: **Laurence Bradbury Design Associates**
Illustrations: **Andrew Popkiewicz**
Production Controller: **Audrey Johnston**

Half-title page:
Rio Grande cottonwoods (*Populus fremonti* var. *wislizeni*) in gypsum sand dunes, White Sands National Monument, New Mexico, in April

First published in 1988 by Pyramid
an imprint of the Octopus Publishing Group
Michelin House
81 Fulham Road
London SW3 6RB

Text and photography © Heather Angel
Design © the Octopus Publishing Group

ISBN 1 871307 35 X

Printed in Spain by Graficas Estella

CONTENTS

INTRODUCTION

The first images of natural subjects produced by the action of sunlight on light-sensitive paper were made by Henry Fox Talbot in 1834. Before he could obtain his photogenic drawings of natural objects, he first had to make his own light-sensitive paper by dipping it in common salt solution and sensitizing it with silver nitrate. Fox Talbot found objects with intricate outlines – such as feathers and ferns – produced the most interesting life-size negative images on his paper. He was later able to copy the negative photogenic drawing to produce a positive image.

After this beginning, nature photography evolved slowly at first but recent years have seen rapid advances with many innovative techniques made possible by sophisticated gadgetry. The equipment and filmstock used more than a century ago limited the type of picture which could be taken. The slow speed of the black and white film plates necessitated long exposures of static animals and the weighty equipment led some people to adopt dubious short cuts to get their pictures. These included the photography of dead or stuffed animals and using a revolver to locate the position of seabirds' nests as they lifted off! Such techniques would certainly never be contemplated by any self-respecting nature photographer today.

Reginald B. Lodge was a professional photographer who took up bird photography around 1890. He and his brother George, who was a famous bird artist, used to manhandle an enormous 'twelve-by-ten' (30 × 25 cm/12 × 10 inch) plate camera round the countryside in a wheelbarrow! A paper Lodge read to The Royal Photographic Society, published in 1898, explains how he came into photography and highlights some of the many problems encountered along the way. He was not amused when other photographers of the time thought his bird pictures were snap-shots taken with a Kodak (the original camera introduced by the Eastman Company in 1888). He retorted:

... a Kodak is an impossible instrument for this kind of work, because one of the chief difficulties of bird-photography arises from the small size of the object to be photographed. A bird is often a very little tiny thing, and when you photograph a bird with an ordinary lens, and develop your plate, you wonder where the dickens the bird has got to – you can't find it.

Lodge also pointed out that the shadows cast from the overhanging foliage meant longer exposures were necessary than his normal $\frac{1}{8}$ second; but if a bird was at a nest he could get away with an exposure of up to four seconds! Another major problem was the prevalence of collectors, so that even then many birds were becoming very rare.

In 1895 Richard and Cherry Kearton produced the first natural history book to be illustrated throughout with authentic wildlife photographs. *British Birds' Nests* contained 130 illustrations of nests, eggs and young. Two years later saw the publication of *With Nature and a Camera*; the 180 plates included some of birds in flight, and a barn owl taken by magnesium flashlight.

The Keartons used a half-plate camera specially built for them by Dallmeyer. It had

► The Kearton brothers resorted to some ingenious methods to get their wildlife studies. This picture, taken in 1900, shows one brother standing on the other's shoulders to peer through a camera on a very rickety tripod!

◄ This study of a sparrowhawk adding sticks to her nest was first published in 1905 in *Pictures from Nature*, by Cherry and Richard Kearton. It was taken from a 'hiding tent' erected on top of a pile of tree trunks behind a pair of hazel bushes.

a pneumatically operated silent shutter between the lens and the sensitized plate, in addition to a focal plane shutter. They also used a so-called 'miniature' camera for taking pictures of flying birds or restless animals. A double-sided glass negative in its wooden holder, as used by the Keartons, weighed 400 g (14 oz). Today the equivalent weight of film would be 14 rolls of Kodachrome – or more than 500 frames.

Like many other early wildlife photographers, the Keartons devised ingenious ways of camouflaging themselves inside natural objects so as to get close-up photographs of breeding birds. Their hiding tents, as they called them, included artificial rocks and tree trunks, a stuffed sheep and even a dummy bullock. On one occasion, Richard Kearton became dizzy from peering through a small peephole for a long time, thereby losing his balance. This resulted in the dummy bullock falling over and landing upside down. Cherry Kearton recorded the incongruous sight of the bullock resting on its back with six legs in the air – four of the bullock's and two of Richard's – by taking a picture as he came to the rescue.

The whole approach to wildlife photography at that time was brilliantly summed up in a Punch cartoon of 1907. It depicts two wildlife photographers – one inside a model giraffe, the other inside a hippopotamus – showing disgust and disappointment at having stalked each other for hours!

Sometimes the Keartons took pictures of nests without a hide. They would resort to every conceivable way of getting up above the ground, such as standing on one another's shoulders to peer through a tripod with extended legs, or perching precariously on top of a ladder held by hand against the branches of a tree.

The quality of the Kearton animal portraits, whether of birds at the nest or mammals resting on the ground, compares very favourably with birds and mammals photographed in similar stances today. Their pictures have a timeless quality: the composition of the sparrowhawk shot is especially pleasing to the eye. It is doubtful that photographs like this could be portrayed in similar poses in a better way today.

Since the pioneering days of nature photography, the techniques for stalking wild birds and mammals have not changed as dramatically as the equipment and film used to photograph them. When we purchase a synchronized electronic flash off the shelf we should remember the primitive flash techniques naturalists had to use in the first few decades of this century.

To boost the level of available light for taking active subjects, photographers working even as late as between the World Wars had to use chemical flash. Douglas P. Wilson, a marine biologist working at the Plymouth Marine Laboratory in Devon, pioneered the photography of live planktonic organisms using flash. Like Lord Alanbrooke intent on photographing birds, Wilson had to resort to using the open flash technique with magnesium powder providing the flash of light. Sometimes, when Lord Alanbrooke ignited two pounds of magnesium powder for a single picture, the surrounding vegetation caught fire and all the wildlife was so frightened by the huge explosion that they failed to return after the first exposure.

It was Eric Hosking, more than 40 years ago, who pioneered the development of the photography of bird flight in Britain using high-speed flash. His flash pictures revealed detailed studies of wing movement during take-off and landing as well as the array of food items parents brought back to their

nest for the young. Hosking was suprised to find that many of the other leading bird photographers at the time were hostile to his high-speed flash pictures.

Today, no serious nature photographer would be without at least one electronic (although not necessarily high-speed) flash. This will be used in conjunction with either a 35mm or a 6 × 6cm ($2\frac{1}{4} \times 2\frac{1}{4}$-inch) single-lens reflex system with a variety of lenses and probably at least one motor-drive. Compared with the cost of equipment and travel, film is cheap. Unlike amateurs, no true professional adopts an economic approach when it comes to exposing film, for a series of original frames will always be of a much higher quality than duplicates made from an original and even a picture of a commonplace subject may be unrepeatable.

The pursuit of nature photography has taken me to some remote corners of the world, among them many isolated oceanic islands, notably the Galápagos archipelago – a biologist's paradise. China also holds a great fascination for me. On one of my many visits I worked in a recently-discovered gorge in Sichuan province, where there are lakes filled with brilliant blue water, bifurcating waterfalls and surrounding hills that are transformed by a kaleidoscope of autumnal tints.

Today we all take colour film for granted;

▲ **Subject:** Beech trees (*Fagus sylvatica*)
Location: New Forest, Hampshire, England
Month: May
Time of day: Early morning
Lighting: Direct side
Lens: 60 mm on Hasselblad
Film: Ektachrome 64

▲ Shortly after dawn broke, dramatic low-angled sunlight threw a beam of light down the length of one side of the ancient beech trunks. For a few brief moments the atmosphere was further enhanced by an owl heard hooting in the forest.

but what a thrill it must have been when nature photographers, previously limited to producing black and white prints, viewed colour films of natural subjects for the first time. The speed of the original Kodachrome was 10 ASA (ISO 10/11°) – much slower than monochrome films used by nature photographers at that time. Now we have colour tansparency film available at speeds ranging from ISO 25/15° to ISO 1600/33° (or even ISO 3200/36°).

Although we all use colour film daily now, do we ever stop to consider how we interpret colour? Whenever the sun's rays are dispersed by droplets of water in a rainbow or a bubble it becomes evident that sunlight is composed of the colours of the spectrum. Every object reflects and absorbs light of different wavelengths to varying degrees.

At one extreme, black velvet absorbs most of the incident light falling on it, which makes it a useful studio background for shells and fossils. Snow, on the other hand, reflects nearly all the incident light. Coloured objects selectively absorb some wavelengths and reflect others. The proportion of light which is reflected depends on the tone and texture of the surface; rough or hairy leaves, for example, will reflect less light than smooth, shiny leaves.

Many colours in the natural world arise from pigments; melanins give rise to browny blacks, anthocyanins to the red of a poppy, carotenoids to the brilliant array of yellows and oranges in autumnal leaves and also the pink feathers of flamingos. While animals synthesize most pigments, flamingos derive carotenoids from the food they eat, so captive birds lose their brilliant colours unless their diet is rich in carotenoids during the time they moult. The colour of white petals and feathers, however, derives from an internal structure which reflects light across the entire spectrum.

Among the most spectacular colours in the natural world are the beautiful iridescent hues on some feathers, butterfly and beetle wings, and shells. These are also all structural colours and the intensity of the colours changes depending on the angle of the light striking them.

With the exception of deserts, mountain tops, cave interiors and polar regions, there are few habitats which do not feature green vegetation. It is therefore important that green areas in a colour photograph are reproduced authentically. If the greens look wrong then the rest of the nature photograph will look unnatural.

All photographers working with colour filmstock need to know and understand the nature of colour and the principle of complementary colours. When a coloured filter is used on a camera it transmits light of its own colour and absorbs light of a complementary colour. The colours seen on colour negative film are complementary to the slide film colours. Hence red and green are complementary, as are yellow and blue.

I use two well-tried camera systems (which will be obvious from the captions in this book) because my equipment needs to be rugged enough to withstand accidental knocks in rough terrain. Cameras and lenses are the tools of my trade, so they must be reliable. I would, however, stress that buying expensive equipment is not a guaranteed means to gaining stunning pictures. Even though features such as through-the-lens metering, and off-the-film

metering for flash, are now commonplace on single-lens reflex cameras, these alone will also not ensure a striking photograph. When questioned, the majority of people would specify patience as the single most important attribute of a nature photographer. While I certainly would not disagree with this, I have repeatedly argued that an important factor towards achieving a memorable nature photograph is the ability to *see* a picture and to compose it in the viewfinder as a harmonious study.

Being a good naturalist first and foremost will aid the location of subjects, but it will not necessarily lead to the production of arresting photographs. Having judged many competitions of nature photography for well over a decade, I have no doubt that some people have a 'seeing eye' while many others, alas, do not. Throughout my life I have never had any desire to paint pictures but by repeatedly bringing my eye down to a viewfinder, I have become so much more aware of lighting and composition. Once I have seen a subject, I rarely hesitate about which focal length lens to use or where to position the frame around the picture. Composition has to be instinctive when working at speed, taking large mammals or birds rapidly moving out of shot.

Nobody will succeed as a nature photographer if they adopt a ruthless attitude, where a picture must be taken regardless of the disturbance caused. The welfare of the subject must always be given top priority.

◄**Subject:** Bumblebees (*Bombus* sp.) foraging in poppy flower
Location: Author's garden, Surrey, England
Month: July
Time of day: Early morning
Lighting: Back
Lens: 150 mm + extension on Hasselblad
Film: Ektachrome 64

◄I noticed that by midmorning the bumblebees had stopped foraging on the poppy flowers in our garden. So one morning, I got up early to photograph them flying in to the flowers as the petals began to open and reveal the fresh pollen inside.

◄**Subject:** Trees changing colour beside lake
Location: Giuzhaigou, Sichuan, China
Month: October
Time of day: Afternoon
Lighting: Direct sun
Lens: 80 mm on Hasselblad
Film: Ektachrome 64

►**Subject:** Edible winkles (*Littorina littorea*) on old shoe
Location: Intertidal zone, Cornwall, England
Month: March
Time of day: Early afternoon
Lighting: Direct sun
Lens: 50 mm on Exakta
Film: Kodachrome X (ISO 64/19°)

Among the pictures chosen to illustrate this book are a few old favourites, where the lighting and composition were perfect and I know instinctively that they can never be improved. The others include a mixture of pictures taken on my worldwide travels, as well as many that were specially taken to illustrate techniques described in the text. When an animal is photographed in the studio this should always be declared in a caption if the picture is published. There are, for example, two pictures of foxes in this book. The frame-filling portrait on page 44 was taken in captivity to illustrate the effect of a diffusing screen over the flash head; the one on page 127, on the other hand, clearly shows a fox in the wild.

Throughout this book emphasis is placed on the importance of appraising the lighting. There are some occasions − invariably early or late in the day − when the lighting makes the picture; all that is required then is fast reflexes to expose the film before the light changes. I can recall some magical moments at dawn when the rising sun began to break through mist, painting a pink or orange expanse on water or a sea of clouds in a valley. A view across a succession of peaks backlit by sun early or late in the day gives a series of tones receding into the distance. For me, these moments live forever. They are worth the extra effort involved in rising early to be on site before dawn. An example of how the angle and quality of light influences the end result can

be seen by comparing two of my pictures taken in Hampshire's New Forest at different times of the year. I arrived in the Forest at dawn early in May 1988 just when the sun was breaking through a gap in the trees, to see the trunks become spotlit by a ribbon of light down their length from the direct, low-angled sun, which also emphasized the fresh spring foliage. In exactly the same part of the Forest in late autumn 1987 I found an ancient beech severely damaged by the October storm. It was standing in a poignant way on a windless, overcast day, with one of its severed limbs lying on the forest floor; the resulting photograph is reproduced on page 124.

A seeing eye and the ability to isolate the picture from the mêlée of potential images all around you, are both essential factors which contribute to producing a memorable picture. Appraising the background is all part of the selection process. Whenever I move into a new habitat, I quickly scan the view ahead of me from the ground up to the horizon or tree tops and beyond, looking for shapes or an area of light and shadow which will arrest my roving eye. Successful nature photography is a combination of being in the right place at the right time and grasping lucky chance events. An observant naturalist is also able to read field clues as short cuts to finding subjects.

For me, simple uncluttered photographs make the most memorable images − pictures such as the eider dwarfed by icebergs

in a glacier lake (reproduced on page 10). Opportunist pictures − such as the winkles browsing algal growths on an abandoned shoe which I discovered on the shore − are an extra bonus, because they are unplanned. With time man's rubbish discarded into the sea has provided a solid substrate for algae to settle and grow on an otherwise unstable sandy beach.

When authentic nature photographs are taken by observant people − whether professionals or amateurs − they may add to our knowledge of animal behaviour or the method of pollination or seed dispersal of a plant. Today, photographs play a vital part in communicating to the general public, making them aware of what needs to be conserved as well as the complexity of natural food webs. Thanks to extensively illustrated nature books and, of course, the superb natural history films on television, children today are much more knowledgeable about wildlife, not only in their own country but also all over the world, than they were a couple of decades ago.

Those of us today who earn a living as nature photographers owe much of our inspiration to the pioneer nature photographers working almost a century ago. It was their still photographs which aroused the interest of so many people long before nature films appeared on television. I hope my pictures will also stimulate a greater awareness of the splendour and diversity, as well as the fragility, of life on earth.

Subject: Eider
(*Somateria mollissima*)
dwarfed by icebergs
Location: Glacier lake,
Breidarlon, Iceland
Month: July
Time: Afternoon
Lighting: Cloudy, but
bright
Lens: 150mm on
Hasselblad
Film: Ektachrome 64

CHAPTER ONE

THE NATURAL WORLD

Even though much of the natural world has been affected by the hand of man, it still offers endless scope for photography. Sweeping open vistas contrast with restricted views within forests, canyons and caves; there are still life studies and dynamic action shots, detailed close-ups as well as patterns and designs at varying scales. The continuous cycle of the temperate seasons, and the alternating wet and dry seasons of the tropics, produce an overall scene that changes constantly throughout the year. Water is not only essential to life on earth, it also enhances the mood and atmosphere of many natural scenes.

LIGHT ON THE LANDSCAPE

The infinite variety of landscapes and the changing pattern of light on them present fascinating and challenging subjects to the outdoor photographer. Indeed, there are many professionals who spend their entire life taking nothing else. Landscape photographs *should* be one of the easiest of all nature subjects for, unlike wary birds and mammals or detailed close-ups, they can be taken with basic non-reflex camera systems with a fixed lens. Landscapes are so often disappointing, however, either because the exposure is incorrect, the light is uninspiring, or the angle of view of the lens inadequate to reproduce the broad vista.

The type (direct or diffuse) and direction (front, side, overhead or back) of the lighting are even more critical to success or failure in capturing a landscape at a particular moment, than they are to a portrait of a plant or animal. Until this essential has been grasped, disappointments will inevitably arise.

Cameras which automatically expose and focus make the mechanics of photographing a uniformly lit view so easy that invariably no time is spent on critically appraising the direction of the light before the shutter is released. Artists, on the other hand, spend hours or even days producing their reproductions (or impressions) of landscapes and so they look much more critically at the lighting. Care must be taken when exposing for a scene which is part land, part sky; since meters tend to take an average reading, the foreground will tend to be under-exposed. The solution here is either to meter off the foreground landscape and use this exposure, or to use a graduated filter to reduce the skylight reflection.

On days when lighting conditions change rapidly — for example, as storm clouds race across the sky interspersed with rare flashes of sunlight — luck can play a vital part in getting a rare scoop picture when the composition and lighting are in perfect harmony. This happened to me once at the end of December in southern Utah in the United States. The sky had been overcast all day until late afternoon, when we approached the Arizona border and a band of blue sky suddenly appeared above the horizon. The low-angled light threw a line of sandstone hills — still partially covered by snow from a snowfall a few days earlier — into sharp relief. As we drove nearer and rounded a corner, a band of lower red sandstone hills appeared in view, glowing a fiery red in the low-angled sun. Unfortunately, a line of telegraph wires cutting across the hills was also clearly picked out by the sun, so it was a race against time to drive across a dirt track and run several hundred metres to find a camera position where the lines were out of shot. By the time I had set up my tripod and camera, I could take only a few frames before the sun sank and the hills lost their fiery magic.

Lucky shots such as this cannot be planned and so should be regarded as a bonus. A higher percentage of striking landscape pictures will be achieved, however, by working in a familiar location and studying the changing patterns of light throughout the day as well as during the seasons. In this way, it is possible to seek the best viewpoint and anticipate the optimum lighting.

If time is short — especially during a holiday abroad — it is well worth locating a map with scenic viewpoints marked on it. Even without this asset, advance planning can be done by studying a map with the elevation contours marked so as to predict where shadows will fall at different times of day. A map can also be useful for seeking high viewpoints to obtain an overview of a flat landscape.

The approach to landscape photography is quite distinct from that required when taking animal or plant pictures. Quick reactions coupled with long lenses are invariably required for photographing animals in action, while acute eyesight is essential for selecting close-ups from the broad landscape vista. It is difficult to fail with the classic landscape situation of a snow-capped mountain perfectly reflected in a calm lake, but taking landscape photographs is not simply a question of selecting a wide-angle lens. Camera manufacturers tend to give the impression that a particular lens can be neatly pigeon-holed for a specific subject, so long or telephoto lenses tend to be synonymous with wildlife and wide-angle lenses with landscapes. In fact, landscapes can be taken with a lens of *any* length. Indeed, I have used my whole gamut of lenses for a 35 mm system — from an 8 mm fisheye to a 400 mm telephoto — for taking landscapes; but the lenses I prefer to use are the 50 mm, 85 mm and 105 mm and it is no coincidence that none of the pictures repro-

▶ **Subject:** Snow-covered hills
Location: Near Mexican Hat, Utah, US
Month: January
Time: Almost sunset
Lighting: Oblique
Lens: 200 mm on Nikon
Film: Kodachrome 25

The direction and angle of light on the landscape have a marked effect on a scene. These two pictures were both lit with low-angle direct sunlight, one early and the other late in the day. Although they were taken eight years apart, they lie comparatively close to each other in neighbouring states in the southern part of The United States.

◀ **Subject:** Saguaro cacti (*Cereus giganteus*)
Location: Organ Pipe National Monument, Arizona, US
Month: February
Time: Early morning
Lighting: Back
Lens: 105mm on Nikon
Film: Kodachrome 25

duced on this spread was taken with a wide-angle lens. Long lenses enable a proportion of a landscape to be highlighted; for example, a 300 mm lens used from a high viewpoint, looking down on to a mosaic of multi-coloured fields or into a canyon, offers scope for a variety of quite different horizontal or vertical pictures to be taken from the same place.

If the light is good, landscapes can be taken with a hand-held camera, but a tripod will be needed for photographing scenics with a long lens – especially in windy, exposed locations – where it is difficult to brace the body to keep a steady hand hold. I also find a tripod useful when using wide-angle lenses, since the camera can be panned round to find the best viewpoint. Although wide-angle lenses offer a limited range of

pictures from a single viewpoint, they are invaluable when the camera-to-subject distance cannot be increased simply by moving backwards – for example, in dense forests or caves (p. 40).

The distinctive quality of light associated with particular climates often makes it possible to locate landscape photographs instantly. Although harsh, direct tropical light produces heavy shadows, it also gives a brilliant luminosity to strong colours, notably the red flowers so abundant in the tropics (p. 25). Shafts of sunlight piercing the forest canopy can dramatically spotlight a feature on the forest floor. In temperate regions, such as Britain, France and Japan, the soft, muted light associated with misty winter scenes helps to create a moody atmosphere. Pale unitoned landscapes, such

as sand dunes or snow-covered hills, can be enlivened with side lighting casting shadows of trees across them. The floor of a deep canyon may be lit for only a short time each day and so the timing for photographing a meandering river or a rock pinnacle within the canyon is particularly critical.

One of the most useful filters for colour landscape photography is a skylight to remove haze at altitude and to protect the lens from corrosive sea spray at the coast. A polarizing filter will increase the contrast between white clouds and a blue sky as well as removing skylight reflections on the water surface and from leaves – especially shiny ones. As illustrated on p. 43, a graduated filter can be an asset for reducing the contrast between a colourless sky and a foreground landscape.

PLANTS IN THE LANDSCAPE

In recent years, there has been an increasing tendency among wildlife photographers to show nature in context with its habitat. A picture which immediately conveys where a plant is growing or where an animal lives is much more informative than, for example, a close-up of a single flower or an animal portrait against a sky backdrop. As illustrated later in this book (pp. 82–97), however, close-range studies of plants or animals are extremely useful for revealing structural details which relate to a particular species.

Contrary to popular belief, taking pictures of nature in the landscape is not an easy option, since the subject has to be well lit in relation to its surroundings. Providing a plant is growing in an accessible place, it will be possible to walk around it to find the best camera position, whereas this will rarely be feasible when taking wild animals (p. 16). Even then, if a plant is found to be inadequately lit, it may well be worth returning later in the day or even on the following day to photograph it under a more flattering light.

Larger plants, such as trees and shrubs, are comparatively easy to show in a landscape setting, although care does need to be taken with appraising the light on the foreground subject. Smaller plants, such as flowers and fungi, need to be boldly coloured so that they contrast well against green vegetation, if they are to show up clearly when reproduced as a small part of the frame. Green ferns or mosses present more challenging subjects, although they can often be separated from the background by use of light and shadow (p. 34).

Wide-angle lenses are essential for showing plants in their habitat. Often a 35 mm lens will be adequate, but a 28 mm or even a 20 mm lens can be useful for giving a wider angle of view of the terrain or vegetation behind the plant. If you are buying a lens and are uncertain which length is going to be most useful, try looking through a short zoom lens (such as 25–50 mm) in a shop and practise zooming in and out to see how the angle of view increases and the scale of distant objects is reduced as the focal length is reduced.

The choice of camera viewpoint will depend on the height of the plant and type of habitat. For example, a low viewpoint is needed in a forest to show a ground plant such as a tree seedling, a fungus or a flower, together with towering trees behind. By wading into a stream or river a novel angle of view can be gained for bankside plants or emergent plants flowering above the water. Small plants growing in flat, sandy desert expanses also need a low camera angle. It is therefore worth buying a versatile tripod which will adapt to low-level work, either by having legs which can spread out or simply by reversing the centre column so that the camera is suspended below.

On the other hand, a high viewpoint is essential for showing a plant on the rim of a crater or canyon and the depression below, or clifftop plants and the sea. The lush growth typical of tropical rain forests makes it virtually impossible to gain a good vista at ground level, but high-level walkways erected between trees above the herb layer provide excellent scope for longer-range photography of plants in their habitat. In swamps such as Okefenokee in Georgia, tower lookouts at the end of raised boardwalks give a marvellous overview.

On an even larger scale, overhead or oblique aerial photography – whether from a light aircraft or a hot air balloon – is invaluable for revealing the make-up of trees in tropical rain forests, especially when one particular tree is flowering, or for showing the extent of hurricane windblow in a forest which has become impenetrable by foot. A striking visual effect of the hurricane which blew up from the south coast of Britain in 1987 could clearly be seen a week later from a hot air balloon. The south side of all the hedges had been burnt brown by the salt-laden winds, whereas the north sides were still green.

When you are working on the ground, excessive tilting of the camera skywards or earthwards will result in perspective distortion. Where the terrain has no obvious vertical lines this effect may not be noticeable, but a plantation of symmetrically planted straight-boled conifers will appear to converge towards the centre of the picture. This effect can be reduced or even

◄**Subject:** Slipper flower (*Calceolaria* sp.)
Location: Mountains, at 3700 m, at Colca Valley, Peña Blanca, Peru
Month: May
Time: Morning
Lighting: Back
Lens: 35 mm on Nikon
Film: Kodachrome 25

◄By selecting a suitable camera angle and using a wide-angle lens, larger plants can be shown in context with their natural habitat.

◄**Subject:** Beech tuft
(*Oudemansiella mucida*)
Location: Beech Wood,
New Forest, Hampshire,
England
Month: October
Time: Morning
Lighting: Overcast
Lens: 20 mm on Nikon
Film: Kodachrome 25

◄When groups of fungi appear on the ground or on fallen trunks, they can be photographed with a wide-angled lens to show the type of habitat in which they occur. In this case, the beech trees help to convey the scale of the fungi.

Compared with a standard lens, a wide-angle lens has the advantage of an increased depth of field for any given aperture. Thus, if a 35 mm lens is focused on a clump of flowers 2 metres (6 feet) away and stopped down to f16, everything from 2 metres (6 feet) to infinity can be brought sharply into focus by ensuring the focusing ring is positioned so the infinity and 2-metre (6-feet) marks lie within the range for f16. Modern lenses have a depth of field (p. 85) scale inscribed on the lens mount and the depth of field can also be checked visually by depressing a depth of field preview button or lever.

It is obviously important to ensure the foreground subject is sharply in focus. If it is not possible to stop the lens fully down when working in dull light with a slow-speed film, or windy conditions dictate a fast shutter speed, the camera should be focused on the plant itself and distant hills, mountains or trees will still be discernible, even if they are not perfectly in focus.

Composition is always a matter of personal choice, but a brightly coloured flower or fungus – especially if it is red or yellow – will immediately attract the eye so it often helps to position the subject to one side of the frame rather than always placing it in the centre foreground. As well as individual clumps of flowers, an expansive drift of wild flowers growing perhaps beside a road can make a striking landscape picture when a wide-angle lens and a low viewpoint are used, so as to include a large expanse of blue sky with an attractive cloudscape.

On the other hand, mat-like scabweeds growing flush with the dry river bed near Mount Cook in New Zealand presented me with more of a problem. I needed to have a higher viewpoint, so I scouted around for a rock on which to stand. When working in Britain, I have used a stepladder to gain a higher viewpoint for photographing expansive fungi growing flush with the ground and I find the boarded-in roof rack of my estate car invaluable for looking over hedges to take a tree in the context of its landscape beyond.

Among the most successful subjects for this type of nature photography are alpine plants with a dramatic mountain backdrop behind them.

eliminated by using either a view camera with the ability to swing, tilt or shift the lens, or a special wide-angle lens on a 35 mm camera. Often used by architectural photographers and known as a perspective correcting lens, it corrects distortion by off-centring the lens. Short wide-angle lenses – in particular from 24 mm down to 16 mm – may also distort the shape of objects at close range to the camera.

ANIMALS IN THE LANDSCAPE

The trend towards increasingly faster long-focus lenses and high-speed colour films makes it relatively easy and tempting to take frame-filling portraits of even timid wild birds or mammals; such pictures convey nothing about the animals in their habitat and could equally well have been taken in captivity. I have used and encouraged the ecological approach for some time now, pointing out that this kind of nature photography should be intermingled with more detailed action and behavioural shots when illustrating a lecture or a magazine article.

Since wild animals cannot be approached at such close range as plants, the camera-to-subject distance will invariably be considerably greater and so the focal length of lens longer. The choice of lens for photographing animals in their natural setting will depend on the size of the animal and how close it will tolerate the presence of a stalking photographer.

Wide-open habitats are obviously easier places to work than forests where animals can so easily take cover, although it is possible to take deer in glades and forest clearings. The types of terrain in which I particularly enjoy showing animals in context include mountainous areas for mammals; coastline or estuary for waders; inland wetland sites for birds; savannah grasslands for game and shallow-water lagoons for whales breeching.

Knowing when and where animals are likely to appear will obviously help to ensure a higher success rate, but I often find this kind of picture simply appears without any pre-planning. When working in Iceland some years ago I particularly wanted to photograph glacial lakes with icebergs, so I visited the south-eastern part of the island. After exposing several rolls of film, a few eider swam into view, completely dwarfed by the huge icebergs. Because I wanted to emphasize this discrepancy in size, I delib-

erately refrained from using a longer focal length lens. This was an easy picture to take since it involved no stalking on foot, whereas to reach the chamois in the Gran Paradiso National Park in the Italian Alps involved a climb up to 2500 metres (8200 feet). Unlike the ibex which also occur here, chamois are fairly timid and will not tolerate a close approach. The best time of year for seeing them is in the autumn, when they come down from higher elevations. Note that this environmental picture was taken with a 200 mm lens which is often the one I select when photographing groups of birds away from their nests, whereas for groups of game animals in the African savannah I tend to select a shorter lens such as an 85 mm or even a standard 50 mm.

The marabou storks were taken with a 400 mm lens using a jeep as a hide, after our main objective had failed. We had driven down to the river to look for crocodiles, but found none. As we drove up the bank on to

the main track I noticed the birds standing on the island further upstream.

There is no set formula for photographing animals in the landscape, but more thought will be needed in composing the picture within the frame, compared with taking a frame-filling portrait of an animal. If a single animal occupies a fraction of the frame, it can be positioned in the middle, at the bottom or top, or to the left or right of the frame. Pictures reproduced on pp. 33, 100 and 127 show how I have varied the position of the animal in the frame.

Many landscape photography and painting books write about using the Rule of Thirds to compose a picture. The frame is mentally sub-divided into thirds – both horizontally and vertically – so as to give nine rectangles on a 35mm frame. The 'ideal' position for the main subject is regarded to be at one of the four places where two of the lines cross, left and right above the centre and left and right below.

▶ Subject: Chamois (*Rupicapra rupicapra*)
Location: Montane scree in the Grand Paradiso National Park, Italy
Month: October
Time: Mid-afternoon
Lighting: Overcast
Lens: 200 mm on Nikon
Film: Kodachrome 64

Some element of luck helps in gaining a picture of animals in their habitat, since they may decide to move out of shot. Portraits of individual marabou storks could never be described as attractive, but the tonal range in this distant group has a painterly quality.

◀ Subject: Marabou storks (*Leptoptilos crumeniferus*)
Location: Uaso Nyiro River at the Samburu Game Reserve, Kenya
Month: August
Time: Late afternoon
Lighting: Overcast
Lens: 400 mm on Nikon
Film: Kodachrome 64

Personally, I have never bothered with any such theoretical formula; I am a firm believer that for a composition to succeed it must be completely instinctive. Any attempt to produce a picture to a formula is courting disaster or, in the case of an action subject, no picture at all! When an animal is viewed from the side, however, the framing should ideally position the animal off-centre so that it is looking out towards a larger area of space than appears behind it.

It is worth remembering when photographing any animal in early morning or late evening light, that it will cast a long shadow on a flat, uniformly coloured landscape – notably a desert or snow-covered ground – thereby conveying a third dimension to the picture. A single tall animal, such as a giraffe or an ostrich, can then produce a most spectacular shadow.

Purist naturalists will argue that photographs of wild animals in the landscape should always be taken as and when the animals naturally move into the field of view rather than artificially baiting them to a convenient spot for photography. Nesting birds return to a known fixed point, which can be useful for planning a picture showing the habitat of a common nesting bird such as some sea birds or possibly a heron from a high hide. Since this necessitates a much closer camera-to-subject working distance than when taking the conventional portrait

nest picture, it is not advisable for the majority of birds and it should never be attempted for timid or rare species.

No mention has yet been made about photographing fast-moving animals in the landscape. Composing the ideal picture becomes even more of a problem and may be a lucky accident. (See chapter 7 for more details on 'Nature in action'.)

The ethics of wildlife photography in general are outlined at the end of this book, but it is perhaps worth mentioning here that in the very early days of wildlife photography, when film speed was extremely slow, nature photographers did have to resort to desperate measures. In The Royal Photographic Society's historic print collection there is an 1852 photograph by J D Llewelyn showing a heron in a pool. On close examination it can be seen that the heron is pin-sharp, but the reeds behind it are blurred. The reason for this apparent anomaly is that during the long exposure, the wind blew the reeds, but the stuffed heron remained static!

Skeletons and larger fossils are static animal subjects which can be highlighted in their surroundings by using a wide-angle lens in a similar way to the approach for photographing plants within their habitat (p. 14). In particular, a bleached skeleton looks very dramatic when lying on parched ground.

SEASONAL CHANGES

In temperate latitudes, people frequently complain about the vagaries of the weather, but these variations make nature photography more of a challenge. Each season has a distinct mix of weather and proportion of daylight to darkness. After the long winter nights, which many small mammals survive by hibernating, spring is a season of feverish activity in the natural world. Catkins open so their wind-blow pollen is dispersed before the trees leaf out. Amphibians return to water to spawn. Resident birds begin nest-building, while winter visitors return to higher latitudes as food becomes more plentiful and winter relaxes its icy grip.

All this increased activity is stimulated by an increasing number of daylight hours. On 21 December 1987, London had less than seven hours' daylight. At the beginning of the following March, there were eleven hours of daylight and by the end of May, sixteen hours. This changing pattern of light and dark affects the growth of plants and activity of animals, and also determines the number of hours a photographer can work using available light. During an Icelandic summer, photography by available light is possible twenty-four hours a day.

Accompanying these changes of light, is a change in temperature which triggers the spawning of amphibians and many freshwater fish. Whether spring comes early or late, the succession in which plants come into flower is remarkably constant. Spring comes later at higher latitudes (further north in northern hemisphere countries such as Britain and the USA, and further south in Australia and New Zealand) so if a plant has faded at one latitude it can still be

▲ **Subject:** Mixed woodland in autumn
Location: Near Blue Ridge Parkway, North Carolina, US
Month: October
Time: Afternoon
Lighting: Slight haze
Lens: 200 mm on Nikon
Film: Kodachrome 64

◄ **Subject:** Blooming desert with brittle bush and lupins
Location: Organ Pipe National Monument, Arizona, US
Month: March
Time: Morning
Lighting: Partially diffused
Lens: 24 mm on Nikon
Film: Kodachrome 25

found by moving further north (or south) within its known distribution area.

I have kept a nature calendar in Britain for a couple of decades, recording the date when I first see each kind of flower in bloom or butterfly on the wing, or hear each migrant bird singing. This is my bible for calculating expected dates – regardless of whether the season is early or late.

Some landscapes look their best at a particular season, but an enjoyable long-term project is to photograph precisely the same scene in all four seasons. You will need to make careful notes of the focal length of the lens used and the main landmarks in the picture to ensure the angle of view remains the same. Even then, I know from experience, it is easy to forget small details, so now I always use a previous photo for easy reference.

The leafing out of deciduous trees typifies spring. Each kind of tree sports a subtle variation of green: beech (*Fagus sylvatica*) is

As summer ends, the days shorten, the flowers fade and fruits ripen. Inaccessible fruits high up on trees can be photographed so they fill the frame by using a long-focus lens. But it is invariably the rich colours of the deciduous trees which catch the photographer's eye in autumn as the green of the chlorophyll is broken down into a variety of yellows and reds. The best colours appear when warm days are interspersed with frosty nights; this is a weather pattern which occurs regularly in New England, hence the fall colours are always spectacular here. Autumnal shades appear earlier in higher latitudes. They are a prelude to deciduous trees shedding their leaves as a precaution against water loss when the ground is frozen. Once the leaves have turned, an overnight gale can strip the branches bare, transforming an attractive autumnal scene into winter. Each North American state with regular spectacular fall colours has a telephone hotline telling you where to view fall colours — an enormous help to photographers, although the best places tend to become very crowded!

Autumn is also a time for fungus forays, since the majority of toadstools or brackets are produced when warm autumnal days coincide with showers. Fungi cannot synthesize their own food and so most are saprophytes, living on dead and decaying plants or animals, but a few are parasitic, feeding on living animal and plant hosts. At ground level, fungi are best photographed either with a wide-angle lens to show their habitat (p. 14) or with a standard or macro lens, while fungi growing at a high level in trees may require a telephoto lens.

Misty mornings are often associated with autumn and this is a particularly good time to take close-ups of spiders' webs sparkling with dew or action shots of male deer calling during their rut.

Once winter sets in, the range of nature subjects diminishes, but there is still ample scope for wintry landscapes, tree portraits and frosty fantasy close-ups, as well as bird and mammal studies, including animal tracks. The robin sitting on a snow-covered branch illustrates how the type of season can be portrayed by taking a plant or animal in an obviously seasonal setting. During prolonged cold spells, as food becomes short, many wild birds lose their typical shyness towards man and are easily baited (p. 76). The special problems associated with cold weather photography are discussed on pp. 26–27.

There are also distinct seasons in the tropics too. The length of the African dry season has a great effect on the vegetation and wildlife, as well as on man. After rain falls, parched savannah grasslands become transformed to a luscious green and dry rivers become raging torrents. The quantity of rain which falls on the Arizona deserts in December influences the extent of the flowering in the following spring.

▼ **Subject:** Robin (*Erithacus rubecula*)
Location: Oak tree at Frensham Little Pond, Surrey, England
Month: December
Time: Afternoon
Lighting: Back
Lens: 200 mm on Nikon
Film: Kodachrome 64

▼ During a prolonged cold spell, I came across this puffed-up robin sitting on a branch. The longest lens I had to hand was a 200 mm, but the snow-covered branches make a more seasonal picture than a tightly-cropped portrait would have done.

a delicate pale green, whereas oak (*Quercus robur*) is a distinctly lime green, and walnut (*Juglans regia*) has a bronze sheen. These subtle tones are unfortunately short-lived, for as the leaves mature they soon become a uniform dark green. Before the trees leaf out, wild flowers carpet the woodland floor; then the leafy canopy closes out the light.

As the days lengthen, spring merges — often imperceptibly — into summer. By now, woodland interiors are relatively dark and it is the more open habitats, such as meadows, heathlands and wetlands, that provide a plethora of flower and insect subjects. Close-ups can be taken by available light at any time of day; avoid the harsh midday light when taking landscapes. Stalking active insects, such as butterflies, with a monopod can be very time-consuming and it is often quicker to use a flash set-up with a hand-held camera (p. 92), selecting subjects with an adjacent background which will also be illuminated by the flash.

FRESHWATER HABITATS

Water in all its three phases – liquid, vapour and solid – presents magical qualities for the photographer. It embraces a huge range of subject scales, from photomacrographs of water-drop lenses (p. 108) to broad vistas of open oceans. Well over half (some 70 per cent) of the earth's surface is covered with water, which is essential for all life. The liquid phase is easily the most accessible to photographers all over the world in the form of ponds, lakes, streams, rivers, canals, dams, coasts and oceans.

Mist and fog, as well as the fumaroles and geysers of thermal regions, form when water becomes dispersed as droplets into the atmosphere. The ability of mist to create moody atmospheric scenes by diffusing the natural daylight is outlined and illustrated on pp. 38–39.

Supercooled water droplets and ice particles combine to produce hail; snow forms when these droplets freeze at −12 to −16°C (3 to 10°F) and hoar-frost forms when water vapour freezes. At high latitudes and high elevations, permanently frozen rivers of ice – glaciers – inch their way forward, gouging out the valley floors. The problems of working in cold weather are outlined elsewhere (p. 26); this spread

looks at freshwater habitats and the following one examines marine locations.

Calm water, as well as wet sand, mirrors its surroundings. Large open expanses simply reflect the sky colour – deep blue on a clear day or grey on a dull day – whereas waterside trees and plants, or animals moving down to drink are themselves reflected. When deciduous trees appear as a galaxy of colours in autumn, they are especially attractive if mirrored in calm water. Should skylight reflections on the water surface spoil the picture, they can be removed by using a polarizing filter. Perfectly calm water is comparatively rare, for even if there is no wind to ripple the water a surfacing fish or falling raindrops send out radiating ripples. However, ripples can help to transform a perfect reflection into an intriguing abstract picture, thereby adding interest to an otherwise dull sheet of water. Some photographers will even resort to creating their own ripples by throwing stones into the water! Any objects – leaves, pieces of wood or feathers – floating on water will also spoil a perfect mirror image if they happen to float across the reflection. I had to wait some time for the stilt's reflection to appear without interference from the copious white feathers. Notice how the backwash from the bird's legs has caused a slight rippling of the water, thus creating a distorted reflection of the legs.

The silvery skylight reflection which appears when water is viewed against the light can be useful for simplifying the surroundings of emergent subjects by obliterating objects below the water surface. The focus of attention can then be concentrated on an emergent plant or any aquatic animal – such as a frog or an alligator – which projects its head out of the water.

Close-range studies of aquatic plants growing some distance from the bank can be made either by using a long focus lens or wading out into a shallow stream – having checked the depth of water and any potential hazards (such as alligators!) first. Birds or mammals obviously need a more stealthy approach (p. 52).

Large wetland sites need both a high viewpoint and a wide-angle lens to do them justice. A high-level bridge is ideal for looking up or down the river it crosses. When I drove over the River Bandon in Ireland, the water was not visible, but instinctively I stopped the car and walked back on to the bridge to find an idyllic lowland river scene in May. The view I saw is not quite as it appears in the photograph, for I selected a very wide-angle lens and used a polarizing filter. This removed the skylight reflections on the trees and on the water in the lower half of the picture, so the colour of the green

bands of submerged water crowfoot plants was enriched. The effect of using such a filter can quickly be gauged by rotating it in front of the eye or by wearing Polaroid sunglasses as fishermen do to locate fish under water. A polarizing filter removes skylight reflections from leaves most effectively if the sun is shining at right angles to the direction of

▲ Subject: Black-necked stilt (*Himantopus mexicanus*)
Location: Salton Sea, California, US
Month: January
Time: Afternoon
Lighting: Diffused
Lens: 400 mm on Nikon
Film: Kodachrome 200

▲ On wind-free days, it is worth looking out for reflections of waterside plants and animals in calm water – without debris or emergent plants.

makeshift way of eliminating the sky reflections falling on to a small area of water is simply to hold a black umbrella around the camera, mimicking the way herons sometimes use their wings as an umbrella when fishing.

Where shallow water flows over rocks, the surface becomes agitated and if it is viewed against the light, spots of sunlight appear to dance on the water. Distant out-of-focus highlights will appear in the picture in the shape of the lens iris diaphragm (usually polygonal but circular in the case of mirror lenses). By stopping down the lens manually, you can see how the highlights change in size as the lens is opened up or stopped down. The final effect of moving water in a photograph will depend on the shutter speed used to record it. Every drop of highly turbulent water can be frozen in mid-action by using a fast shutter speed of 1/500 second or more.

However, I much prefer using a slow shutter speed of $\frac{1}{2}$ or I second to create soft continuous lines of tumbling or falling water which suggest movement. For this, slow speed film, such as Kodachrome 25, is essential and working in dull overcast light is preferable, although the film speed can be reduced by using a neutral density filter (p. 43). When I saw the Svartivoss waterfall plunging over a black basalt outcrop in Iceland, I knew I wanted to produce the effect of a white curtain. With a tripod this was no problem.

Using the same technique for taking ice floes floating down a river produces an abstract picture of short white lines appearing against the darker river water. If dripping water is taken using a long exposure, it appears as continuous white lines. This can be especially dramatic if they are lit from the side and viewed against a dark background. Exposures of a $\frac{1}{4}$ or $\frac{1}{2}$ second record falling raindrops or snowflakes as short white streaks.

A rainbow develops when sun shines on rain, spray from a waterfall or a spouting whale. The water drops refract and reflect the sunlight to create the spectral colours, visible only when the water drops are in front, and the sun behind, the direction of view. Often rainbow pictures are disappointing because the spectral colours appear rather faint; better colour saturation can be gained by slight under-exposure.

◄**Subject:** River Bandon
Location: Inishannon, County Cork, Ireland
Month: May
Time: Morning
Lighting: Direct, with polarizing filter
Lens: 20 mm on Nikon
Film: Kodachrome 25

Water, whether moving slowly over lowland plains or cascading as a waterfall, offers exciting challenges for creative photography.

the angle of view. This filter can also be useful when taking close-ups of plants, seaweeds or life in pools by looking down through the water, but the camera will then need to be used at an angle of approximately 37° to the water. The main disadvantage of fully polarizing a scene is that the exposure is reduced by as much as 1½ stops. A useful

►**Subject:** Svartivoss waterfall with columnar basalt
Location: Skaftafell National Park, Iceland
Month: July
Time: Late afternoon
Lighting: Overcast
Lens: 35 mm on Nikon
Film: Kodachrome 25

MARINE LOCATIONS

Coastlines include intimate sand coves, broad beaches where a succession of rollers continually break, jagged rocks pounded by surf, vast deltas where silt-laden water meets the seas, shallow-water lagoons inside coral reefs and mangrove swamps. The colour of the rocks (and sand) also varies from golden, grey and red to black or white.

Wide-angle lenses are useful for showing broad vistas as well as the situations of seaweeds or rock pools. A low camera angle with a wide-angle lens gives a dramatic · viewpoint for a stranded jellyfish, crab or turtle with waves behind. If you have ever tried focusing a low-level camera on a wet, sandy beach using a standard pentaprism,

you will appreciate the benefits of right-angle viewfinders!

A high viewpoint, such as a cliff top, and a long lens allow the dynamic patterns made as the sea creeps over a flat beach to be tightly framed. This kind of lens also allows a greater – and therefore safer – working distance for taking backlit waves with copious fine spray; for, as highlighted in the section on special problems associated with working at the coast (p. 132), sea water is highly corrosive.

Try experimenting using different shutter speeds when photographing moving water (p. 23) to see which effect you prefer. If wide-angle views only are required, a

weatherproof compact camera will survive wetting by a shower or salt spray. Waterproof compacts are ideal for taking pictures of breakers from the shallows as well as when rafting on white-water rivers; they can even be used down to a depth of 4 metres (13 feet).

Dramatic coastal scenery occurs in places where the sea has sculpted the rocks into arches, stacks and caves. Natural arches can be used for framing coastline views, while stormy seas crashing against rocks give plenty of scope for dynamic pictures as the white surf breaks. Sheer-sided cliffs will prove difficult to photograph from the land – unless the coastline sweeps around into a curve. Often the only way of photographing vertical cliffs and coastal waterfalls is from a boat at sea.

For most marine work a flash is unnecessary, but it is essential for lighting the interior of sea caves. Sometimes access to caves can be gained by foot at low tide, but before venturing out with cameras, be sure to consult tide tables and note the time the tide will turn. Entry into larger caves by boat will extend the time available for exploration.

Locations with high-ranging tides which have expansive inter-tidal zones offer opportunities for taking a pair of pictures comparing the same view covered by sea and exposed to the air. Relatively sheltered rocky shores with a large inter-tidal zone are rich hunting grounds for exquisite marine invertebrates such as sea anemones, feather stars, sea urchins, sea slugs and sea squirts.

Expansive sandy beaches without rocks offer no natural dry place for putting down a gadget bag, so a thick polythene sheet or a lightweight camping mat provides a useful barrier to sea water and sand. Never wander far from your gear, since the tide comes in fast up a gentle gradient and can easily take you by surprise while you are engrossed with the camera. On rocky shores, a raised flat-topped boulder is a good base for gear.

A close-up lens, or preferably a macro lens, is essential for taking close-ups of life in rock pools. The shape, size and number of pools relate directly to the geology of the shore. They form wherever sea water remains trapped after the tide recedes. Pools low down on the shore, which are exposed for only a short time each day, have a much greater variety of life than high-level pools which soon warm up on a hot day. Shallow pools are much easier for photography, since only a small depth of field is required to get everything, from the floating seaweeds to encrustations on the floor of the pool, in focus. A polarizing filter (p. 42)

▲ Subject: Squat lobster (*Galathea strigosa*)
Location: Rocky shore in Devon, England
Month: August
Time: Afternoon
Lighting: Direct sun
Lens: 55 mm micro-Nikkor
Film: Kodachrome 25

◄ Subject: Brown seaweed (*Ecklonia* sp.)
Location: Rock pool at Leigh Marine Park, New Zealand
Month: January
Lighting: Overcast
Lens: 80 mm, Hasselblad
Film: Ektachrome 64

can be useful for eliminating skylight reflections and enriching the colours of underwater life.

On windy days, persistent ripples blowing across a pool make photography impossible. They can be eliminated simply by using a wooden frame slightly larger than the field of view, although without an assistant it may be difficult to prevent the frame from floating into the picture.

Other close-up subjects worth taking on the shore are shells and pebbles washed up in the strandline. Their colours are always enriched by wetting, so it may be worth taking dry shells or stones down to the water's edge. Seaweeds are without doubt the least popular of all plants for the nature photographer – perhaps because they are exposed for only a limited period each day – yet they come in a range of colours: blue-green, green, red and brown. The latter are particularly difficult to reproduce as an authentic colour on transparency film, invariably appearing green. All seaweeds contain green chlorophyll which is masked by other pigments, notably in the red and brown seaweeds. Many colour slide films

appear to be more sensitive to the green than the brown pigments, but I have found Agfachrome 50S gives the most authentic colour for exposed brown seaweeds.

Visiting the shore during a low tide at night is infinitely more exciting than a daytime visit, since without the drying action of the sun, crabs clamber over rocks, while worms and limpets move at a more leisurely pace. Feeding crabs and limpets can be observed by using a torch covered in red cellophane. Photography at night is more difficult here than in most terrestrial habitats since there are so many wet surfaces to produce distracting highlights from the flash. When a flash is used for photographing life in a pool, it should be held at an angle of about 45° to the water and *never* on the camera.

A long lens is useful for taking seabirds (pp. 50–51), marine mammals and wary ghost crabs on tropical beaches. Seals and sea lions can be photographed in the water or when they have hauled themselves out on land. In remote parts of Scotland, otters live along the coast, swimming amongst the brown oarweeds in much the same way as

▲ **Subject:** Sea lions (*Zalophus woolebaeki*)
Location: Galápagos
Month: March
Time: Afternoon
Lighting: Overcast
Lens: 200 mm on Nikon
Film: Kodachrome 64

Coastal habitats offer expansive landscapes as well as seabirds and mammals. Colourful close-ups of flowers and marine life also abound. Exploring the seashore with a camera adds a new dimension to nature photography.

the sea otters play among the giant kelp forests off the Californian coast. Out in the open ocean, dolphins will playfully leap close to the bow waves of a boat, providing excellent opportunities for taking action pictures with a standard or even a wide-angle lens.

On remote coastal roads which run parallel with the coast or a sea water loch, the car can be used as a hide to photograph herons intent on stalking fish, rafts of duck or playful otters.

Any large expanse of water – marine or freshwater – also offers wonderful opportunities for taking magical reflections of a rising or a setting sun (p. 112).

TROPICAL CONDITIONS

Within the tropical regions lie rivers, lakes, beaches, mangrove swamps, mountains and grasslands, but it is the lush rain forests and the arid deserts which present special problems for the photographer. In open locations such as deserts, continuous bright sunlight from dawn to dusk for weeks or even months on end is not only wearing, but also results in stereotyped lighting. Early or late in the day, however, elongated shadows will help to reveal wave patterns (p. 34) or animal tracks in sand dunes. On palm-fringed beaches there are plenty of opportunities for getting striking silhouettes of coconut palms standing out against the brilliant blue or orange sky.

The pattern of atmospheric circulation leads to the tendency for deserts to form around the 20° latitude bands both north and south of the Equator. It is the erratic, as well as scanty, rainfall (less than 25 cm/10 inches a year) in these bands which results in hostile desert conditions occurring in four continents.

Deserts are by no means a solid expanse of sand; they may consist of gravel, rocks, boulders and even mountains. Desert rocks have no clothing of vegetation to protect them from the elements, so they are constantly under attack from sun and wind and, at high elevations, frost in winter. In places where sand storms occur, rocks are sculpted by natural sand blasting and can make intriguing shapes for photography.

The deserts in California and Arizona are among the most easily accessible, for they lie only a short drive from an airport. Death Valley in California is the most consistently hot place in the world, with a highest temperature of 56°C (134°F) and an average of only 4 cm (1½ inches) of rain a year.

Although cacti and yuccas thrive in the Sonoran and Mojave deserts, vegetation is typically scanty and may be non-existent in other desert areas. This means that without any clouds, there is no shade for man and little for animals during the days, which are extremely hot in summer yet quickly lose their heat overnight when temperatures plummet. Desert plants and animals manage to survive in such extreme conditions through being able to exploit rain when it falls and developing a variety of water retention mechanisms.

The most spectacular time for visiting the Sonoran and Mojave deserts is when they are in bloom around March. The exact time and the extent of the flowering depends on the rainfall a few months earlier. If time is short, it is worth calling the desert hotlines for regular updates of the best places to see the flowers. Little rain falls on deserts during the year, but when it does flash

▼ **Subject:** Coconut palms (*Cocos nucifera*)
Location: Mahé, Seychelles
Month: May
Time: Morning
Lighting: Direct sun
Lens: 35mm on Nikon
Film: Kodachrome 25

Harsh tropical sunlight may create problems when taking landscapes, but it can produce some dramatic close-ups of flowers. Care needs to be taken to ensure that the sun does not shine directly into the lens.

floods can appear extremely quickly, so there are repeated warnings not to park a vehicle or camp in dry washes.

Large expanses of ground colour come from the yellow brittlebush flowers – a perennial plant which looks very drab for most of the year – and the annual desert poppies, which are a deeper yellow. In amongst these yellow carpets, a host of different-coloured flowers – including cacti – also bloom. The spectacular flowers of the large saguaro cacti appear later on in May and open out at night.

Wide-angle lenses are essential for general vistas of the blooming deserts, which are best taken with a low-angle sun early or late in the day. For revealing the detail of the interior of small cacti flowers, a macro lens will be essential, while a medium tele-photo will be useful for reptiles, for the elevated saguaro flowers and for animal tracks in sandy areas.

Since animals tend to burrow into the ground, crawl under stones or hide in hollowed-out cacti by day to keep cool, there are not many opportunities for

subject. Sometimes a mirror can be used to beam the sun on to a flower or a fern to highlight a particular feature. Within a general forest interior, however, no colour film has the latitude to expose both dark shadows and bright sun spots correctly. Such broader views are therefore always something of a compromise.

Travellers on luxury holidays may face an additional problem if they stay in an air-conditioned hotel and go straight from a cool interior into the hot and humid atmosphere outside: condensation will form on the cooler camera. When lenses steam up it becomes impossible for any pictures to be taken for several minutes until the condensation gradually evaporates and the lens clears. Attempting to clean lenses with a lens cloth or a handkerchief does not help since condensation will continue to form until the camera warms up. Precisely the same effect will be noticed in temperate winters when moving from a naturally cold environment into a tropical glasshouse or an aquarium. The solution is to allow the camera to warm up beforehand.

◄**Subject:** Tiger's claw (*Erythrina indicata*)
Location: Cultivated on Kauai Island, Hawaii
Month: January
Time: Late afternoon
Lighting: Back
Lens: 105 mm micro-Nikkor
Film: Kodachrome 64

▼**Subject:** Sifaka lemur (*Propithecus verreauxi*)
Location: Tamarind forest, Madagascar
Month: May
Time: Afternoon
Lighting: Overcast
Lens: 250 mm, Hasselblad
Film: Ektachrome 200

photographing desert wildlife during the daytime, but the excellent Arizona–Sonora Desert Museum at Tucson has many live captive desert animals on display. Desert reptiles – including various chuckwalla lizards – bask in the sun on trunks in walled open-air enclosures.

High temperatures have a detrimental effect on colour film (p. 131), so a camera (especially a black body) should not be left on a tripod in the full heat of the tropical sun. To save constantly taking my camera on and off a tripod I use a white padded tea cosy to insulate my camera, but a white towel would be almost as effective. Pale-coloured gadget bags will reflect the sun better than dark ones and padded bags will help to keep equipment and film cooler than a thin canvas bag. Above 60°C (140°F), the surface of a liquid crystal display turns black, making it impossible to read the exposure on many fully-automatic cameras.

By contrast, tropical rain forests are hot and steamy, with a very high relative humidity. Unlike deserts, the temperature remains remarkably constant throughout the day and the year. In recent years tropical rain forests have been felled at an alarming rate, but there are still large areas remaining in the Amazon Basin, Zaïre and Sumatra – the home of the orang-utan.

Although rain forest harbours a wealth of plants and wildlife, it is one of the most difficult habitats for working that I know. As well as the excessive heat, the high humidity can cause damage to both films and lenses. High-speed film and exposed film are more sensitive to heat than slow film and unexposed film. All films should therefore be kept in their original packaging until required for use. Exposed films should be kept in airtight containers packed with silica gel crystals. These are bright blue when dry, but after absorbing moisture they turn pink. Gentle heating will remove the moisture and restore their blue colour, so that they can be used again.

Shafts of sunlight streaming down through the forest canopy momentarily spotlight plants and animals; if the gap is small, the sun soon moves behind a branch or a trunk, casting a shadow over the chosen

OUT IN THE COLD

Ice and snow can transform a drab landscape into a winter wonderland. Exhilaratingly cold, wind-free days with a clear blue sky above snow-covered ground offer plenty of opportunities for striking photographs. Temperatures around freezing present relatively few problems to the outdoor photographer, yet surprisingly few people seem prepared to make the effort to spend any length of time working in winter.

Snow acts like a huge reflector, so exposure readings tend to be high and problems often arise in determining the correct exposure (p. 33). Shadows on snow tend to have an obvious blue cast which can be counteracted by using a UV or a skylight filter (p. 42).

A light fall of snow is ideal for finding animal tracks and it is always surprising to have proof of the wealth of birds and mammals which have passed through an area in a short time. Tracks show up best if photographed into a low-angled light so that shadows are cast in the impressions. The best tracks will be found immediately after a fresh snowfall, before they become confused by others crossing over them.

Moving around on deep snow is extremely tiring without skis or snow shoes, as I found to my cost years ago when attempting to stalk reindeer in the Scottish Cairngorms. Some people argue that using a tripod in deep snow is a waste of time, but if fully extended legs are pushed down hard into the snow, it is reasonably stable for all but very long lenses. Recently, I devised some tripod snow shoes using raffia mats (with a central hole for the leg spikes) to help spread the weight. The other problem with deep snow is the real danger of losing objects – such as a cable release or filters – if they are accidentally dropped. A wading bag which can be strapped around the waist is useful for snow work because, unlike a rucksack, it can be opened without having to be put down on the ground. In fact, it is inadvisable to rest a gadget bag on frozen ground for any length of time – unless it is extremely well padded.

When the light level drops during a snowfall, some form of camera support becomes essential for taking slow exposures which record snowflakes as short white lines. While driving towards Salt Lake City in a snow storm one January, I spotted an eagle sitting on the branch of a tree fairly near the road. The quickest way to support a 400 mm lens was to use a thick sweater in place of a Tri-bag (p. 136) on the window frame of the car, which allowed me to use a $\frac{1}{4}$ second exposure.

In high latitudes where the air temperature remains below freezing even when the sun is shining, frost can be preserved for days on end. In milder climates, such as that of southern Britain, the warmth from the first rays of the sun invariably begins to melt the frost fantasies, so it pays to get up early on cold mornings before the ephemeral frost begins to disappear.

The scale of the pictures can be varied by taking wide landscapes, middle-distance views with animals, and close-ups. If hoar frosts form early in a temperate winter, there will be opportunities for taking frosty spiders' webs, as well as colourful autumnal fruits coated in frost. Evergreen leaves such as holly, as well as fallen deciduous leaves, are clearly defined when etched with frost. Seedheads of large umbel flowers are particularly striking when viewed from a low angle against a blue sky; the contrast between the white frost and the sky can, of course, be enhanced by using a polarizing filter. As with all close-ups (p. 84), a tripod will ensure crisp images, but great care needs to be taken not to knock one of the tripod legs accidentally against the plant about to be photographed.

If you live at a latitude where snow rarely falls in winter and you want to be sure of getting some exciting winter pictures, it is worth spending a few days at a higher latitude or altitude where snow and ice are guaranteed. When sub-zero temperatures persist for several days, the open water of ponds and lakes diminishes as they begin to freeze over. Perpetual swimming by water-fowl will keep a small patch of water open so they can can continue drinking. A long lens is essential for taking shots of water-fowl in this situation, since it can be far too dangerous to walk out over the ice.

Unless special precautions are taken, temperatures of several degrees below freezing can hamper or even prevent photography. Excessively cold weather reduces the efficiency of camera batteries, although lithium ones function better than silver oxide and alkaline. If batteries become too cold, they cease working altogether, which means it is impossible not only to take a light reading, but also to take a picture with a battery-dependent camera. A spare set of batteries can obviously be kept warm in a pocket, but it is awkward to change them in cold weather.

Even at temperatures as low as $-15°C$ (5°F), it is possible to keep an electronic camera operational by tucking it inside a padded anorak and taking it out for one or two quick hand-held exposures. A mechan-

▶ **Subject:** Immature bald eagle (*Haliaeetus leucocephalus*)
Location: Roadside tree, Circleville, Utah, US
Month: January
Time: Afternoon
Lighting: Diffuse, low light (during snow)
Lens: 400 mm on Nikon
Film: Kodachrome 200

▶ This opportunist picture of an eagle in a blizzard was taken using the car as a hide.

◀ Orb webs coated with frost are not often seen because adult spiders die at the onset of winter after the females lay their eggs under cover.

◀ **Subject:** Frost on orb webs and holly leaves
Location: Author's garden, Surrey, England
Month: December
Time: Morning
Lighting: Diffuse
Lens: 80 mm with extension tubes on Hasselblad
Film: Ektachrome 64

camera baseplate rapidly chills. A cold-weather battery pack is made by several camera manufacturers for use on their better SLR models. The Nikon anti-cold battery pack weighs only 92 g (3¾ oz), complete with two 1.5 volt penlight batteries. The normal camera batteries are removed so the basal plug of the pack can be screwed into the camera body. The plug connects via a rubber-coated cable to the battery pack kept warm inside an anorak. I have used this to expose many films over a period of several hours at −20°C (−4°F) in Harbin, north of Beijing in China.

It is not easy to change films in these temperatures. When wearing several pairs of gloves, I find it impossible to manipulate the film, so I remove an outer pair and keep on thin silk gloves. Care needs to be taken when loading and unloading film, since it becomes very brittle at low temperatures and can easily break. For this reason (as well as the battery problem) it is sensible *not* to use auto-winds or motor drives at sub-zero temperatures in case they tear the sprocket holes in a 35 mm film. Although this problem will not arise with a roll film, any slight advantage is offset by having fewer frames and therefore having to change the film more frequently. Anyone contemplating working for extended periods at sub-zero temperatures would be advised to have one of their camera bodies winterized (p. 133).

On *no* account should bare skin come into contact with very cold metal on a camera or a tripod. Since moist breath condenses on to a cold camera as ice, it is sensible to cover the whole of the back of the camera — especially over the hinges — with the gaffer tape used by professional photographers.

Continuous frozen conditions silence the mighty roar of waterfalls by transforming them into impressive walls of ice. At Valdez in Alaska, waterfalls remain frozen from November to May and mountaineers climb the near-vertical ice faces. When photographing a subject like this, a reflected light reading will be reasonably accurate if there are portions of dark rock visible between the pale ice.

Try to avoid rapidly moving a camera from a very cold temperature to a very warm environment (or vice versa) since condensation will tend to form on the camera surfaces (this will turn to ice if the camera body has been out in sub-zero temperatures) and may result in corrosion and malfunctioning of the electronics. A wise precaution is to keep the camera in a plastic bag with silica gel crystals to absorb any moisture (p. 25) until the camera has cooled or warmed up to match the ambient temperature.

ical SLR is clearly more practical for use in cold weather, but it will have to be used in conjunction with either a Weston meter, or a battery-operated meter kept warm inside an inner pocket.

If an electronic camera needs to be used for prolonged tripod work in freezing weather, it is essential to use an alternative power source for the camera; even if the tripod head is insulated with tape, the

CAMOUFLAGE AND MIMICRY

Throughout the animal kingdom there are many ingenious ways in which animals have evolved colours, and sometimes shapes as well, to enable them to blend in with their surroundings. Disguise not only allows a proportion of animals in each community a better chance of survival against attack by predators, but also enables predators to pass undetected by their prey. Camouflage is effective only when the animal is viewed in its natural habitat. It breaks down when the animal is transferred to a unitoned background.

Animals which simply merge in with the colour of their surroundings are cryptically coloured. Many night-flying moths which rest among leaves or tree trunks by day have mottled brown upper wings, whereas butterflies, which generally close their wings on alighting, often have cryptically coloured underwings.

Predatory animals which stealthily stalk their prey are also masters of disguise. The chameleon is usually regarded as the prime example for illustrating colour change, but compared with octopuses, cuttlefish and squid the several minutes required by a

chameleon are slow. Other predators — including crickets, frogs, lizards and snakes — retain a single colour to match their surroundings: green in green vegetation or sandy-coloured in deserts and sand dunes.

In northern latitudes — especially in the arctic region where snow blankets the winter landscape — the mottled brown summer coloration of mammals and birds, such as the arctic hare and fox as well as ptarmigan, is replaced by a white winter coloration. This lack of colour may also function as an adaptation against heat loss.

During the two world wars, the outlines of buildings and tanks were disguised visually (but not from infra-red films) by irregular 'dazzle' painting. This method of disruptive coloration, which breaks up a uniformly coloured surface by means of contrasting tones, is found in many wild animals. Very simply, an animal's outline shape is broken down most effectively when one or more of the patches blend in with the surroundings.

Disruptive coloration is widespread among ground-nesting birds — not only on the adults and the young chicks, but also on

the eggs. Very often no attempt is made at nest building: the eggs are simply laid among pebbles on a shingle beach (oyster-catcher) or among grass or heather (red grouse). In these examples the egg outline is broken up by darker mottled patches. The concealment of the birds is effective only when they crouch or lie on the ground since a shadow cast by an upright bird immediately gives away its position.

The young of many mammals are also cryptically coloured: the dappled coat of roe deer kids simulates the dappled sunlight so typical of the forests they frequent. Bottom-living fish — including the freshwater bullhead and the marine blenny — have cryptic colours to match the bottom substrate. Flatfish go one stage further by flicking sand over the edges of their body to obliterate all trace of a shadow.

A beady eye contrasting with the overall body pattern could ruin all attempts at camouflage. Many amphibians, birds and fish have a vertical or horizontal eye stripe extending on either side of the eye.

Photographing camouflaged animals requires a critical approach to both lighting

◀**Subject:** Roe deer kid
(*Capreolus capreolus*)
Location: Surrey, England
Habitat: Deciduous
woodland
Month: June
Time: Afternoon
Lighting: Overcast
Lens: 250 mm on
Hasselblad
Film: Ektachrome 64

For animal camouflage to be effective, the subject should not be tightly framed. The visual effect will be more convincing if there is plenty of background visible all round the animal. The mottled coat of this new-born roe deer kid helps to break up its body outline as it rests amongst the leaf litter.

Both these pictures were taken by available light as the harsh shadows of direct flash would have spoiled the camouflage.

and picture composition; convincing pictures will be achieved only by studying the behaviour of each animal in relation to its surroundings.

Since animal disguise has to function in natural lighting, it is logical to use only available light to photograph this biological phenomenon. Camouflaged animals at rest can be photographed using a long exposure with the camera supported on a tripod, but active animals, such as a tiger stalking its quarry through grass, will require a faster shutter speed and possibly a faster film. Mention has already been made of the way some animals conceal their body shadow; direct flashlight – unless very carefully positioned – will cast some body shadow, so it is not suitable for illustrating camouflage.

The angle of the light used to photograph animals with counter-shading is even more critical. If any uniformly-coloured object is lit from above, it will appear light above and dark below. When an eyed hawk-moth caterpillar stops feeding, it adopts a resting position, clinging with its false legs upside down beneath a willow branch. In this attitude, the available light first strikes the darker underside of the caterpillar and blends in with the paler upper side below. The camouflage is further enhanced by diagonal markings resembling leaf veins on each side of the body. If the caterpillar is inverted so that the paler upper side is uppermost, it immediately becomes conspicuous among the leaves. This dramatically demonstrates how important it is to

ensure that the subject is behaving naturally in its proper ecological context, before any photography is contemplated.

Many mid-water fish such as mackerel exhibit counter-shading with a dark back and a light stomach, but the upside-down catfish shows, like the hawk-moth caterpillar, reverse counter-shading with a dark stomach and a light back. It lives in central Congo streams, feeding upside-down on algae growing on leaves of water plants.

A classic example of the way in which natural selection arises from the interaction of the predator with its prey is demonstrated by the peppered moth. Before 1850, this moth was pale-coloured with dark speckles, merging perfectly with lichen-covered trunks. Then a black (or melanistic) form appeared in Manchester. Gradually, as atmospheric pollution blackened buildings and trees and all the lichens were killed, the proportion of black to pale forms increased. By 1900, 99 per cent of the peppered moths in Manchester were black. When large numbers of both forms were released in rural and industrial areas, it was found that the birds detected and ate more of the pale forms in the smoke-ridden areas, but more black forms in the country. Since the introduction of smokeless zones, the pale forms have begun to increase in industrial areas.

The obvious way of illustrating this graphic example of evolution in action for a biological textbook, is to use a picture of a pale lichen-covered trunk with both normal and melanistic forms of the moth. The odds

▲ **Subject:** Eyed hawk moth caterpillar (*Smerinthus ocellata*)
Location: Willow tree in Surrey, England
Month: August
Time: Morning
Lighting: Overcast
Lens: 55 mm micro-Nikkor
Film: Kodachrome 25

▲When resting, the eyed hawk moth caterpillar mimics the coloration (as well as the venation) of the willow leaves on which it feeds. Later in its life-cycle the mottled brown wings of the adult moth blend in with the bark of the tree trunks where it comes to rest.

of coming across this naturally in the wild are remote, so the only way to get a photograph is by attracting moths to light at night and transferring them to a suitable trunk for photography by day. Be sure to return the moths to a camouflaged background after photography.

Some animals go one step further in their disguise by mimicking natural objects such as twigs (stick insects), leaves (katydids and toads), thorns (plant hoppers) and even bird droppings (caterpillars and moths). Flat-topped winkles abound on sheltered rocky shores in Europe with copious brown seaweeds. Their shells are the same size as the air bladders on the bladder wrack and some are precisely the same colour. They can be photographed *in situ* only when the bladder wrack is exposed to the air.

If any indication has to be made to show the position of a camouflaged animal within a photograph, then surely both the animal and the photographer have succeeded in portraying camouflage to its limit?

Subject: Quaking aspens (*Populus tremuloides*)
Location: Dixie Forest, Utah, US
Month: January
Time: Afternoon
Lighting: Direct sun from side with polarizing filter
Lens: 50mm on Nikon
Film: Kodachrome 25

CHAPTER TWO

APPRECIATING LIGHT

The quality of light and the duration of its influence on the film emulsion is the basis of all aspects of conventional photography. The light level governs the choice of film speed, which in turn affects the quality of the final image. Static nature subjects such as landscapes and plants permit time for the careful appraisal of natural lighting so that the optimum moment can be selected. With action shots this is rarely possible, for lighting is then of secondary importance. When taking a localized scene or a close-up, the natural light can, if necessary, be modified or completely over-ridden by the judicious use of flash.

Natural light

Over the years, I have tended to use my flash less and less frequently as I developed a distinct preference for using natural light wherever possible when working on location. Only when it is impossible to take a picture by available light, do I resort to using flash (pp. 44–45). The reason for this change in approach is that I want my pictures to appear as natural as possible. This is particularly important when illustrating the way in which a camouflaged animal blends in with its surroundings (p. 28). Also, small lightweight flashguns may fit into a gadget bag very conveniently, but they are suitable only for taking close-up studies. Large professional flash units are practical if a vehicle can be driven close to the location site; otherwise I much prefer to carry another lens or more film when working in the field during the day.

When the available light is poor and using flash is impractical, fast films would seem to be the obvious solution, but most of the high-speed colour transparency films tend to give unnatural colours when used in dull light, as well as showing a pronounced grain. There is no point in me taking a picture with obvious grain, since this would be unsuitable for reproduction as a high-definition nature photograph.

Traditionally, professional nature photographers prefer using slow-speed films with fine or virtually no grain, notably Kodachrome 25 and 64. Adopting a slavish attitude to natural light and using slow-speed films can present problems, however, often necessitating the use of a tripod for static subjects and maybe missing out on an action shot. The recent introduction of Kodachrome Professional 200 has expanded the scope for action shots by low light, for this film has good colour saturation and surprisingly little grain, as can be seen by looking at the captions to pictures on pp. 39, 64 and 68.

Natural light varies with the time of day and the season. Getting to know and being able to predict the type of light which best suits the subject is an enormous help in achieving the desired picture. Photographers and artists who concentrate on landscapes look first and foremost at the quality of light; naturalists tend to spend much more time and thought on locating yet another species of plant or animal to add to their photographic collection than on critically appraising the lighting. Having found the desired subject, queries – such as 'is it a typical or perfect specimen?', 'does it stand out or blend in with its surroundings?', 'do the direction and type of lighting help to enhance or detract from the subject?' and 'would it look better from a different camera angle?' – should be instinctively posed and answered before you attempt to make a single exposure.

Early morning is a good time to look for birds or mammals in wilderness areas which are well endowed with boardwalks and hides and so tend to be frequently visited. Many a time I have risen before dawn and been rewarded with some good pictures lit in an exciting way, well before breakfast and before other visitors have begun to arrive on the scene.

An early morning winter visit I made to the Suwannee River in Florida was distinctly moody, with mist rising so thickly from the water I could not see any wildlife at all! As the mist gradually cleared, an egret flew in and began wading upriver to feed. I resisted the temptation of using my longest lens so the egret filled the frame; instead I waited until the bird stretched out its wings so that its curving neck and wings were lit along one side against the dark water. The boles and knee roots of the swamp cypress trees behind are also lit down one side.

There are also those unplanned shots where a dramatically lit subject will immediately catch my eye, and providing the light does not suddenly change, cannot fail to make an eye-catching picture.

Finding a subject and appraising the lighting are unfortunately not the sole factors involved in clinching a good picture. Selecting the focal length of the lens and determining the correct exposure, as well as selecting the appropriate shutter speed or aperture, are all vitally important. So often mistakes over one of these factors cause a disappointing picture. Through-the-lens (TTL) metering is both quicker and easier than using a hand-held meter for the vast majority of nature subjects. It is, however, important to know how the TTL meter works on your particular camera system, to avoid some incorrect exposures.

The correct exposure is achieved by using the right combination of shutter speed and aperture, or f-stop, for a given amount of light and a particular film speed or ISO rating. Most single lens reflex (SLR) cameras have a centre-weighted system which measures most of the light from the centre of the frame as well as taking into account light reflected from outside this area. Spot-measuring allows a reading to be made from within a defined central area. Many SLR cameras now offer the option of manual or automatic metering. There are great advan-

► **Subject:** Common egret (*Casmerodius albus*) **Location:** Swamp cypress grove at Manatee Springs State Park, Florida, US **Month:** January **Time:** Early morning **Lighting:** Low-angled oblique **Lens:** 250 mm, Hasselblad **Film:** Ektachrome 100

These pictures both illustrate how low-angled lighting can dramatically separate a subject from its surroundings.

◄ **Subject:** Bigelow cholla (*Opuntia bigelovoii*) **Location:** Joshua Tree National Monument, California, US **Month:** February **Time:** Late afternoon **Lighting:** Back **Lens:** 50 mm on Nikon **Film:** Kodachrome 25

tages in using automatic metering for action nature shots. With shutter priority cameras you select the desired shutter – say 1/250 second – and the camera will then automatically use the correct aperture for the film speed setting and amount of available light. If the maximum depth of field (p. 85) is important, aperture priority cameras allow the aperture to be selected and the appropriate shutter speed will be used. Some cameras have a multi-mode system allowing you the option of selecting whichever mode is most suitable for the particular subject. Still greater sophistication is available on a few cameras which provide the option of up to eight separate spot readings of the frame which can be averaged out by the

electronics contained within the camera.

Some cameras meter the light directly off the film (OTF). This method measures the light reflected from the film throughout the length of the exposure and has the advantage that it will react to the sun suddenly appearing from behind a cloud during a long exposure, by closing the shutter immediately the film has been correctly exposed.

Only by understanding your metering system will you be able to get consistently correct exposures for difficult shots, such as thin backlit subjects against a shadow background or sunlight shining through a few leaves viewed against the sky. Since the camera meter is calibrated to give a correct reading for an 18 per cent Kodak grey card,

highly reflective subjects (including snow and pale sand) filling most of the frame will be under-exposed, whereas large areas of shade will tend to be over-exposed. The solution is to open up one or two stops for pale subjects and close down a stop or two for dark subjects. Where the subject occupies only a small part of the frame, try to meter from a subject lit in the same light nearby. It does not matter if it is outside the picture area, providing the lens is not re-focused. If in doubt, it is worth bracketing the shot by adjusting the exposure by $\frac{1}{2}$-stop increments either side of the meter reading. After all, when you have spent time, effort and money tracking down an elusive subject, it is pointless being mean about film.

LIGHT AND SHADOW

Days when the sun shines and shadows are cast offer some marvellous opportunities for dramatic and imaginative lighting. Low-angled direct light from the side or back casts conspicuous shadows which repeat the shape of the subject. If a tall tree or rock rising out of pale-coloured ground is backlit, a shadow will be cast forward towards the camera and may make more impact than the tree or rock itself, whereas the shadow cast by front lighting extends behind the subject. Front lighting never gives any modelling to a subject and, when low-angled, may cause your shadow to impinge on a wide-angle shot.

A landscape will have a greater three-dimensional feeling if it is lit from the side so that long shadows are cast across it. In open habitats with hot climates, shadows cast by trees and buildings will provide welcome shade for animals to rest in during the heat of the day. This is particularly noticeable around midday during the dry season in the African savannah (pp. 60–1).

Large animals will themselves cast shadows which need to be considered in the composition of a picture. Since tall-necked animals (ostriches and giraffes, for example) cast elongated shadows early and late in the day, these animals can be fairly small in the frame. If they are lit obliquely from behind or in front, they can be positioned near one corner of the frame so their shadows run diagonally across it.

If shadows are to be featured in the picture, it is important to consider the most appropriate lens and camera angle as well as the framing. In a similar way to silhouettes (p. 36), shadows repeat and simplify shapes of plants and animals. A small plant growing on a sand dune takes on a completely different appearance when the leaf and stalk shadows appear beside it. Morning or afternoon light on aerial views looking down on to a flock of birds will show their shadows repeated on a unitoned background such as water, grass or pale soil.

Using light and shadow is an excellent technique for making a subject stand out from the background. For a few brief moments, as sunlight breaks through a stormy sky, trees appear spotlit against a threatening backdrop. Flowers and ferns will appear to glow if they are spotlit by sun against an unlit background. If both the plant and the background are lit up by the sun, a background shadow can be cast by an assistant holding up a strategically positioned coat or rug but keeping out of the field of view.

It is well worth looking at published nature photographs to see how other people have used light and shadow; not so you can mimic their pictures, but to make you think about the images which are particularly striking and why they arrest attention.

Shadows can help to emphasize the relief of geological features, especially when the rocks are of a uniform colour and tone. Strong cross-lighting helps define fissures,

▲ Subject: Sallylightfoot crab (*Grapsus grapsus*)
Location: Galápagos
Month: December
Time: Early evening
Lighting: Direct sun
lens: 105 mm micro-Nikkor
Film: Kodachrome 64

► Subject: Ripple pattern
Location: Gypsum sand dune at White Sands National Monument, New Mexico, US
Month: April
Time: End of day
Lighting: Oblique
Lens: 50 mm on Nikon
Film: Kodachrome 25

► Subject: Skink (*Mabuya wrightii*) basking
Location: Palm Forest on Cousin Island, Seychelles
Month: May
Time: Afternoon
Lighting: Dappled
Lens: 135 mm on Nikon
Film: Kodachrome 64

The crab and the skink illustrate how low-angled light, or a narrow beam of light, help to spotlight the subject against an unlit background.

tion of pointing the meter or camera and taking the reading. Since the amount of light reflected by subjects is so variable, hand-held meters and those in SLR cameras are calibrated so all the tones equate to a middle tone reflecting 18 per cent of the light shining on it. Thus a camera will want to expose a snowy landscape or a pale sky as a mid-tone and therefore tend to under-expose it.

When taking very dark or very pale subjects, many SLR cameras have a compensation dial. On the Nikon F3 this is graduated in one-third stop increments, allowing the film speed to be adjusted for extra-dark or pale subjects. The minus settings reduce the exposure and so apply to dark subjects, while the plus settings increase the exposure for pale subjects.

If a spotlit subject is surrounded by a large area of shadow, the camera will tend to give a low reading and a tendency to over-expose. I came across this situation when I visited Cousin Island in the Seychelles where skinks were basking in sun spots beneath trees. As the sun spots moved, so the cold-blooded reptiles moved with them. It was, therefore, important to show the localized sun spot and to resist the temptation to fill the frame with the reptile. By panning the camera round I managed to find a place where the sun was filtering through overhead leaves giving a middle-toned reading which I metered, and I used this exposure for the picture. There is nearly always some mid-toned subject nearby, but if there is not, a Kodak 18 per cent grey card or even the palm of your hand can be used instead. Before using your hand, it is important to check how much light it reflects compared to a mid-tone. For Caucasian skin, this is normally one stop more and so the reading will need to be increased by one stop.

If the available lighting does not show the desired features on a large-scale scene, there is no alternative but to return later in the day or even on another day. For close-range shots it is worth considering adding supplementary lighting. A reflector can help to ease unwanted shadows and the precise effect can be seen by looking through the camera. The effect of using a flash, on the other hand, has to be guessed, although a torch strapped on to a flash will help to indicate the direction of the light source and to avoid flare on the lens.

Some photographers argue that it is better to work early in the day if you wish to use long shadows, while others prefer the other end of the day. It is worth remembering that in the morning the shadows will be shortening all the time, whereas at the end of the day the shadows are increasing.

faults, folds and cross-bedding in rocks.

Ripples on a sandy beach or on sand dunes look nothing on a dull day or around midday in equatorial light, but low-angled grazed lighting from the sun throws the ripple pattern into three dimensions, as well as casting shadows of any grasses growing in the dunes.

When sunlight falls on a scene or a subject, it is absorbed or reflected to varying extents. Snow and pale sand act like a huge reflector bouncing the light skywards, whereas black basalt rocks or a dense coniferous forest reflect very little light. These extremes, with all the variations in between, affect the way we see and meter a scene. If both shadows and highlighted areas are included, a decision must be made about what parts should be correctly exposed. For instance, if detail is required in the dark areas – including shadows – it is necessary to expose correctly for the shadows; to avoid burning out the highlighted areas, it is necessary to expose correctly for the highlights. Sometimes the best solution is to take the average between the two, but this is invariably a compromise.

Judging the correct exposure for a scene with extremes of lighting is by no means straightforward, for it is not simply a ques-

BACKLIGHTING

Using natural backlighting can help to produce dramatic nature pictures as well as highlighting hairy or spiny subjects. The structure of both cacti and fine grasses are shown up to advantage by backlighting, so I aim to photograph them early or late in the day when the spines and hairs appear to glow against the dark background.

Determining the correct exposure for backlighting can be tricky, for if the camera is simply aimed at the subject, a false low reading will be obtained which will result in an over-exposed picture. My usual technique is either to walk round to the other side of the subject and meter the light reflected off it, making sure to use the same lens focused at the same distance as the final shot; or, in the case of the grasses, look for a similar-toned but broader subject which I can also meter from the sunlit side.

The shape of tree leaves as well as their venation pattern show well when lit from behind. Not only the leaf shape, but also the arrangement of the leaves around the finer branches – spiral, alternate or opposite – is distinct for each kind of tree. This avoids leaves overlapping so that they receive the maximum amount of sunlight possible. The leaf patterns, known as mosaics, make striking backlit subjects.

Young leaves of both deciduous and evergreen trees are translucent and appear to glow when photographed with the light shining through them. Leaves of deciduous trees become translucent again when they change colour in autumn. A medium long lens – such as 135 mm or 200 mm – is ideal for taking dramatic autumnal pictures of trans-illuminated leaves on high-level branches. Trees with low-hanging branches may not appear to offer any scope for this kind of photography, but a walk underneath the branches will often often reveal a spectacular shot of the leaves against the sky.

Seeds and fruits with fine white hairs, such as dandelion and milkweed, appear more striking when backlit. The contrast between the brightly lit seeds and the front of a milkweed pod can be reduced by using a small reflector – a piece of aluminium foil will do – to reflect some light forward.

Until I visited Sri Lanka with a Japanese film crew who were making a documentary about my work, I had never seen a live cobra. When we first saw it, clouds masked the sun, so I decided to wait until they passed, hoping I could photograph the cobra rimlit from behind. In fact, I was delighted to find the expanded hood was thin enough to allow the light to shine through it, thereby enhancing the distinctive pattern as well as the dark scales.

Solid subjects such as mammals, birds and trees can also be made to stand out from their background by lighting them from behind. There are two possible approaches. If the subjects cannot be silhouetted against the sky, it may be preferable to show them fairly small in relation to their surroundings, for if the light is then metered from the ground (remembering to open up a stop for snow or pale sand), the animals appear brightly rimlit. If, however, I want to meter the correct backlit exposure for animals, I obviously cannot walk round to the front of them, so I then turn round 180° and meter off a similar-toned frontlit subject. When animals on snow or pale sand are backlit, they may not always appear completely silhouetted, for quite a lot of light will be reflected off the ground on to their bodies.

If subjects are photographed against a light-toned or bright background – especially using extreme backlighting so they appear as solid black shapes – they are known as silhouettes. This name originated from a French government official, Étienne de Silhouette, who made portraits from cutting profiles out of black paper. This art is still practised in many parts of China, where a silhouetted portrait is produced in a matter of seconds. Photographic silhouettes are most dramatic when they are taken against a colourful sunrise or sunset. Indeed, skyline silhouettes are most frequently taken, but plants, birds and mammals also appear as equally striking silhouettes against brightly lit water.

Solitary trees or small groups of trees – especially if they are growing on raised

◀Subject: Cobra (*Cobra cobra*)
Location: Captive specimen, Sri Lanka
Month: May
Time: Afternoon
Lighting: Back
Lens: 105 mm on Nikon
Film: Kodachrome 64

▼Subject: Joshua trees (*Yucca brevifolia*)
Location: Joshua Tree National Monument, California, US
Month: February
Time: Sunset
Lighting: Back
Lens: 35 mm on Nikon
Film: Kodachrome 25

ground so they are viewed against a clear, uncluttered sky – work well as silhouettes. The branching pattern of deciduous trees is best appreciated in winter and a silhouette taken at this time of year provides all the information needed for identification. Tree fruits, especially large tropical ones such as the long pods of the flamboyant tree, also make good silhouette subjects.

To avoid the problem of flare when shooting against the light, make sure the sun's rays do not shine directly on to the lens by always using the correct-sized lens hood. A multi-coated haze or UV filter (p. 42) can also help to reduce flare. If the lens hood is not long enough for long focal length lenses, it can be extended simply by laying a hand level with the edge of the hood. If possible, try to shield the camera from the direct rays of the sun by moving it so that the sun is hidden behind a tree trunk or branch.

A low camera angle may help to isolate against the sky a tree which appears with a distant hill behind it in the normal viewing position. Mist can be useful for blotting out an unwanted background yet still revealing the shape of the tree.

Larger birds and mammals, either singly or in groups, can make effective silhouettes, notably animals with long necks (giraffes, ostriches and flamingoes) and also large carnivores such as leopard or lion gazing from a bare stone outcrop. Groups of animals standing in front of each other do not make good silhouettes, since it is unclear where one animal ends and another begins. However, a well-spaced line of giraffes or flamingoes (preferably not feeding with their necks down) can work well. Determining the correct exposure is easy for silhouettes: simply meter directly off the sky or water. This will ensure no surface detail is recorded of trunks, stems, fur or feathers. Long exposures may be needed at sunrise or sunset, which present no problems with static plants, but can result in a blurred image of a moving mammal or bird. The profile of these will be more easily recognized if the animal is standing side-on to the camera.

Some people argue that a silhouette is not a true nature picture, but merely a pictorial representation of a nature subject. But silhouettes are a natural (albeit short-lived)

▲ **Subject:** Great blue heron (*Ardea herodias*) in live oak
Location: Biddens Water, Florida, US
Month: April
Time: Evening
Lighting: Back
Lens: 200 mm on Nikon
Film: Kodachrome 64

▲ The tree above is festooned with epiphytic Spanish 'moss' – a familiar site on trees and telegraph lines in the wetter areas of the south-eastern United States.

way of viewing subjects in the field and they can be photographed without any gimmicky accessories. I believe photographic silhouettes work well for certain subjects and, indeed, can convey information most effectively by forcing the eye to focus on the shape instead of being distracted by the colour, form or texture.

Some Chinese photographers closely follow the style of traditional brush and ink paintings, using simple silhouettes of natural subjects such as cranes in cedar trees. The final effect may be achieved by using two or more negatives and building up the picture in the darkroom.

Diffused light

When a cloud passes over the sun, the nature of light reaching the earth changes dramatically. Most obviously, the sharply defined shadows from the sun's direct rays disappear, as do conspicuous reflections on water, shiny leaves and fruit. Instead, a soft even light shines from the whole sky, casting soft shadows or none at all. The colour temperature of light changes with the seasons and the time of day and it also varies between direct and indirect sunlight. This can often be detected by eye and, on a day when clouds are racing across the sky, it is easy to take the same landscape lit by bright sunlight one moment and by soft diffused light the next. The way in which the colours, as well as the modelling, change can then be compared at leisure.

Elsewhere in this chapter there are many pictures taken in direct light showing effective use of light and shadow, of silhouettes and backlighting. Although diffuse light may be much less dramatic, the softness is infinitely preferable for certain subjects, notably pale-coloured flowers. Misty conditions help to isolate trees from unsightly backgrounds, as well as providing atmospheric landscape pictures.

Haze – natural and man-made – diffuses sunlight. Dry haze is caused by dust, smoke (from aerial pollution or a forest fire) or sand mixing with the atmosphere. Often this results in a bluish cast to a scene, which may help to add atmosphere, but more often than not it detracts from the picture by restricting the vision. A UV filter can help to penetrate haze caused by pronounced ultraviolet light as occurs at the coast or on mountains.

Mist and fog form close to the ground when warm, moist air mixes with cold air. Fog can form in coastal areas of Britain throughout the year, whereas the fog that develops over lakes and rivers is associated with autumn and winter. At these times of year when the air temperature drops rapidly at night, the comparatively warm water visibly 'steams' early in the morning. This is a marvellous time to be out with a camera to get some moody scenics.

The reason why pictures appear soft and muted on misty days is that the water droplets in the atmosphere scatter light in all directions. Instead of the light being unidirectional, it falls on a subject from all directions. The thickness of the mist alters the whole mood of the picture. When a thick fog descends, the landscape is completely blotted out, except for subjects in the immediate foreground. This can be useful for obliterating unsightly buildings, pylons or power stations from an otherwise rural scene or eliminating distracting plants behind a dew-covered spider's web. To make the foreground as distinct as possible, the camera-to-subject distance needs to be minimal and so a wide-angle lens is more suitable for this kind of shot than a telephoto or even a standard lens.

A thin mist coupled with a thick cloud cover makes the scene look very flat, but if sun breaks through a thin mist, it immediately adds interest. Ancient stag-headed oak trees which have begun to die back appear even more sinister when seen looming out of the mist rather than viewed in full light on a bright sunny day.

Thin mist or haze over a series of hills or mountains – especially when viewed against the light at dusk or dawn – produces a

striking series of recession planes whereby the nearest hills are silhouetted and each line of hills beyond appears successively paler in tone with increased distance from the camera.

There are some high-elevation forests which are able to thrive in locations where little rain falls because sufficient moisture is gained from the persistent mist which blankets the hills. Providing no wind is blowing, photographing inside these mist or cloud forests is easier than inside a tropical rain forest with bright sun spots and shadows, because the correct exposure is much easier to judge with a more uniform lighting. The low light levels, however, will necessitate using a tripod to obtain crisp pictures. Using flash to light any subject in a misty situation ruins the natural effect of mist and so should be avoided at all costs.

A dust storm, a forest fire or an ash cloud from a volcanic eruption can suddenly transform a clear sunny day into a dull (and quite dark) one, as it did on 18 May 1980 when Mount St Helens, a volcano in the southwest of Washington state, erupted. As dawn

◄**Subject:** Stag-headed oak trees (*Quercus robur*)
Location: Bradgate Park, Leicestershire, England
Month: October
Time: Early morning
Lighting: Misty
Lens: 20 mm on Nikon
Film: Kodachrome 25

◄Some of the branches of these gnarled oak trees – planted several hundred years ago – are no longer living.

◄**Subject:** Mule deer (*Odocoileus hemionus*)
Location: Bryce, Canyon, Utah, US
Month: January
Time: Early morning
Lighting: Overcast
Lens: 300 mm on Nikon
Film: Kodachrome 200

Dull, overcast days need not preclude nature pictures from being taken. Providing the wind is not blowing and the subject is stationary, a long exposure – with the camera firmly supported – can be made when the light level is low.

►**Subject:** Beetle in cultivated cactus flower
Location: Wilpattu Park, Sri Lanka
Month: May
Time: Morning
Lighting: Overcast
Lens: 55 mm micro-Nikkor on Nikon
Film: Kodachrome 25

or a piece of white muslin. If you are working on your own and there are no convenient saplings to string the diffuser between, come prepared, having fixed a pair of bamboo canes to its sides. A vertical screen can then be erected by pushing the canes into the ground. The circular white diffusers available at good photographic shops can be held easily in one hand while taking a picture with the other, but you should be aware that they reduce the light transmitted through them considerably more than either trace or muslin.

When dark-coated mammals on snow-covered ground are lit by bright sunlight, they present too great a contrast for colour film to expose correctly, and compromises will have to be made. Soft diffused light reduces this problem, although a faster film speed may be required to ensure there is no subject blur.

The longer the focal length of a lens, the greater the working distance, so the light has to travel further to reach the film. It is therefore more likely to be scattered by dust or moisture. For this reason, the contrast of a photographic image may appear to decrease when using a long focus lens during certain atmospheric conditions.

broke the sky was clear, but after the early morning eruption ash from the huge ejected cloud began to settle and visibility was so bad in nearby towns that cars had to drive on full headlights. Working in such extreme conditions is highly hazardous to both photographer and camera. It is impossible to prevent the fine dust from penetrating a camera unless it is completely insulated, like the waterproof compacts and the Nikonos. When working in persistently dusty atmosphere, it is advisable to wear a gauze mask over the nose and mouth.

Atmospheric pollution, such as the renowned Los Angeles smog which hangs over the city for days on end, also reduces the amount of light reaching the ground. The effect is exacerbated by the temperature inversion when heat is lost during autumn and winter nights with clear skies and the ground cools beneath the warm layer above. During the day a clear cut-off can be seen between the haze below and the clear blue sky above. During the winter in China's capital, Beijing, coal bricks burnt for heating and cooking produce abundant

smoke which creates hazy conditions for long periods; for this reason film-makers tend to work in Yunnan province in southwest China, where the air remains clear.

Techniques used by commercial photographers for creating soft muted colours for scenics or outdoor portraits on a day when the sun is shining include breathing on the lens, smearing it with Vaseline and using a fog filter. None of these approaches in fact precisely simulates natural mist or fog because the subject nearest the camera is merely reproduced as a soft focus image; on a misty day it is the subjects further away which appear most indistinct.

A slightly overcast day is ideal for photographing white or pastel-coloured flowers to show the surface texture of petals. On sunny days, local areas of diffused light can be produced by using a diffuser to soften the direct light. The way in which the diffuser alters the nature of sunlight depends on its size, thickness and distance from the subject. You can make your own diffuser using either the white translucent trace sold off the roll at professional photographic dealers

LOW-LIGHT PHOTOGRAPHY

When working early or late in the day (pp. 112–115), on overcast days or in dark habitats (such as forests and caves), the level of light is low. For static subjects, long exposures will be possible even with slow-speed film, providing a steady tripod is used; moving subjects will usually require either fast films or flash (p. 44). If soft blurred lines of movement are desired for cascading water, natural dull light is a positive advantage for ensuring the $\frac{1}{2}$ or 1 second exposure required (p. 21). In low light a camera with internal illumination for the viewfinder will be invaluable, otherwise a torch may be needed to read the exposure.

For taking long exposures, the camera must have several essential features. The range of shutter speeds needs to include at least $\frac{1}{4}$, $\frac{1}{2}$ and 1 second exposures – prefer-

ably longer. Exposures of several seconds can be made using the bulb (B) setting to open the shutter with a locking cable release. The shutter is closed by unlocking the release. The longest exposure I have ever made was 8 *hours* for recording the bioluminescence of honey fungus mycelium (p. 118). Cameras with a time (T) setting do not require a locking cable release, for the shutter is opened when the shutter release button is first depressed and closed when it is depressed again. Long exposures are a big drain on the batteries of electronic cameras, but the mechanical (T) setting uses no power at all.

Even if a cable release is used for releasing the shutter, the rising mirror can cause vibrations. It is therefore preferable to lock up the mirror prior to taking a long expo-

sure, to eliminate any chance of camera shake, particularly with a long focus lens.

It is no good taking all these precautions, however, unless the camera is rigidly supported. Extending the legs on a lightweight table-top tripod so they wobble in the slightest breeze is a complete waste of time. Full-sized tripods with a short centre column are good for low-level work, but I use the versatile British-made Benbo. The unique design allows each leg, as well as the centre column, to be angled and locked into any position.

Unlike flowering plants, fungi contain no chlorophyll and so do not need sunlight to photosynthesize. Invariably they are found growing in dark places where available light photography without a tripod is impractical. Direct flash photography is not to be recommended, since a brightly lit fungus looming out of a nocturnal-looking background is unnatural. Flash can be used to advantage, however, either by being bounced off a flash umbrella or by being balanced with available light so that the background colours are correctly exposed. Even then, care has to be taken not to get distracting highlights reflected off wet caps or leaves.

The most natural-looking pictures of fungi are those taken by available light, with a reflector to boost the light on the underside of the cap or bracket. Since small apertures are essential for gaining the maximum depth of field, and slow speed film is necessary for sharp grain-free images, exposures of several seconds will be needed when working in many woodlands.

When film is exposed for more than a second, the normal relationship between shutter speed and aperture no longer applies, because the film becomes less sensitive to light at very long (and also very short) exposures. Allowance must therefore be given for this reciprocity failure by exposing the film for longer than indicated. For example, using Kodachrome 25, a calculated 4-second exposure should in reality be nearer 6 seconds. Until you are familiar with the effects of using long exposures on the film of your choice, it is probably worth experimenting and keeping careful notes for each subject, its length of exposure and

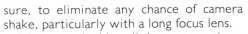

◀**Subject:** Bracket fungus (*Coriolus versocolor*) on mossy stump
Location: Yarner Wood, Devon, England
Month: November
Time: Morning
Lighting: Overcast
Lens: 50 mm on Nikon
Film: Kodachrome 25

◀**Subject:** Papoose Room Cavern
Location: Carlsbad Caverns, New Mexico, US
Month: March
Lighting: Artificial   20 second exposure
Lens: 20 mm on Nikon
Film: Kodachrome 64

◀Cave photography is a particularly challenging aspect of low-light photography. Only the larger cave systems open to the public will be lit with a continuous light source: elsewhere lights or flash will have to be brought in to get any pictures at all.

◄**Subject:** Stream in winter spate
Location: Islay, Scotland
Month: January
Time: Afternoon
Lighting: Overcast
Lens: 50 mm, Hasselblad
Film: Ektachrome 64

◄This picture of a peaty stream shows virtually the entire area of the square format. Notice how the colourless sky has been almost completely excluded.

be taken without using some form of artificial lighting. Extensive cave systems which are open to the public and lit by continuous lights can be photographed by using long exposures with the camera on a tripod. The subdued lighting system installed in the Carlsbad Caverns, New Mexico, in 1976 not only enhances the beauty of the cave system, but also avoids raising the temperature excessively and thereby drying out of the caves.

The imaginative backlighting at Carlsbad offers good opportunities for taking some exciting pictures using a variety of lenses. For showing details of stalactites, a medium telephoto such as 85 mm is useful, whereas for the larger set pieces, such as stalactites reflected in the Green Lake and the Papoose Room, wide-angles of 35 mm or even 20 mm will be needed. Exposures as long as half a minute with Kodachrome 64 may be needed to allow for reciprocity failure. Since the lighting is not natural, it is debatable what the 'correct' colour balance should look like.

In some cave systems, completely artificial lighting is used, as for example in the Reed Flute Cave near Guilin in China. In one area a whole galaxy of colours – blue, red and green – is switched on in succession. In another part, where a photographer takes visitors against a spectacular formation, a light is switched on for 3 seconds and it is possible to utilize this light (without people) to take a 2-second exposure.

In unlit caves, pictures will have to be taken using flash. A single flash mounted directly on the camera is far from ideal since it may well result in distracting highlights appearing on wet surfaces. A more creative approach is to set up the camera on a tripod and use the open flash technique. The camera shutter is opened using a locking cable release and a flash (which can be fired manually using an open flash button) is used remote from the camera. Keeping the shutter open, make sure not to shine a torch directly into the camera lens and fire off the flash from different positions around the cave. Alternatively, multiple flashes can be strategically positioned to be fired simultaneously using slave units. Either way, painting a scene with light takes time, but the results make it well worth the effort.

the amount of extension used for a close-up. Another problem associated with reciprocity failure when using colour film is that the colour balance tends to shift. I find this is barely detectable with a yellow fungus on Kodachrome 25, but green mosses and ferns tend to show a bluish cast, which is even more pronounced on wet leaves taken with Ektachrome.

When stalking crepuscular animals active only at dawn and dusk, a fast film may be required to allow a fast shutter speed to be used. On dull days I therefore always carry one camera body loaded with Kodachrome 200 for such contingencies. If you are using any E6 processed film – including Ektachrome, Fujichrome and Agfachrome – it is possible to 'push' these films by rating them to a higher speed than normal. For example, Ektachrome 100 can be double-rated to ISO 200/24° or triple-rated to ISO 400/27°. Once the decision has been made to uprate the film, the whole film has to be exposed at the higher speed. The processing laboratory must be notified about this speed change so

the film can be correctly processed – this will usually involve a surcharge. Uprating a film is not to be recommended as standard practice for nature photography, since it will result in an increase in grain, although I have pushed Ektachrome 100 to ISO 200/24° on many occasions and barely noticed the difference. Excessive 'pushing' may also result in an incorrect colour balance, and as there are lots of high-speed films now available on the market it is preferable to use one of these instead. Ektachrome P800/1600 Professional film has an emulsion especially designed for low-light photography and to be 'push-processed' with optional speeds of ISO 400/27°, 800/30°, 1600/33° or even 3200/36°. All these speeds are clearly printed on the film cassette, for marking before use for correct exposure and later processing. It is not possible to uprate any Kodachrome films.

Apart from the entrance to a cave, which can be used as a silhouetted frame to an outward view, the available light in this habitat is so poor that no photographs can

USING FILTERS

A filter alters the nature of light reaching the film. This change may be almost imperceptible and there will be no need to alter the exposure from the unfiltered picture, or it may be dramatically different and require an exposure increase of several stops. Since the aim of all bona fide nature and wildlife photographers is to record their subjects as naturally as possible, filters should be used with discretion to balance light, and to remove haze or flare or unwanted reflections.

Filters are usually placed in front of the lens, but long lenses with a large front diameter often have a filter mount at the rear of the lens. Gelatin filters, although cheap, are easily damaged – by fingerprints and water – so they are best used in a special gel filter holder which screws into the front of the lens. Before going to the expense of buying a glass filter, it can be useful to experiment using a gel of the same type to see the effect it produces.

Glass filters, which also screw directly into the lens, are much more robust but, like lenses, will get scratched if misused. Step-up and step-down rings allow them to be used on different diameter lenses. Plastic filters are available as part of a universal filter system which makes it possible to use a single filter on different diameter lenses, simply by using an adaptor ring. Cokin and Hoyarex both produce these systems, consisting of an adaptor ring which screws into the front of the camera lens, a filter holder, the filter and, if required, a filter hood. Plastic, although more permanent than gelatin, will scratch more easily than glass but, being relatively inexpensive, these filters can easily be replaced.

When using colour film in the field, skylight, ultraviolet (UV), polarizing, neutral density, gradual colour and a few pale-coloured, light-balancing filters are most useful. A skylight IB filter balances natural light on coastal or mountain scenery by removing a bluish cast in open shade when the sky is clear. A UV filter absorbs the ultraviolet rays which can cause a distorted hazy image. Both these filters are usually multi-coated to reduce flare and ghost images. They also help to protect a lens against corrosive salt spray at the coast.

Under certain lighting conditions, a polarizing filter is particularly useful for both nature and landscape photographers. It can be used (for both colour and black-and-white film) to increase the contrast between blue sky and white clouds, providing the camera is used at right angles to the sun. A pola filter will also remove reflections from non-metallic surfaces such as water, leaves and glass.

Comparison of the pair of pictures of water-lily leaves taken with and without a polarizing filter shows the dramatic transformation. Providing the camera is used at an angle of 30°–40° to the water surface and the maximum polarization is used, the silver skylight reflection disappears and the colours of both the floating and submerged leaves are enriched. This technique is particularly useful for taking underwater life in shallow water ponds, streams and rock pools with a calm surface.

On land, a pola filter also enriches the colour of leaves and shiny fruits by removing skylight reflections. When photographing through glass-fronted enclosures, as at zoos and public aquaria, a polarizing filter can help to remove unwanted reflections on the glass. The main disadvantage of this filter, however, is that, when it is used fully polarized, it will reduce the exposure by $1\frac{1}{2}$ to 2 stops, which may be a problem when using slow-speed film and taking shots of moving subjects.

The effect of using a polarizing filter can be seen by slowly rotating it in front of the eye. This preliminary is essential when using a non-SLR camera (such as a Hasselblad Superwide): the orientation of the filter at the maximum polarization is noted by a letter on top of the lens mount, or by scratching a mark on the outside of the mount, so the filter can be positioned correctly on the camera lens.

The majority of polarizing filters used today are linear, which allow only linear light rays to pass through. Circular pola filters (allowing the passage of circular rays) were previously used to counteract incorrect exposures resulting from light being partially polarized on TTL cameras with a fixed mirror.

If a polarizing filter is used on a wide-angle lens of 24mm or more, it will not darken the sky evenly across the frame. The fall-off in intensity furthest from the sun can be seen by eye when looking through an SLR camera.

Neutral density filters reduce the overall light reaching the film plane. Grey in colour, they are available in a variety of strengths, with the darkest filter cutting out the most light. The prime use of a neutral density

◀**Subject:** Water lily pads
Location: Pond in Jardin Botanico, Oporto, Portugal
Month: March
Time of day: Morning
Lighting: Overcast
Lens: 105 mm micro-Nikkor on Nikon
Film: Kodachrome 25

▶Here the camera was kept in the same position as for the above picture, but this time a polarizing filter was placed over the lens so as to remove the skylight reflections and enrich the colour of the lily pads.

filter for nature photography is to reduce the film speed so that a slow shutter speed can be used as, for example, when taking moving water. They will also reduce the depth of field, but the aim of most nature photographers is invariably to gain as much depth of field as possible. The effect of using two polarizing filters and rotating each independently is to form a variable neutral density filter. Such a filter is used for fading out scenes on movie cameras and is known as a pol-fader.

As the name suggests, a graduated (or gradual) filter gently fades the coloured strip into the rest of the transparent filter. This gives a much more natural appearance to the colour zone than the abrupt change from colour to no colour on a half-colour filter. When taking landscapes with colourless skies it is impossible to get a correct exposure for both the highly reflective sky and the less reflective land. There are two solutions: either crop the sky completely out of the picture, or use a graduated filter to reduce the contrast between sky and land. The most natural-looking filters are gradual grey and gradual blue; the tobacco and magenta filters so popular in advertising for producing 'special effects' are highly unnatural and are not to be recommended for natural history work.

Graduated filters are square and, since they are part of a universal system – unlike screw-in glass filters – the extent of the colour in the frame can be adjusted simply by moving the filter up or down in its mount. Care should, however, be taken not to move the filter so high that the bottom edge cuts across the frame. This problem can be avoided by attaching a step-up filter holder to the front of the lens, thereby using a slightly larger filter.

On days when the cloud cover is complete, the indirect sunlight tends to give a blue cast. Warmer colours can be produced on colour film by using one of the 81 series of light-balancing filters. Known as warming filters, they are straw-coloured and are readily available in three strengths – 81A, 81B or 81C: the 81A, being the palest, produces the least amount of correction, while 81C gives the most. These filters will, of course, warm up winter scenes, but this is not to be recommended since they will then look unnaturally warm!

More colour film is probably wasted on striving to produce blue flowers as an authentic blue than on any other natural subject. The reason why many blue flowers appear pink or magenta on colour film is that they reflect red and infra-red wavelengths at the far end of the spectrum, which our eyes are barely able to detect, but which are recorded on colour film.

I have found that if a blue flower fills the frame with few or no green leaves, a pale-blue colour correcting (CC) filter such as a CC20B or CC30B will help to produce a truer blue. When taking multi-coloured flowers, the blue filter is clearly not suitable. Kodak recommends a filter pack of its Wratten gelatin filters for counteracting the pink cast. The pack consists of numbers 66 (very pale green), 85B (amber), CC50M and CC20M (both magenta), but the increase in exposure is six stops!

▲ **Subject:** Teddybear cholla cacti – graduated grey filter across sky
Location: Joshua National Monument, California, US
Month: January
Time of day: Afternoon
Lighting: Overcast
Lens: 50 mm on Nikon
Film: Kodachrome 25

▲ I find a neutral density or a grey gradual filter gives the most natural colour to a cloudless sky in a natural scene. Any other colour immediately looks erroneous and resembles the style of advertising shot which often has a tobacco-coloured strip across the sky.

FLASH

The art of using flash during the day in the field is to produce a picture which does not appear to be obviously flashlit. Lighting with flash is rarely fully understood, yet with care flash can be more than a means of simply illuminating a poorly lit subject; it can be very creative.

Even though the extremely fast films now available make it possible to take pictures in very poor light, flash will ensure better definition by allowing fine-grain, slow-speed films to be used. Most obviously, flash is used to illuminate a dark location such as a narrow crevice, a cave or a forest; to photograph nocturnal life (p. 116); to arrest fast movements; to increase the depth of field for close-ups; and to boost the available light in the foreground of a synchro-sunlit shot (see below).

During the last decade, the size and weight of electronic flashguns have considerably diminished, and this has aided the field photographer who may have to carry equipment for some distance. The limited power of very small flashes, however, makes them practical only for close-ups (p. 92) or for providing a catchlight to enliven dark eyes.

The trend of camera manufacturers has been to produce cheaper SLR models which have only a hot-shoe to connect a flash to the camera; this precludes any possibility of creative lighting with the front-directed flash-on-camera. Also, if a front flash is used to light a mammal looking straight at the camera, it will be reflected off the retina at the back of the mammal's eye, resulting in the phenomenon know as 'red-eye'. The solution is to use a hot-shoe synchronization (sync) cord and move the flash off to one side of the camera.

When flash is used for taking active subjects, pictures will be lost if time is spent deciding where to position it. If both camera and flash are attached to a right-angle flash bracket (p. 70) they can be carried around as a single unit.

A single side flash will give better modelling than a front flash, but it may cast unwanted heavy shadows. When taking static subjects, the photographer can soften these shadows by using a reflector, by bouncing the flash off a silver umbrella (p. 138) or by using a second flash on the opposite side from the main one. Multiple flash heads are fired simultaneously either by linking each directly to the camera via a flash extension lead and a multiple flash connector; or by using a single flash linked to the camera and attaching a photosensitive slave unit to each of the additional flash heads.

If electronic flash is frequently used in the field, it will be worth acquiring recharge-able batteries. Although initially more expensive, powering a flash by a rechargeable nickel cadmium battery pack will give a faster re-cycling time, and often more flashes, than disposable batteries. Separate rechargeable packs (which can be hooked on to a waist belt) are available for medium-sized flashguns that do not have their own rechargeable packs.

Top-of-the-range medium-sized guns have facilities such as a tilting head, a zoom head, a diffuser and variable power settings. A tilting head allows the flash to be bounced off a reflector or a flash umbrella, while a zoom head allows the angle of light to be adjusted for use with a wide-angle, a standard or a medium telephoto lens. A variable power setting allows the output of the flash to be reduced; at the same time the speed of the flash is increased (p. 108).

Computerized flashguns with a built-in sensor may not always give a correct exposure for, with the exception of models with a zoom head, they make no allowance for the focal length of the lens. The recent development of dedicated flash allows precise TTL metering off the film plane (OTF). The sensor inside the camera quenches the flash when the film has received enough light, reflected off the subject. Providing the correct auto TTL connectors for your system are employed, multiple flash heads can be used with an OTF system.

If an event you are photographing is short

▶ The dense undergrowth enabled me to take this picture of a marsh tit returning to its nest with food, without a hide. All I had to do was string up a camouflage net between trees.

The clarity and depth of field of these pictures have been enhanced by the use of flash, for they were all taken with slow speed film in poor available light.

▲ **Subject:** Snakelocks anemonies (*Anemonia sulcata*)
Location: Rock pool, Isle of Wight, England
Month: March
Time: Morning, low tide
Lighting: Direct flash
Lens: 55 mm micro-Nikkor on Nikon
Film: Kodachrome 25

▲ Special care must be taken when using flash systems in a marine environment. Since sea water is so highly corrosive, it is a wise precaution to cover the connection between the flash sync cord and an extension with protective tape.

lived and may not happen again for another year, it can be reassuring to check the flash exposure with a flash meter. This can also be done using a Polaroid back on medium-format cameras, which has the added advantage of allowing the photographer to see the precise position of shadows or of flash reflections on wet or shiny surfaces and to make adjustments where necessary.

When flash is used as the prime light source in the field, it will override the daylight, producing a black distant background. This problem will not arise when photographing directly on to the ground since the background is virtually in the same plane as the subject. A nocturnal-looking background can be avoided, however, by balancing the flash with the available light. Some cameras have a metering system which ensures that the flashlit foreground is perfectly balanced with the background. If flash is to be used creatively off the camera, this synchro-sunlight technique is appropriate only for static subjects such as plants and rocks, or for animals which are guaranteed to return to a fixed place such as a perch

beside a bird's nest, a drinking place or a baited spot.

When using non-dedicated flash, first meter the ambient light and select the desired aperture, making sure the shutter speed it couples with is practical to use with a focal-plane shutter. Then divide the guide number (GN) for the particular flash and film speed by the chosen aperture, to determine the flash-to-subject distance which will give the same light intensity as the daylight. For example, using a flash with a GN of 128/40 (feet/metres) and an aperture of f16, the distance will be 8 feet/2.5 metres. With sky as the background, it may be preferable to under-expose it by using a slightly faster shutter speed, yet keeping the aperture constant.

To avoid a ghost image, caused by the subject moving after the flash has been fired, use the fastest shutter speed which will allow a focal plane shutter to synchronize with flash. Many 35 mm SLR cameras synchronize at 1/250 second, but the Hasselblad Compur shutters synchronize at any speed up to 1/500 of a second. The Olympus full-synchro flash F280 synchronizes at all focal plane shutter speeds.

When flash is combined with dappled sunlight, there is a tendency to over-expose the sunspots, so it is prudent to bracket the flash expose in these circumstances by under-exposing by $\frac{1}{2}$ and 1 stop.

Even the smallest of flashguns can add a catchlight to the dark eye of a bird or mammal on a dull day without affecting the available light exposure; for there is nothing so lifeless as a dark eye lacking any sparkle surrounded by dark feathers or fur.

Specialized flash techniques covered elsewhere include ring flash (p. 139) and high-speed flash (p. 108).

Subject: Marbled godwit
(*Limosa fedoa*)
Location: Muir Beach,
California, US
Month: February
Time: Afternoon
Lighting: Overcast
Lens: 400mm on Nikon
Film: Kodachrome 64

CHAPTER THREE

USING LONG LENSES

A long lens alters the perspective by which we normally view a subject, because it takes in a narrow angle of view. Usually, the prime reason for a nature photographer to use such a lens is to increase the image size of a timid animal, but another important use is to separate the subject – be it an animal or a plant – from its background or to exclude unwanted elements of the scene. By using a long lens in a hide, it is possible to get even closer to a wary animal than by stalking. However, when a camera is fitted with a long lens, it is far more prone to camera shake, so a firm support is even more important.

PLANTS AND LANDSCAPES

Long lenses are invariably associated with the photography of wary birds and mammals, but their use should not be regarded as exclusive to these subjects. I find a medium long focus lens (135 mm or 200 mm) invaluable for photographing certain plants – for example, when taking subjects which are too high up to allow a reasonable-sized image with a standard lens – or when locations of plants or geological features are too dangerous for close access on foot.

Any slight camera shake is magnified when using a long lens; if it is impossible to use a tripod or monopod to steady the camera, blur can be reduced by using a fast shutter speed. A useful rule-of-thumb guide for gauging the slowest shutter speed to use when hand holding a camera with a long lens, is to choose the one nearest to the reciprocal of the focal length of the lens. Thus when using a 250 mm lens, the shutter speed should be 1/250 second, but when using a 105 mm or a 135 mm lens, the exposure time can be lengthened to 1/125 second, and so on.

When a long lens is used to photograph plants or landscapes, there will usually be time to set up the camera on a tripod. If the light is rapidly changing, however, it may be necessary to hand hold the camera supported by either a shoulder pod (p. 137) or a bean bag or Tri-bag (p. 136) on a convenient rock or the branch of a nearby tree.

Parts of trees are good examples of subjects often impractical for taking with a standard lens. Most obviously, these may be flowers, fruit or leaves, but parasitic or epiphytic plants growing high up among branches can be even more inaccessible. Using a long lens helps to bring out shape, colour and texture to better advantage.

When using a standard lens to photograph parts of trees there is a natural tendency to position yourself at the shortest possible working distance by standing directly beneath whatever you are taking. *Dombeya cacuminum*, a native of Madagascar, is one of the few trees with flowers that open out towards the ground; they are therefore best taken by standing directly beneath them – particularly if an overhead sun shines through the leaves and petals so they appear to glow. Normally, with flowers that open upwards, it is better to stand further back and to use a longer lens so the lower angle of elevation gives a side profile of the flower. When a tree's flowers or fruits are produced on the ends of branches they can be taken with a long lens against a sky backcloth. If the camera is at right angles to the sun, the intensity of a blue sky can be increased by using a polarizing filter. This is particularly effective when

taking white or pink magnolia flowers before the stark branches of deciduous forms leaf out.

The striking flowers of even a relatively common tree such as horse chestnut can seldom be seen at close range from ground level – especially when stock have maintained a high browsing line. The increased image size gained by using a long lens, however, reveals the exquisite details of each individual flower.

While many tropical trees flower at the extremity of their branches, others bear their flowers and fruits directly on the trunk. The cannonball tree from tropical South America has large showy flowers which open early in the evening and fall the following morning; from these develop hard, 15–20 cm (6–8 inch) cannonball fruits. Both the flowers and the fruit make excellent long lens subjects.

In urban environments, opportunist annuals and perennials often grow high up on ruined buildings. It is worth looking for an elevated viewpoint, such as a bridge or a building, so these plants can be taken on

their own level with an obvious urban background of either traffic or high-rise buildings. Details of urban trees can also be taken in the same way; for example, the flowers and fruits of plane trees bordering the River Thames in London can be taken with a 200 mm lens from bridges spanning the river.

Emergent aquatic plants which cannot be reached by boat or by wading can be taken from the water's edge using a long lens. Firm ground will also support the camera on a tripod better than a rocking boat. When I am hiking long distances I usually leave binoculars behind in preference to carrying another lens and I then use a 300 mm or a 400 mm lens for searching out and photographing plants on inaccessible mountain ledges, unstable scree slopes or slippery rock.

Using a wide-angle lens is the obvious way of recording a broad landscape, but then a large expanse of sky is also likely to be included. A long lens can produce more powerful images than the 46° angle of view of a standard lens by narrowing the perspec-

◄ **Subject:** Flowers of *Dombeya cacuminum*, a Madagascan tree
Location: San Diego Zoo, US
Month: February
Time: Morning
Lighting: Trans-illuminated direct sun
Lens: 85 mm on Nikon
Film: Kodachrome 200

◄ The detailed structure of tree flowers – often high above eye level – can be much better appreciated by photographing them with a long focus lens. A firm camera support is every bit as essential for taking these flowers as when taking close-ups at ground level.

strata or as inclined cross-bedded planes. The continual action of rain water on limestone rock produces intriguing, naturally weathered, sculptured forms as can be seen in China's Stone Forest in Yunnan Province as well as in Utah's Bryce Canyon, where frost action in extreme winter conditions accelerates the erosion.

Unstable and inhospitable landscapes which are unsafe to approach at close range on foot – such as those created by volcanic or geothermal activity – are examples of cases where a long lens is obligatory. Avoiding erupting red-hot lava is an equally obvious example, but even less dangerous thermal features, such as fumaroles, mud pools and sulphur vents, often require a long lens to do them justice.

At the opposite temperature extreme are glaciers, which cannot easily be traversed without using specialized gear. When working in Iceland, I often used a 400 mm lens for revealing details of the surface as well as the snout of a glacier.

◄**Subject:** Willow growing among weathered limestone rock formations
Location: Stone Forest, Yunnan, China
Month: March
Time: Late afternoon
Lighting: Back
Lens: 135 mm on Nikon
Film: Kodachrome 25

▼**Subject:** Fruit of cannonball tree (*Couroupita guianensis*)
Location: Foster Gardens, Ohau, Hawaii
Month: January
Time: Morning
Lighting: Top
Lens: 250 mm on Hasselblad
Film: Ektachrome 64

tive. When we view a landscape with our eyes, we take in an angle of view similar to that of a standard lens, but by using a 200 mm lens on a 35 mm format the angle of view is reduced to 12°, and with a 400 mm lens it is reduced still further, to 6°.

Long lenses focused on a broad vista offer lots of picture opportunities – both horizontal and vertical – by dissecting the landscape and making the eye focus on a selected portion. Among the many large-scale patterns I have taken are ice floes moving down a river, braided streams criss-crossing over broad flood plains in Iceland, a succession of hills with snow on one aspect, and a mosaic of deciduous trees and conifers (p. 18). Long lenses are especially useful for highlighting patterns and textures in the geological landscape; for example, where sedimentary layers are laid down as multi-coloured

SEABIRDS

Seabird colonies offer excellent opportunities for tackling all aspects of bird photography – birds in their habitat, groups of birds, birds on the nest, courtship behaviour, mating, preening, adults feeding their young and flight shots. With good weather and plenty of film, it is possible to expose many rolls in a single day.

The most extensive colonies develop in places where they are least disturbed – either on offshore islands or precipitous cliffs and stacks. The techniques used for taking animals in their habitat are described on pp. 16–17. If you are taking a boat trip out to an offshore island, be ready to get some pictures showing the distribution and density of bird nests on vertical seaward-facing cliffs. Although the cliffs are static, movement from the boat, as well as the birds flying past the cliffs, means that an exposure of at least 1/250 second will be needed but an extra-long lens certainly will not be necessary and a standard lens may suffice. The colour of the rocks on which the seabirds choose to nest, as well as lichens or sea flowers, can add additional interest to a habitat or a nest picture. Many seabird colonies occur on the old red sandstone rocks on the south-west coast of Wales and on the outlying islands.

A boat will also give closer access to seabirds on the water. The auks – razorbills, guillemots and puffins – typically raft along on the water and for this reason are particularly susceptible to the hazards of oil pollution in coastal waters.

Each kind of seabird tends to favour slightly different specifications for its nest site. Kittiwakes often nest on very narrow ledges of precipitous cliffs, for they can build their substantial nest out over the rock ledge. They will also utilize window ledges of warehouses fronting on to tidal water. Guillemots nest on ledges of vertical cliffs as well as on offshore stacks. Northern gannets do nest on cliff ledges, but large-scale gannetries develop on flattish islands such as Grassholm off the South Wales coast.

The first things you notice when approaching a seabird colony are the noise and the smell, but these initially powerful impressions soon begin to pale into insignificance with the excitement of seeing so many birds at close quarters. When the adults are incubating their eggs, care must be taken not to get so close that the birds desert their nests. Increasing intrusion by selfish and thoughtless photographers has resulted in access being restricted on some British island reserves until after the chicks have hatched. Repeated disturbance by visitors among some Antarctic penguin colonies has resulted either in the penguins deserting their eggs which the skuas then attack or in the birds failing to lay.

When approaching a tern colony, great care must be taken to carry a stick (or a monopod) above your head so that it is protected from injury as a result of dive-bombing birds.

Before attempting portrait studies, it is worth using a standard (or even a wide-angle) lens to show the extent of the nesting colony and, in a gannetry, the even distribution of the nests. With care, however, many nesting seabirds can be approached close enough for portrait studies to be taken of one or two birds without using a hide or any form of cover.

The best behavioural studies will be taken by sitting down quietly and using a long-focus lens – supported either on a monopod or a shoulder pod – to isolate one or two nests. A zoom lens can be a great help in framing the picture exactly as you want it. In a dense colony such as a gannetry, the main problem associated with portrait shots is getting a clear image without lots of birds behind. Sometimes, when the birds are nesting on a ledge, the sea, beach or sky can be used as a contrasting background; otherwise differential focus will help to isolate foreground birds from the background.

Many seabirds such as gulls, gannets and tropic-birds, have white or cream bodies. On sunny days details of feather texture may be lost in the bright light. Portraits of birds with dark eyes set in dark plumage – such as white-fronted terns, guillemots and razorbills – need to have a catchlight in their eye (either from the sun or a small flash) to

◄**Subject:** Puffins (*Fratercula arctica*)
Location: Cliffs at Reynishnerfi near Vik, Iceland
Month: July
Time: Afternoon
Lighting: Overcast
Lens: 350 mm on Hasselblad
Film: Ektachrome 64

▲**Subject:** Red-tailed tropicbird (*Phaethon rubricaudus*) nesting
Location: Round Island, Mauritius
Month: April
Time: Morning
Lighting: Indirect
Lens: 150 mm on Hasselblad
Film: Ektachrome 64

◀**Subject:** Blue-footed booby (*Sula nebouxii*) sky pointing
Location: Española (Hood) Island, Galápagos
Month: December
Time: Afternoon
Lighting: Diffuse
Lens: 135 mm on Nikon
Film: Kodachrome X (ISO 64/19°)

▲**Subject:** Masked booby (*Sula dactylatra*) with chick
Location: Española (Hood) Island, Galápagos
Month: December
Time: Afternoon
Lighting: Diffuse
Lens: 150 mm on Hasselblad
Film: Ektachrome 64

convey its position. The plumage of all seabirds is in prime condition at the beginning of the breeding season.

Gannets provide plenty of interesting behavioural studies for the photographer. These include plunge-diving to feed, aggressive lunging attacks with outstretched bill on a neighbour, diving on an opponent from the air, playful neck biting of a mate, and mates greeting by facing each other and fencing with their bills outstretched towards the sky. Boobies are closely related to gannets and they will also sky-point. The blue-footed booby performs a comical dance displaying its blue feet to its mate.

Birds such as puffins and shearwaters which nest in burrows underground make the surface very friable and it is all too easy to collapse the burrows by walking over a colony. It is therefore important to stick to well-worn paths. With a 300 mm or 400 mm lens it is possible to take portraits of puffins arriving at the nest hole with a beakful of neatly arranged sand eels, or flying towards the land with their wings and webbed feet outstretched.

Taking portrait studies of birds in colonies which are used by scientists for research can be a problem, since many of the birds will be marked with coloured rings which may appear more conspicuous than the bird's own coloration. For aesthetic-looking pictures, try to avoid taking ringed birds.

The constant movement of birds back and forth as they leave their nests to feed provides lots of scope for flight photography (p. 54). It is worth spending time carefully watching to determine the direction in which birds take off from, and return to, their nest. After appraising the lighting, it may be necessary to change the camera position. White birds with outstretched wings or in flight can look especially striking if they are taken against the light so they appear rimlit. The contrast between their plumage and a blue sky or sea can be increased by using a polarizing filter, although the resulting loss in film speed may be a problem unless a fast film is used. Dark-winged petrels flying against pack ice in Antarctica, on the other hand, present an inverse contrast.

STALKING

There is nothing to compare with the excitement of being out in the wild and stalking your quarry with a camera. Success will be achieved only by knowing the behaviour of your subject and the times of day when it is most likely to be seen. Inevitably, the failure rate will be fairly high, but with patience and perseverance, you should be rewarded with some thrilling pictures.

As mammals have an acute sense of smell, it is essential to stalk them from downwind so the wind is blowing *towards* you. They can also react to sudden and unusual sounds, as well as to sudden movements, so avoid wearing squeaky shoes, outer nylon gar-

ments which create a noise as you walk, and Velcro fastenings. Some animals may react to the noise of a motor drive or auto-winder, while others may be disturbed by the sudden movement of a thumb re-cocking the shutter on a manual camera or a hand changing a lens. For this reason, it is sensible to carry a motor drive and a manual camera, each fitted with a different focal length lens. Deer and antelopes have an acute sense of sound for they can direct their outer ear towards a noise. When a bird starts uttering an alarm call, there is no point in attempting a closer approach.

If the camera lens and camera support do not have a matt black finish, all reflective

parts should be covered with black tape. Shooting through a curtain of out-of-focus foliage can aid camouflage as well as lend an impression of depth to the photograph.

Before setting forth over open ground, look for natural cover and work out the best route for stalking. Often this will mean zigzagging your way forward from one bush or rock to another. I find the best way to stalk is to move slowly forward when a bird or mammal has its head down to feed and to freeze immediately it looks up. If the ground is fairly flat, it is better to approach in a crouched – or even a prone – position than in an upright one with your body silhouetted against the sky.

Clothing worn when stalking should always be subdued and blend in with the dominant colour of the landscape. By day, camouflage clothing breaks up the body outline of a photographer, in the same way as disruptive coloration aids the disguise of animals (p. 28), but in many African countries it is illegal to wear such clothing because it is army uniform. Khaki safari clothing is appropriate in the African savannah during the dry season, whereas white clothing is preferable when stalking on snow and ice.

A camouflage net can be put to many uses for field photography: it can be strung up as a screen between two trees; it can be draped over a photographer crawling on the ground; and it can be festooned over a hide or a photographer working in an open boat. A lightweight variation of the camouflage net is the Lastohide (p.140). This is actually worn by the photographer, the ultimate in portability!

When stalking, it is quite impractical to set up a tripod each time you stop, but if the camera is attached to a monopod or a

◄ **Subject:** Ring-tailed lemur (*Lemur catta*)
Location: Berenty, Madagascar
Month: May
Time: Early morning
Lighting: Side
Lens: 135 mm on Nikon
Film: Kodachrome X (ISO 64/19˚)

▼ **Subject:** Ghost crab (*Ocypode ceratophthalma*)
Location: Upper shore, Aride Island, Seychelles
Month: May
Time: Afternoon
Lighting: Direct
Lens: 200 mm on Nikon
Film: Kodachrome X (ISO 64/19˚)

◄The fresh spring growth on the trees overhanging the water add colour as well as conveying a third dimension to this portrait of a mute swan. A large bird such as a swan offers plenty of variations on a theme when composing the picture.

shoulder pod, the viewfinder can quickly be brought to the eye as the camera is steadied. When choosing a monopod, check that the leg sections can be extended or contracted quickly and securely locked at any height. A shoulder pod is positioned by bracing a shoulder butt tight against the shoulder at one end and by grasping a hand grip at the other. The shutter is released by means of a cable release extended into the hand grip. With practice, a shoulder pod will allow a 400 mm or a 500 mm lens to be used at slower shutter speeds than the conventional 1/500 second normally recognized as the slowest speed at which it is safe to hand hold such lenses safely without getting camera shake.

The substantial Cam support (p. 137) designed for video cameras, has the advantage of leaving both hands free to write notes or climb a ladder. A curved shoulder support is connected to an adjustable, pivoted and spring-loaded arm complete with camera mounting. A nylon webbing strap secures the support around the chest.

If a monopod is too high for supporting the camera from the prone position, then a shoulder pod can be used with both elbows firmly on the ground or by using a bean bag. This loosely filled bag will fit into the contours of the ground or a tree stump and at the same time cradle the lens in a central depression. A lighter version of the bean bag is the Tri-bag (p. 136), which is filled with

lightweight synthetic granules. It weighs only 100 g (3½ oz) – less than the weight of an average 50 mm lens – and can also be used for protecting equipment in a camera bag against damage from bangs or scratches.

Lizards basking in the sun can often be stalked with a greater degree of success than birds. They also have a good sense of vision, however, so a gentle unhurried approach is best. Even if a lizard is disturbed, the instinct for these cold-blooded reptiles to bask in the sun will tend to overcome fear of a human intruder.

Frogs and toads which spawn during the day can be approached close enough to work with a 105 mm or 135 mm lens. Even if they initially duck below the surface of the water, they soon re-appear. As the muscles used for bracing a hand-held camera begin to suffer from fatigue, it becomes difficult to support it; it is therefore easier to photo-

graph amphibians using a tripod. Even then, special care needs to be taken when focusing the lens by hand and especially when changing a film. I have found frogs will accept a hand being slowly moved into position if it is run down the lens barrel or over the back of the camera body.

Tropical ghost crabs are even more wary. When danger threatens, they make a hasty retreat down their burrows. Their eyes – on elongated stalks – emerge first from the burrows to check the coast is clear. After two abortive weeks I finally managed to photograph a Seychelles crab by standing motionless for some time and using a 200 mm lens.

When photographing damselflies resting on emergent plants in streams (p. 135) I wear waders so I can test the depth of the water before pushing tripod legs firmly into the stream bed. I then pre-focus the camera on a plant and wait for a damselfly to settle. I find the proportion of successful frames achieved by standing and waiting is much greater than by dashing back and forth along the stream bank.

▶ Because I wanted the two pairs of beady eyes to be the focus of attention, I made a deliberate decision *not* to use a polarizing filter for the frogs. This meant that the grey skylight reflection was used to advantage, blotting out any distracting detail of the frogs' bodies underwater.

BIRDS IN FLIGHT

In recent years, there has been an increasing trend among bird photographers to take pictures of birds away from the nest. This can be done by stalking birds on the ground (p. 53) or by taking birds in flight. Getting a pin-sharp image of one or more birds in flight presents a real challenge, so it is especially rewarding when the exposure, focus and composition are all faultless and the end result is a prize-winning picture.

When taking flight shots there will inevitably be a high proportion of wasted frames: the bird may suddenly change direction or the plane of focus may not be spot-on. It is therefore no good attempting flight photography with any thoughts of economizing on film, for a motor drive set at a rate of five frames per second will expose a whole roll of 36 exposures in a few seconds! This is not always the best way of guaranteeing a higher proportion of good pictures, since at this rate it is impossible to check focus in between frames. If a large bird, such as a swan, keeps a constant distance by flying side on in front of the camera, however, a motor drive will illustrate the sequential change of wing movements as it takes off.

The easiest way to photograph birds in flight is to practise focusing the camera as birds fly at a fixed distance from it, following in the wake of a ship or using the updraught along a cliff face, perhaps. The camera can then be pre-focused and the shutter released as the bird appears in the viewfinder. This technique can also be used for birds flying towards the camera; by using an auto-wind or motor drive on single-frame mode and adjusting the focus, it is possible to take several frames of a large bird coming in to land. I have done this many times in Africa with vultures arriving to feed on a corpse (p. 98). A bird is located as a dark speck high in the sky and followed down to a distance where the bird appears a reasonable size with a 300mm lens, before a series of shots are taken which are sufficiently different to make a striking sequence.

When taking any action shot, the focusing screen should be as bright as possible. A plain ground glass screen is easier to use than one with a split image, as half of the central area tends to darken, making quick and accurate focusing difficult.

If a bird suddenly appears in the sky without warning, very fast reflex actions are needed to frame and focus the picture before the bird disappears. Geese flying in formation, however, are much easier to take since they give an audible warning of their approach.

Cameras with a shutter-priority metering system are an asset when photographing birds in flight – although if the sky is lacking in colour it will be necessary to adjust the meter by one stop to avoid under-exposing a dark bird. An auto-focus lens is a hindrance rather than a help when taking birds in flight, for unless the bird is kept in the centre of the frame, the lens will keep on tracking in and out of focus.

Taking flight shots of a single bird will usually require a long lens with a focal length of at least 300mm – often more. This means that even when using a high-speed film, some form of camera support, such as a shoulder pod or a Cam support (p. 137), will be needed. Both will help you achieve a continuous smooth action when tracking a bird in flight (p. 106).

Shooting against the light and metering off the sky can give some bold silhouettes (p. 37) but it cannot convey any feather detail or coloration. A flock of small waders or a single bird with a large wing span work equally well as silhouettes. Black-winged frigate birds, which pirate other seabirds' food, appear even more menacing in silhouette.

If the aim is to freeze all trace of movement of the flying bird, fast shutter speeds are essential. With experience of photographing different kinds and sizes of birds in flight, you will be able to judge the desired speed. As a rule of thumb, birds with a large wing span and a slow wing beat, such as swans, do not require such a fast shutter speed as smaller birds with a rapid wing beat. As a bird hovers to maintain its position, it faces into the wind. The vigorous wing actions of a hovering tern may still appear blurred even when using a shutter speed of 1/1000 second. Humming-birds

hovering at a flower beat their wings so quickly that high-speed flash will be needed to freeze all trace of movement.

The direction in which the bird is flying relative to the camera also makes a difference to the minimum shutter speed which can be used. If a bird is flying head-on towards the camera, a slower speed is required than if it is flying from one side of the frame to the other — although if the camera is panned (p. 106), it is possible to use a slower speed than if it remains in a fixed position.

There is, of course, another approach to photographing birds in flight which will appeal to anyone with an artistic eye. As described at some length on p. 21, a suggestion of movement can be conveyed by using a slow shutter speed to create a somewhat

◄ **Subject:** White-fronted terns (*Sterna striata*) lifting off	▲ **Subject:** Brown pelican (*Pelecanus occidentalis*)
Location: Firth of Thames, New Zealand	**Location:** Fernandina, Galápagos
Month: December	**Month:** March
Time: Afternoon	**Time:** Afternoon
Lighting: Overcast	**Lighting:** Overcast
Lens: 200 mm on Nikon	**Lens:** 200 mm on Nikon
Film: Kodachrome X (ISO 64/19°)	**Film:** Kodachrome X (ISO 64/19°)

blurred image. The first time I tried this I was working in a permanent hide using Kodachrome 64 in very poor light, so I had no option but to use a slow shutter speed. A group of oystercatchers was resting on a sandy spit in a Welsh estuary with the tide rising fast behind them. I pre-focused the camera and took several shots of them lifting off — at 1/60 second.

Where large concentrations of waders frequent popular beaches, they are repeatedly disturbed by humans and animals so there are plenty of opportunities for taking a massed flock in flight. In this situation, keep checking the focus, for a low-flying plane, a horse-rider or a stray dog may suddenly cause the birds to lift off with little or no warning. At the moment of lift-off — before the birds start to wheel away — it is often possible to get a mass of birds in flight completely filling the frame. Anticipating such a moment with the camera pre-focused ensures at least one good shot. Using a jeep as a hide in Wikpattu Park in Sri Lanka, I noticed that conventionally noisy whistling teal, congregated around a pond, had suddenly become very quiet. The cause was a spotted deer moving down to the water to drink; a moment later I took several shots of the dark-winged teal lifting off against a contrasting white backdrop of massed water crowfoot flowers.

ANIMAL BEHAVIOUR

Pictures portraying some aspect of animal behaviour are more interesting than a static portrait, but there are problems associated with fast action (see Chapter 7) which make this kind of photography particularly challenging. Sometimes dramatic or unusual behaviour can be recorded quite by chance, simply by being in the right place at the right time.

Some years ago, I was working in the Galápagos off the coast of Ecuador. Shortly after I stepped ashore on to James Island, I came across several Galápagos hawks fighting over a recently dead goat kid. They were so intent on defending their portion of food that I was able to work at fairly close range behind a bush, using a medium long focus lens. Focusing on the action, I failed to notice some 20 hawks perched on rocks and trees awaiting their turn to move in on the corpse. There seemed to be a definite pecking order, since any bird which attempted to jump the queue was immediately attacked by the dominant hawks. Animals

can, of course, be attracted by baiting (p. 76) but this particular incident was a completely natural occurrence.

Also in the Galápagos, when walking over the brow of a hill towards the shore, I found an endemic flightless cormorant standing drying its stunted wings. I regard both these lucky chance encounters as a bonus. Usually I do my homework beforehand to find out when and where a particular species is likely to be behaving in an interesting way as it courts, mates, or breeds.

Many birds and mammals often display striking colours and also adopt elaborate behaviour patterns to attract their mate. For example, the male frigate bird inflates his throat pouch into an over-sized red sac which he waggles from side to side at females flying overhead. Wild peacocks in their natural haunts in India and Sri Lanka, as well as captive ones in gardens all over the world, erect their magnificent fan of tail feathers to attract their peahens. The brilliant colours of the iridescent feathers —

complete with eye spots – show up to best advantage in bright sunlight.

When a particular animal behaviour is linked to a certain time of day or night (humming-birds feeding at flowers, bats pollinating flowers and feasting on fruit), time of year (hares 'boxing', adders dancing, frogs croaking, deer rutting, grizzly bears gorging themselves during a salmon run and wildebeest and whales migrating), or a particular phase of the moon (massed spawning of marine animals such as grunions and horseshoe crabs), research needs to be done about the most likely time the behaviour will be seen, so that the odds of gaining an interesting picture are increased. Many seabirds congregate in colonies to nest and aspects of their behaviour are described and illustrated on pages 50 and 51.

Good-quality behavioural pictures will be difficult to achieve unless the camera can be handled and used quite instinctively, so that full concentration can be given to the animal. The way a camera is held and, in a location where a tripod is impractical (such as a rocking boat), how it is supported need to be well rehearsed so that you can react quickly to the situation.

Encapsulating the precise moment when fast action reaches its peak in a single still picture is more difficult than letting a video or movie camera run. Blasting away with a motor drive is not always the best solution, for it is possible to run out of film at the crucial moment. I often prefer to load two motor drives, operating them on the single frame mode, but even then some wastage of film is inevitable. Time spent observing animals so that their behavioural pattern can be anticipated invariably pays dividends in the long run.

The choice of which lens to use will depend not only on the size of the animal(s) being photographed, but also on the degree to which they tolerate intruders. Animals which are used to the presence of humans – as in botanical gardens and parks – will be much readier to accept a close approach than animals living in remote places. When I notice a particular form of behaviour for the first time, I always play safe by using as long a lens as possible, gradually moving in and constantly checking that I am not causing any disturbance. Since changing lenses can distract an animal, a zoom long-focus lens is an advantage here.

Photographing deer in one of the many enclosed British deer parks may not give the same sense of satisfaction as stalking deer in the wild, but it does present marvellous opportunities for learning at first hand, without spending hours stalking in the field, the activities associated with the deer's yearly cycle. Within parks, the deer are free

◀ **Subject:** Galápagos hawks (*Bueto galapago-ensis*) feeding on goat kid
Location: James Island, Galápagos
Month: December
Time: Morning
Lighting: Overcast
Lens: 150 mm on Hasselblad
Film: Ektachrome 64

All these pictures illustrate an example of a lucky encounter with wild animals. In each case there was no pre-planning other than carrying a long lens as part of the basic field equipment into locations where I could never be sure exactly what would turn up.

to move at will and so the situation is not comparable with photographing animals in the cramped confines of a zoo enclosure. The best time to get action pictures is during the rut when male stags (or bucks) repeatedly throw back their heads and call. They also clash antlers as they fight for supremacy and the opportunity to cover the female to mate.

The Luwanga Valley in Zambia is one of the relatively few places where it is possible to go on a walking safari, accompanied by a game guard. I was photographing hippopotamuses wallowing in a pond covered with water lettuce – resembling open cabbages – when one animal began to emerge from the water. The enormous size of this amphibious mammal cannot be appreciated until it is seen on land and great care must be taken to keep a reasonable distance. Even though I had already taken many frames of hippos, I was extremely anxious to get a picture showing the water lettuce being carried on the hippo's back. As the hippo headed off into the scrub, I raced around the edge of the pond to glimpse it running across a track where I was able to take a few frames illustrating how large

▲ **Subject:** Hippopotamus (*Hippopotamus amphibius*) carrying water lettuce
Location: Luangwa National Park, Zambia
Month: September
Time: Afternoon
Lighting: Back
Lens: 300 mm on Nikon
Film: Kodachrome 64

▶ **Subject:** Aggressive Southern elephant seal (*Mirounga leonina*)
Location: Kiakoura coast, New Zealand
Month: January
Time: Afternoon
Lighting: Side
Lens: 300 mm on Nikon
Film: Kodachrome X (ISO 64/19°)

aquatic plants can be dispersed from one water body to another.

When a troop of baboons comes down to the ground, it will provide a variety of behavioural studies in a very short time. Activities most often seen are adults grooming one another, mothers suckling their young, adults carrying very young babies slung beneath them or older offspring riding on their back, as well as feeding and drinking.

Using flash to record animal behaviour is obviously impractical for long-distance work, but it is essential for recording nocturnal behaviour (p. 116).

USING HIDES

Animals, notably birds, with a poor sense of smell will tolerate a closer approach by humans hidden inside a hide – especially if it is a permanent structure. Since the latter part of the last century nesting birds in Britain have been well documented by nature photographers using an ingenious range of hides. Richard and Cherry Kearton believed that birds would accept hides only if they resembled natural objects and at the turn of the century they used a dummy sheep and bullock for their photography. In fact, a hide (or blind, as it is known in the United States) can be made of any opaque material which does not flap around in a breeze – preferably camouflaged so that vandals are not attracted to it.

However carefully a temporary hide is erected at any nest site, it will inevitably cause some disturbance to the birds; also, the location of a rare bird's nest in a treeless landscape is precisely pinpointed by a photographer's hide. It is for these reasons that approval must be gained from the Nature Conservancy Council to photograph rare birds at or near their nests in Britain (p. 142).

As photographic equipment became lighter and lenses longer, birds (and mammals) could be stalked further and further away from a vehicle base. It is encouraging to note the current trend for photographing birds away from their nest. Although this can be done by stalking on foot (p. 53), hides – both temporary and permanent – can be an invaluable aid for photographing birds feeding and drinking naturally or attracted to bait (p. 76). On safari (p. 60), as well as in remote traffic-free areas, a vehicle makes an excellent mobile hide, while permanent hides are now a standard feature in many wildlife reserves and safari parks.

A camouflage net makes an effective screen strung up between two poles or covering a body in a prone position. The Lastohide (p. 140) is a more sophisticated version of a camouflage net.

When working from a vehicle, a bean bag or a Tri-bag (p. 136) can be used quickly to support a long lens on the window frame. I have devised a way of using the versatile Benbo tripod in a car by wedging it between the seat and the door. This will not be practical when standing up with several other people in a minibus on safari, so a monopod or a shoulder pod will need to be used instead. Anyone working for more than a couple of weeks on safari might consider fixing a camera-mounting to the framework of a jeep.

Permanent hides are built in places where animals come regularly to drink or feed. This may be a natural wetland site, a man-made scrape for waders or a water hole for game. These hides are usually spacious enough to enable a tripod to be erected in front of a bench. When working in any hide, keep as quiet as possible and refrain from putting a hand outside.

Luck plays a big part in getting a good shot of a small bird from a permanent hide since, unlike at a nest site, the bird is free to settle over a fairly wide area. Therefore it is worth having a selection of different-length lenses to hand. There will be only a limited time of day when the light at a hide is ideal for photography, but on reserves with several hides facing different aspects, it is possible to work them in rotation. The house or garden shed can also be used as a hide for photographing birds attracted to bait or water (p. 74)

A portable hide is the only way of getting photographs of most wild birds. Exceptions are colonial seabirds (p. 50) or birds in winter (p. 19). Portable hides need to be lightweight yet robust enough to withstand wind and rain and completely opaque so the photographer is not silhouetted when the hide is backlit.

Ready-made hides are available in a limited range of sizes and typically consist of four vertical supports with a rectangular cloth cover which has a sleeved opening for the lens and a peep-hole in each side. A standard 1·2-metre (4-feet) high hide is very cramped inside and is useful only for photographing birds at, or just above, ground level. Photographers would welcome a more versatile ready-made hide with adjustable legs – like a tripod – and an optional additional skirt.

Since birds can nest at heights ranging from ground level to the tops of trees, anyone contemplating the erection of hides at varying heights during the year would be well advised to make their own purpose-made models. Lightweight aluminium tent poles make convenient supports for low hides, whereas robust angle-iron supports or scaffolding used by builders (p. 141) will be needed to construct more substantial and high-level hides.

A hide needs to be erected slowly; at each stage the photographer should check, by retreating and looking through binoculars, that it has been accepted by the birds. A low hide can be gradually moved in towards a nest over a period of several days, whereas a high hide needs to be moved in and slowly

◀ **Subject** Fallow deer (*Dama dama*) with summer coats, grazing
Location: New Forest, Hampshire, England
Month: June
Time: Afternoon
Lighting: Overcast
Lens: 300mm on Nikon
Film: Ektachrome P800/1600

◀ By rating Ektachrome P800/1600 at ISO 1600/33°, I could use 1/250 second exposure in poor light to photograph the deer moving around to feed. They continued to graze as I worked behind an elevated platform erected by the Forestry Commission for viewing these wild deer.

built up over a longer period. Even when a hide has been moved up to the final position and accepted by nesting birds, they may take exception to a lens suddenly being poked out. A bottle or a rolled piece of black card can be used as a dummy lens.

Sometimes branches may obscure the view into a nest and so careful 'gardening' may be necessary. This should be left until the last moment and on no account should branches be cut with secateurs; simply tie them back from the field of view using green garden wire. After each photographic session, the wire is untied and the branches repositioned so the nest is not exposed to predators or the elements.

When the hide is ready for photography it is important to make sure all your equipment is at hand – a check-list is given on p. 140. When an isolated hide is approached without covered walkways, birds will accept a person remaining in a hide only if someone is seen to leave. It is therefore important to have a companion see you into the hide (and see you out).

In open situations on a sunny day birds can be photographed using available light, but in dark forests, on dull days or at night, flash will be necessary. Like the hide, flash

▲ **Subject:** Ceylon hawk eagle (*Spizaetus cirrhatus ceylonensis*)
Location: Yala, Sri Lanka – jeep as hide
Month: May
Time: Morning
Lighting: Direct sun
Lens: 400mm on Nikon
Film: Kodachrome 64

▶ **Subject:** Tufted duck (*Aythya fuligula*)
Location: Canal, Sussex, England, car as hide
Month: December
Time: Morning
Lighting: Direct sun
Lens: 300mm on Nikon
Film: Kodachrome 64

stands with dummy flash heads will need to be gradually introduced if they are to be accepted. Most birds are disturbed by a motor drive and some may not accept the whine of a flashgun every time it automatically recharges itself.

With so many keen nature photographers invading the countryside, it is sensible to reduce disturbance to nesting birds to a minimum by teaming up with one person or more to share a common hide in rotation.

ON SAFARI

Photographing game on safari may be the average person's idea of how wildlife photographers spend their working days, but as this book shows, there are many other fascinating and challenging aspects of wildlife and nature photography. Working on safari inevitably brings both excitement and frustration, for you would be extremely lucky to take many spectacular behavioural pictures during a couple of weeks on safari with a package tour. With careful preparation, however, you should be able to get some good pictures of the common birds and mammals.

Try to avoid using too many different lenses; this will save wasting valuable time changing them. A 200 mm (or an 80–200 mm zoom) lens will be adequate for groups of mammals, but a 400 mm (or a 200 mm with a × 2 converter) is essential for taking bird portraits. If you do not have a zoom lens, a separate 85 mm or 105 mm will be useful for landscapes as well as a 50 mm and possibly a 35 mm. A motor drive will enable a sequence of pictures to be taken of animals interacting with one another or moving at speed. Even though there will be little chance of using a tripod inside a mini bus owing to lack of both room and time, I would still recommend bringing a tripod, for there may be opportunities for taking a sunrise or a sunset adjacent to the camp. In areas where walking is allowed, opportunities for taking flowers or fruits in close-up may arise.

Less bulky and easily erected camera supports such as a monopod, shoulder pod or bean bag will help to steady a camera with a long lens in a jeep or mini bus, although the main problem may well be that the driver is unwilling to turn off the engine (in a potentially dangerous situation where he may need to make a hasty getaway) or that other people fail to keep still.

Even though only a small part of the photographer's body may be visible from outside a mini bus, it is still sensible to wear sombre clothing that blends in with the surroundings and to keep as quiet as possible. In some places, notably the Luwanga Valley in Zambia, it is possible to go on a walking safari with a game guard (p. 57). Suitable clothing is then even more important. Whether game is stalked on foot or in a vehicle, sudden movements and noises should be avoided.

The best action pictures will be taken when the game is most active at the beginning and end of the day. These times are also preferable because photographs are less likely to be distorted by heat haze. Around midday the overhead lighting also gives short shadows and poor modelling. To avoid missing the action when it suddenly hap-

pens, always keep a camera loaded with film and the shutter cocked. If possible, use two camera bodies so that when a film is finished one body can quickly be changed for another. A recently killed carcase will attract scavenging vultures from afar, giving plenty of opportunity for taking flight shots of them arriving (p. 98) as well as of their periodic aggressive behaviour.

During the dry season dust is a big problem, so every precaution must be taken to avoid it getting on to equipment and particularly inside a camera body when changing a film. Either keep each lens in its own bag or cover all equipment with a cloth sheet which has been well washed so that it does not shed fluff. Never change a film when in a vehicle following another which is throwing up dust. Each evening, clean all equipment with a blower brush. Film needs to be kept as cool as possible so never leave a camera or rolls of film on a seat in the sun, and before putting down a gadget bag on

the floor of a vehicle, check that it is not on a hot spot. Exposed film in particular, needs to be kept cool. Even without air conditioning films will keep reasonably cool back at your hotel if they are wrapped in clothing inside a drawer or suitcase in the part of the room which receives no direct sunlight throughout the day.

When focusing on a large cat for the first time it is easy, with the adrenalin running high, not to pay careful attention to detail. Notably, the background often makes or mars a picture. In the most popular African parks and reserves as soon as a vehicle stops others are quickly on the scene, like bees to nectar. I have experienced the depressing situation where lions on a kill or a leopard are completely surrounded by such a tight circle of minibuses, that it is virtually impossible to get a picture without a minibus behind. Local drivers should know better, but it only needs a very persuasive group to urge a driver to get closer and then all the

comes down to drink close to a hungry well-camouflaged crocodile, there is likely to be plenty of activity.

In some areas, such as the Masai Mara in Kenya, balloon safaris are available. Although these are not cheap, it is an unforgettable experience to drift gently upwards at dawn so as to obtain an overview of the plains game. A zoom lens spanning focal lengths from 50 mm to a medium long lens will save wasting time changing lenses during the comparatively short flight. To avoid blurred images, a shutter speed of 1/250 second will be needed even for landscapes, and 1/500 second may be preferable for fast-moving animals.

One of the exciting aspects of going on safari is that you never know when something unexpected will happen; for example, two of my best moments were when an elephant charged towards me in Sri Lanka (p. 101), and when a hippo emerged from a pond in Zambia and trotted off transporting water plants on its back (p. 57).

▼This leopard came down from a tree moments before the sun sank behind distant hills and the dramatic backlighting was lost. We found the leopard first, but shortly after we stopped, other jeeps converged on the scene.

▼ **Subject:** Leopard (*Panthera pardus*)
Location: Samburu Game Reserve, Kenya
Month: August
Time: Dusk
Lighting: Grazed, back
Lens: 200 mm on Nikon
Film: Kodachrome 64

other almost inevitably follow suit.

Just before the wet season begins, water is at a premium and so game congregates at the few remaining water holes. At this time of year, in places such as Tsavo National Park in Kenya where a lodge has been built overlooking a large water hole, a continuous stream of game can be seen by day (and by night when the water hole is floodlit). In this situation, where it is impossible to adjust the camera position relative to the background, it is important to vary the length of lens used and to take a mixture of horizontal and vertical pictures so that the shots do not look too smilar.

Both hippopotamuses and crocodiles spend much of the day lying virtually motionless in water or hauled out on a river bank, but if you have time to sit and wait you will often be rewarded with some action. A close-up of a hippo opening its mouth makes a more exciting picture than a complete hippo lying on the bank. If an antelope

▲ **Subject:** White-bearded gnu or wildebeest (*Connochaetes taurinus*)
Location: Masai Mara National Reserve, Kenya
Month: August
Time: Mid-day
Lighting: Overcast
Lens: 85 mm on Nikon
Film: Kodachrome 64

▲ Even though this group of wildebeest gathering beneath a tree in the heat of the day shows no action, it is one of my Masai Mara favourites, since it typifies the August landscape with golden grasslands dotted with green trees.

Subject: Bank vole (*Clethrionoymys glareolus*) on white fork moss (*Leucobryum glaucum*)
Location: In bottomless glass enclosure on woodland floor, Surrey, England
Month: September
Time: Evening
Lighting: Flash
Lens: 80mm + extension on Hasselblad
Film: Ektachrome 64

CHAPTER FOUR

ANIMALS IN CAPTIVITY

When an animal is confined, it may exhibit atypical behaviour. For many people, however, zoos and animal collections provide the only opportunity they have to see and photograph exotic animals. Once the problems of photographing through mesh or glass have been mastered, captive animals offer excellent opportunities for studying their anatomy in greater detail than is possible in the wild where they are free to roam at will. Another advantage of working with confined animals is the increased scope for selecting the best time for optimum lighting. Peak activity is usually associated with feeding times.

Zoological gardens

To the dedicated and intrepid wildlife photographer zoos are anathema, since all the thrills associated with tracking down the quarry in the wild are lost. But zoos should not be completely rejected, since they offer an excellent opportunity for trying out new photographic equipment. They also enable detailed portrait studies of larger animals to be taken – which can be extremely useful for educational purposes.

Many zoological gardens are much more than a series of animal enclosures; they have an attractive garden element outside the enclosures, as well as trees inside providing both shade and somewhere for arboreal animals to climb.

In recent years, the image of zoos has been changing; bare enclosures surrounded by bars or mesh are fortunately now rare. Wherever possible, moats – both dry and wet – or glass are replacing bars and mesh, permitting unimpeded views of the captive animals. None the less, zoo photography is inevitably something of a compromise.

The most useful lens to use at a zoo is a

▼**Subject:** Giant panda (*Ailuropoda melanoleuca*) feeding on bamboo
Location: Chengdu Zoo, China
Month: October
Time: Afternoon
Lighting: Overcast
Lens: 85mm on Nikon
Film: Kodachrome 64

▶**Subject:** Meerkat (*Suricata suricata*), native to southern Africa
Location: San Diego Zoo, US
Month: February
Time: Late afternoon
Lighting: Side
Lens: 300mm on Nikon
Film: Kodachrome 200

medium long focus one, although sometimes a standard lens can be used for a large animal such as an elephant when it moves to the inner edge of the dry moat. A wide-angle lens is not suitable for zoo work, because it will inevitably show far too much of an enclosure.

Animals such as large cats and polar bears, which naturally traverse considerable distances at speed, cannot be expected to behave in a natural way when they are cooped up in a small enclosure. There is nothing more pitiful than seeing a polar bear pacing back and forth across a few square metres of bare concrete, but given a good-sized pool it will enjoy frolicking in water. Some animals, notably primates, learn to react and play up to human on-

lookers, thereby presenting opportunities for taking pictures of facial expressions showing pleasure, annoyance or even rage.

Bars and mesh obviously spoil a photograph, but they can be obliterated from a picture by centring the camera lens between bars or large mesh; in practice, however, this may not be possible if a railing is positioned in front of the enclosure. Should this be the case, it is foolish to ignore the warning notices about climbing inside the railings. It may be only a camera that gets damaged, but it could just as easily be a hand or an arm. The technique for shooting through finer mesh is to hold the camera flush against it, focusing beyond and using a large aperture so the mesh is automatically thrown out of focus. If the sun is shining,

make sure there are no distracting — and misleading — shadow patterns from bars or mesh cast on to the animals.

Having solved any foreground problems, you also need to appraise the background. The presence of obviously artificial walls can sometimes be disguised by waiting until a shadow falls across them. The camera position may need to be altered so that a tree can blot out a coloured door or sign. A large aperture will also ensure that the background walls of an enclosure appear less distinct by being out of focus.

When working in open enclosures bordered by a moat or ditch, there may be more scope for varying the camera angle. For example, arboreal animals, such as monkeys, lemurs and koala bears, can often be taken against the sky by using a low camera angle. Alternatively, animals in sunken pits or pools can be photographed from a high viewpoint with vegetation or water as a naturalistic background.

Different problems arise when photographing animals inside glass-fronted enclosures. Most obviously, ghost-like images of hands, cameras and clothing appear in the glass. For this reason, it is much better to wear sombre clothing instead of white or brightly patterned garments. You can avoid your own reflection appearing in the picture by standing to one side of the subject, but other people's reflections may still appear. I had to wait for people to move away from a glass-fronted orang-utan exhibit at San Diego Zoo, before I could photograph a charismatic mature male with his fat-filled cheek pads. Unlike animals in aquaria (p. 68), the orang-utans were well lit by available light in a spacious enclosure open to the sky. However, during an overcast spell I was glad of the extra speed provided by Kodachrome 200. It was only after the film was processed that I noticed the highlights in the orang-utan's eyes, produced by someone else's flash.

Also at San Diego Zoo, I came across blue-crowned pigeons naturally backlit so that their crowns of grey feathers stood out from the unlit background. Many other people were also attracted by these handsome birds, but I noticed automatic cameras were firing their front flash — completely ruining the effect of natural backlighting!

After an initial visit to a zoo, the optimum time for photographing each exhibit can be anticipated on subsequent trips. For livelier pictures of animals such as sea lions or polar bears, it is worth finding out what time of day they are fed.

Walk-through aviaries are becoming popular, for they provide the visitor with a more intimate feeling of a jungle environment. There may be opportunities for tak-

ing birds feeding on flowers or fruits, although a fast shutter speed will not adequately freeze the motion of a humming-bird's wings as it hovers to feed on a tropical flower.

Small indoor exhibits lit by strip lights will give an unnatural colour cast unless daylight tubes are used. Flash will overcome this problem as well as stopping action. Some zoos prohibit the use of flash, but cameras with a built-in flash will automatically fire when the light is dim. Visitors to London Zoo are encouraged to use flash so the animals become conditioned to it and no longer react. The correct way to position flash when photographing through glass is

explained on p. 68. As with any wildlife photography, it will be obvious if an animal is disturbed by the flash; in this case, it is pointless attempting further pictures.

So that nocturnal mammals are active during daylight hours, days and nights are reversed in the nocturnal house at London Zoo. After the zoo is closed, the house is fully illuminated, so the mammals go to sleep. In the morning, the lights are dimmed as if it were night-time. This makes photography by existing light difficult, unless a high-speed film is used. Using a direct flash is not a possible alternative since it gives an unnaturally high level of illumination for a nocturnal animal.

WILDLIFE COLLECTIONS

In addition to the traditional and long-standing zoos, a plethora of wildlife parks and collections has opened in the last decade or so. Many provide spacious surroundings without bars or glass. When African game was introduced to Longleat in Wiltshire in 1966, it was the first drive-through safari park in the world outside Africa. The one-way route through the 2 square kilometre ($\frac{3}{4}$ square mile) park is divided into distinct areas; in some it is possible to get out of the car to photograph giraffes, camels and zebras, but in the enclosure with elephants, rhinoceroses and eland, visitors have to remain in their cars, although the windows can be left open. In the lion and tiger enclosures all car windows must remain closed, so this means that all photography here has to be done through glass. It therefore pays to clean the windows – inside and out – before setting forth, but on a hot day they will soon steam up. Lions and other potentially dangerous animals have learned to accept cars as being quite harmless.

Royal Windsor Safari Park was the second drive-through park to be opened in Britain. Here Indian tigers, lions, cheetahs and baboons can be seen from the safety of an enclosed car. There is also an area where it is possible to walk around and see white rhinoceroses in a moated enclosure, as well as Indian elephants, giraffes, zebras, chimpanzees, raccoons and wallabies.

Woburn Wild Animal Kingdom – the largest drive-through safari park in Europe – was opened in 1970. Among the game animals to be seen in the $6\frac{1}{2}$-km (4-mile) long drive are Bengal tigers, lions, white rhinos, hippopotomuses, African and Indian elephants and the sole breeding herd of bongos (a rare species of antelope) in Europe.

The pictures on this spread demonstrate the range of subjects available for photography in wildlife parks, where there are opportunities for trying out new camera techniques.

◄**Subject:** Mandarin drake (*Aix galericulata*)
Location: Arundel Wildfowl Trust, Sussex, England
Month: January
Time: Afternoon
Lighting: Direct
Lens: 200mm on Nikon
Film: Kodachrome 64

At Longleat and Woburn the engine can be switched off for photography in the lion and tiger enclosure, but this is not recommended at Windsor where a tiger – aptly named Dunlop – attacks tyres.

An additional attraction at Woburn is the deer park where the herd of Père David's deer, established by the eleventh Duke of Bedford, can be seen. These Chinese deer came to Woburn via European zoos from the Emperor's Imperial Hunting Park outside Peking (now known as Beijing). When the walls of the hunting park were breached by a severe flood in 1894, many deer escaped, only to be killed by starving peasants. At the turn of this century, the Duke of Bedford decided that the best chance of saving the species would be to gather all the deer from European zoos into a single herd at Woburn. By 1939, the original herd of 18 deer had increased to 250 and some were transferred to Whipsnade Zoo where a

attract red deer stags to wallow in the mud.

For anyone who has been fortunate enough to go on an African safari, seeing game amongst English oaks is rather incongruous. But for the many people who will never have the opportunity of visiting Africa for themselves, these substitute safari parks are the next best thing and, compared with zoos, are better for the animals because their territory is expanded.

Spacious deer parks such as Woburn offer excellent opportunities for taking a series of pictures illustrating the animals' complete life history, including birth, suckling, feeding, shedding of antlers, inter-male rivalry, courtship and mating. A tripod, monopod or shoulder pod will be needed for support when using a long lens.

The expansion of wildlife safari parks has necessitated much tighter controls on the movement of wild animals from one country to another. However, increasing emphasis is now being placed on breeding, and not only can livestock born in captivity be used to stock other parks and zoos (instead of importing yet more animals from the wild), but also successful captive breeding programmes enable individuals of threat-

◄ **Subject:** Chameleon (*Chamaeleo* sp.)
Location: Nairobi Snake Park, Kenya
Month: August
Time: Morning
Lighting: Direct sun
Lens: 200mm on Nikon
Film: Kodachrome 64

▼ **Subject:** Californian sea lion (*Zalophus californianus*) swimming
Location: Longleat Safari Park, Wiltshire, England
Month: April
Time: Late afternoon
Lighting: Oblique
Lens: 200mm on Nikon
Film: Kodachrome 200

ened species to be returned to the wild.

The Wildfowl Trust headquarters at Slimbridge in Gloucestershire has had many notable breeding successes. By 1951, when less than 50 ne-ne or Hawaiian geese remained on Hawaii, three birds were dispatched to Slimbridge. Two thousand birds have now been bred there and 200 of them have been re-introduced to Hawaii.

Slimbridge has the largest and most comprehensive wildfowl collection in the world, and there is always something there of interest to photograph. Wildfowl are most photogenic when they are sporting their full breeding dress. They are least attractive in their eclipse plumage when male ducks lose their brilliant coloured feathers (including the flight feathers) and develop a dull camouflage plumage during the time they are flightless.

After courtship, mating and egg laying, young cygnets, goslings and ducklings hatch out in spring. They are especially appealing with their soft, downy plumage. Numerous hides built overlooking pools, scrapes or feeding grounds allow wildfowl to be approached at close quarters via screened walkways. Care needs to be taken when photographing resident birds in collections, however, since many are pinioned to prevent them flying away. The resident population helps to attract large numbers of wild birds to a reserve, especially in winter.

One of the most spectacular avian sights must surely be the huge numbers of wild Bewick swans and other wildfowl which congregate in winter on the Ouse Washes, where they can be viewed from the comfort of a centrally heated hide. When working in the same hide for a long period, a tripod is best for supporting a long lens.

second breeding centre was established. From these two locations, Père David's deer have been sent to zoos all over the world – including Beijing Zoo. The world population of this rare deer is now 1500.

Where walking is allowed in wildlife collections, there are fewer problems involved in photographing the animals because of the absence of the bars, mesh or glass one has to contend with at zoos. A difficulty with large enclosures, however, is that the animals invariably distance themselves well away from the closest point of access.

After making several visits to a park, it will be apparent that some areas are more popular than others. There may be a shady spot favoured during the heat of a midsummer's day, or an open but sheltered area for basking in the sun in cooler weather. A natural stream will lure deer down to drink, while a damp hollow will

AQUARIA AND OCEANARIA

Many zoos have an aquarium section displaying a variety of cold-water and tropical fish; some have glass observation windows built into the side of a penguin or sea lion enclosure so that the skilful underwater acrobatics of these marine animals can be appreciated to the full. When these animals, sharks or turtles are contained in large tanks with clean water open to the sky, they can be photographed through glass using a fairly fast daylight colour film (or by double-rating a medium-speed film if necessary) without flash. Top lighting from the sun is completely natural, but since the red wavelengths are rapidly absorbed by water, the pictures may show a greenish cast similar to underwater pictures taken without flash. This can be corrected by using a red colour-correcting (CC) filter.

The camera should be held as close to the glass as possible so that any scratches will be thrown out of focus. Many pictures taken through glass are ruined either by ghost-like reflections of camera parts, hands and pale-coloured or patterned clothing, or by conspicuous reflections of a flash on the camera. Reflective camera parts can be masked using matt black tape and human reflections minimized by wearing dark clothing and covering hands with a black cloth, but these tactics will not solve the problem of white lettering inside the lens mount being reflected. This is why I attach a matt black mask to the camera, made of cardboard measuring anything from 15 cm (6 inches) to 60 cm (2 feet) square or more, with a central hole cut out for the lens; this prevents any reflection of the camera or photographer appearing in the field of view. First of all I cut a central hole in the board so that any lettering on the front of the lens is hidden, yet the surround does not impede into the picture area. Using impact glue, I then attach a glassless filter mount around the hole on the back of the board. In this way, I can screw the filter ring with the mask on to the front of the camera lens and carry it around as a single unit. I have several masks of different areas to fit both Nikon and Hasselblad lenses. The area of the mask depends on the size of the subject and the working distance – the bigger the magnification, the smaller the size of the mask required. I always use a mask for all my tank photography, whether it be a public aquarium or a small aquarium in my studio.

In small tanks, and all tanks lit entirely by artificial light, the only way to freeze movement of close-up subjects and to override the colour cast from the strip lights is to use electronic flash. Some aquaria prohibit the use of flash, so check first before using it and try to avoid disturbing the animals by knocking the glass with the lens or flash.

Judging from the number of times I have seen people taking pictures in public aquaria using either a camera with a built-in flash or a flash mounted on top of the camera, a large proportion of shots must end up in the waste bin. If you shine a light on to glass in front of you, you will see that it is reflected straight back again, but a flash can be used to illuminate fish in public aquaria if it is positioned to one side of the camera and angled in at about 45° to the glass. For large tanks, two flashes may be needed to give adequate illumination. The first can be either held by an assistant or attached to a lighting stand. The second needs to be positioned on the other side of the camera.

Owing to the refraction of light passing through water, fish swimming close to the inside of the front glass will not be adequately lit by the flash. The ideal position of the fish for photography is somewhere in the centre of a tank so that any imperfections in the front glass or rear wall of the tank can be thrown out of focus and the fish themselves can be well lit.

As with birds and mammals, it is important to make sure that the eye of a fish

Subjects for photography in public aquaria span a wide size range. They include close-ups of tropical fish, larger fish and turtles and even marine mammals such as sea lions and whales.

►**Subject:** Killer whale (*Orcinus orca*)
Location: Sea World, San Diego, US
Month: January
Time: Early evening
Lighting: Warmed by setting sun
Lens: 200mm on Nikon
Film: Kodachrome 200

appears sharply in focus. Laterally compressed fish which are photographed from the side require a very small depth of field, whereas a fish swimming head-on towards the camera with its body curving behind requires a much greater depth of field to get everything, from the tip of the mouth to the end of the tail fin, in focus. In practice, providing the head and eyes are in focus, it will be acceptable if the rest of the body is not pin-sharp.

Fish with large silver scales, such as mirror carp or chub, present a problem when lit by flash from the front or sides of the aquarium, since the silver scales can function like a mosaic of mirrors. When this occurs, the flash is directed straight back into the camera lens and the fish appears greatly over-exposed. This difficulty will not arise if the flash can be directed down-

◄ Subject: Clown anemone fishes (*Amphiprion clarkii*), with background shadows from air bubbles
Location: London Zoo Aquarium
Lighting: Electronic flash from above
Lens: 80mm + extension on Hasselblad
Film: Ektachrome 64

▼ Subject: Sea horse (*Hippocampus* sp.)
Location: Coral Bazaar, Tamworth, Surrey, England
Lighting: Electronic flash
Lens: 80mm + extension on Hasselblad
Film: Ektachrome 64

wards from the top of the tank – which is unlikely in a public aquarium. Fish with small coloured scales, such as many of the freshwater and marine tropicals, can be lit from any angle without the risk of the scales appearing over-exposed.

Try to avoid including a stream of bubbles given off by the aerator in the field of view, as this is both distracting and quite unnatural in a picture of freshwater fish swimming among weeds or marine fish among corals. However, on one occasion when my brief for taking tropical fish for a record album cover was to use a range of plain coloured backgrounds, I experimented with an aerator to create shadows on a pale background in a tank set up behind the scenes at London Zoo Aquarium. The final effect was not unlike an out-of-focus watery cascade.

The techniques for photographing large marine mammals in open oceanaria are quite distinct from those required for small aquatic life behind glass. Leaping sea lions, and more especially a killer whale, can produce a big splash when they crash down on to the water. Since sea water is highly corrosive, it is sensible to sit well back. This will mean that a long lens is required, but with staged seating it will be possible to have an uncluttered background of water filling the frame. In a fast-moving show, the best action shots may be missed by not

knowing from which side of the tank the animals will emerge. Therefore, if I have time, I watch one performance so I can note the direction of the moves and check the framing with a zoom lens; I can then anticipate each move the second time round.

It may be worth waiting for the final performance in the day, by which time the sun has sunk low in the sky and the water takes on an attractive orange glow.

BUTTERFLY HOUSES

Similar to the walk-through aviaries where birds fly freely around you, butterfly houses contain free-flying butterflies. Glass replaces mesh which is impractical for containing butterflies; not only is heat lost to the outside, but also tiny caterpillars can crawl through the gaps. All butterflies, including temperate species, require plenty of sun to warm up their bodies before they can fly to flowers to gather nectar. A cold butterfly will starve to death before it dies of cold. Commercial butterfly houses are outsized glasshouses inside which the humidity, temperature and light are all carefully controlled for growing the plants on which the butterflies feed.

The first walk-through butterfly house in Europe was built in Guernsey; the London Butterfly House was opened at Syon Park in 1981 and the Stratford-upon-Avon Butterfly Farm and Jungle Safari four years later. Between June and the end of September a thousand butterflies and moths can be seen on the wing at Stratford. The main flight area is a hot and humid tropical environment. This means that cold lenses – in both glasses and cameras – will immediately steam up, making photography impossible for several minutes until the consensation slowly evaporates. A picture which is taken through a steamed-up lens appears as though a soft-focus filter has been used. If a warm camera is taken into a heated glasshouse there will be no problems with the lens or viewfinder steaming up.

The main advantage of working under glass is that photography is possible regardless of the weather outside, since rain and wind are excluded, although automatic sprinklers present a hazard when they respond to a drop in humidity and begin to spray the vegetation. Even on a dull day, resting butterflies can be taken using available light, with a reflector to bounce back some of the overhead light. On a sunny day, conspicuous shadows from the struts supporting the glass are cast across plants and butterflies inside, whereas no such problem will arise on an overcast day.

Flash may be needed to freeze the movement of active butterflies. The pictures on these pages illustrate the use of both available lighting and flash inside the Stratford Butterfly Farm. Since the butterflies alight all over the vegetation, not just beside the paths, a medium long focus lens with extension tubes, or a 105 mm or a 200 mm macro lens will be most useful. If a flash is used, it will be much easier and quicker to work if it is carried on a flash bracket as a single unit with the camera (p. 44).

When butterflies alight they often close their wings, revealing the pattern on the underwings. A collection of butterfly pictures will be more interesting if the approach can be varied by photographing some with closed and some with open wings. In either case, the camera needs to be positioned at right angles to outstretched or closed wings so that the film plane is parallel with the wing surface. Pairing butterflies or moths can often be approached with a camera more easily than a solitary butterfly. As well as portraits of complete specimens, a detailed close-up of a butterfly feeding with the uncoiled proboscis probing for nectar makes a good impact picture.

If the butterfly has not moved after the first frame has been taken, check the background for distracting pipes or glasshouse supports. Often a slight adjustment to the camera position is all that is needed to fill the frame completely with vegetation.

I have never found flight shots within the confines of a butterfly house any easier than

▲ **Subject:** Florida atala (*Eumaeus atala*)
Location: Stratford-upon-Avon Butterfly Farm, England
Month: July
Time: Afternoon
Lighting: Available
Lens: 150mm + extension on Hasselblad
Film: Ektachrome 64

Butterfly houses in temperate countries with tropical insects offer opportunities for photographing exotic species, and getting to know their markings, without travelling far afield. Inside glass houses butterflies can be taken by natural or flash light.

in the field, but they are worth attempting using a high-speed film and a fast shutter speed to freeze the action.

As well as the main flight area, Stratford also has a British Wildlife Garden under glass where British butterflies can be seen on the wing. The modern farming practice of fewer, larger fields has substantially reduced the amount of hedgerow boundaries which were valuable reservoirs of butterfly food plants; consequently many butterflies native to the British Isles now have only a localized distribution.

Butterfly houses rear most of their livestock and any surplus is sold to visitors. A small greenhouse or conservatory is quite adequate for rearing tropical butterflies at home. Before buying any livestock, however, make sure you know the preferred food plant(s) of the caterpillars and on which nectar-producing flowers the adults feed. An electric fan heater is a convenient and safe method of maintaining heat. A double door arrangement is sensible not only to avoid losing butterflies as you enter and leave, but also to maintain heat on cold days; in hot weather, however, ventilation will be needed.

If you do not want to run to the expense of heating a tropical greenhouse, native butterflies can be contained in small breeding cages, providing their food plants are changed daily. Eggs can be kept in a

▲ Subject: Giant atlas moth (*Attacus atlas*)
Location: Stratford-upon-Avon Butterfly Farm, England
Month: July
Time: Afternoon
Lighting: Available light
Lens: 150mm + extension on Hasselblad
Film: Ektachrome 64

◄ Subject: Gulf fritillaries (*Araulis vanillae*) pairing
Location: Stratford-upon-Avon Butterfly Farm, England
Month: July
Time: Afternoon
Lighting Electronic flash
Lens: 80mm + extension on Hasselblad
Film: Ektachrome 64

transparent plastic lunch box. When the caterpillars or larvae hatch, make sure they feed on their egg shell before you gently transfer them with a paintbrush to another box lined with paper containing the larval food plant. As larvae are very susceptible to fungal infection, they should never be given wet food plants.

After the larvae have moulted several times, they should be transferred to a breeding cage with fine mesh sides. Sprays of the food plant can be placed in a pot of water with a paper tissue plug wedged in the neck to prevent the larvae from drowning. Some larvae burrow into soil to pupate; others climb up branches and pupate on a stem or a leaf. If you are not sure what they are going to do, it is sensible to add a layer of soil to a shallow tray at the bottom of the breeding cage.

Breeding butterflies (or moths) gives the opportunity for photographing all stages of their life history from eggs, caterpillars and pupae to adults. Eggs need to be photographed at a magnification several times greater than life size with bellows extension. Some eggs have a textured surface, which can be emphasized by using grazed lighting (p. 89). Young larvae also need to be taken with bellows, but mature hawk moth caterpillars are large enough to be taken with a macro lens, as indeed are most pupae or chrysalids.

Perfect specimens of adult moths and butterflies will be gained by captive breeding, and so make a more attractive close-up than a specimen photographed in the wild with damaged wings.

Subject: Frog (*Rana temporaria*) on lily pad
Location: Pond in author's garden, Surrey, England
Month: July
Time: Early evening
Lighting: Oblique
Lens: 105mm micro-Nikkor on Nikon
Film: Kodachrome 25

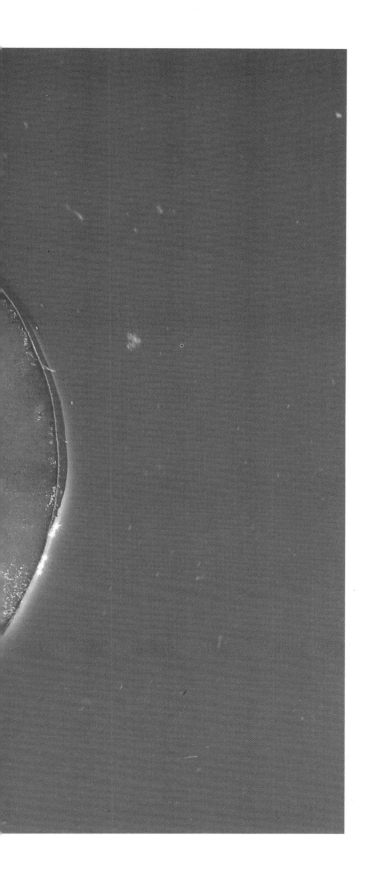

CHAPTER FIVE

ATTRACTING ANIMALS

Luring animals to food or water certainly lacks the challenge and excitement of stalking quarry out in the wild; but it can often be a means of achieving better quality photographs or taking interesting behavioural shots. This is especially true if the camera – with a shorter focal length lens – is supported on a tripod inside a hide. When natural food or water is in short supply animals are much more readily attracted to bait. During a severe winter, birds which are normally timid become quite tame. Likewise, any patch of permanent water acts like a magnet to game during a prolonged period of drought.

IN THE GARDEN

Naturalist gardeners invariably take delight in relaying accounts of unusual wild animals visiting their garden, although they are never quite so enthusiastic when deer eat their roses or squirrels dig holes in their lawn. Many wild animals can be persuaded to visit a garden if their preferred food is provided on a regular basis. Butterflies will be tempted to linger where their favourite food plants – or the food of their larvae – are grown (p. 128). Birds are also attracted by food as well as by water for drinking and bathing (p. 78).

When positioning a bird table for photography, you should give some thought to the time of day when it will be lit by available light, remembering that birds tend to be most active early and late in the day. A bird table with a pitched roof will prevent

snow or leaves covering food, but a flat-topped table is better for photography since no roof shadow will be cast on the feeding birds. Depending on the height of the window you are planning to shoot through and the elevation of the adjacent ground, a bird table needs to be 1·5 metres (4½ feet) or more above the ground. If there is a convenient branch, the table can be suspended from a tree, otherwise it can be fixed to a pole in the ground. Avoid siting a table adjacent to any cover, since cats can easily lurk inside. However, a lone shrub or tree with low branches can be useful for tempting birds to pause amidst photogenic surroundings *en route* to the bird table. Alternatively, a branch positioned near to the table makes a natural perch, provided it is changed frequently so as to vary the composition of photographs.

To deter both squirrels and cats from climbing on to the table, cover the pole (or branch) with a plastic tube like those used by foresters to protect tree saplings from damage by grazing.

Before siting a bird table or perch as a focal point for photography, check there are no eyesores behind it; brightly coloured doors or gates – even when thrown out of focus – will tend to draw the eye away from a sombre-coloured bird. A permanent eyesore can, if necessary, be screened using a row of potted conifers.

Once the location has been selected and the bird table positioned, do not expect the birds to flock in immediately. It takes time for them to build up the confidence to feed for a reasonable length of time. At first, they

will tend to be very wary of any sudden noise or movement, but as their desire to feed overcomes their fear of man, they will learn to accept people walking to and fro inside the house. If you want to take pictures shortly after the table is put up, it will be necessary to use some sort of hide – either a photographic one (p. 140) in the garden or a set-up as simple as curtains drawn across a window. Because of the problems associated with photography through glass (p. 68), I prefer to shoot through an open window when using the house as a hide.

The optimum lens for taking birds feeding in the garden will depend on the distance of the bait from the window, the size of the birds and their tameness. I have managed to photograph fieldfares feeding on crab apples during a severe winter spell by stalking them across a lawn without any cover using a 300 mm lens.

While it is possible to hand hold 105 mm and 200 mm lenses, it is much less tiring if the camera is set up on a tripod inside the house and pre-focused; then pictures can be quickly taken after a fine adjustment to the focus is made. Many birds, especially the more timid ones, will be disturbed by the motor of cameras which have an automatic wind-on.

During the winter months, when birds are more desperate for food, they will literally queue up to feed at a table. If a feeder is used for nuts, birds tend to remain for longer periods as they cannot easily remove food.

A more attractive way of photographing

▲ Subject: Fieldfare (*Turdus pilaris*) feeding on crab apple
Location: Hampshire garden, England
Month: February
Time: Morning
Lighting: Direct sun
Lens: Stalked with 350 mm on Hasselblad
Film: Ektachrome 200

► Subject: Chameleon (*Chamelaeo* sp.) walking through leaves
Location: A garden in Zambia
Month: September
Time: Morning
Lighting: Dappled sunlight
Lens: 105 mm micro-Nikkor on Nikon
Film: Kodachrome 64

◀**Subject:** Starling (*Sturnus vulgaris*) on bird feeder
Location: Surrey garden, England
Month: May
Time: Early morning
Lighting: Side
Lens: 200 mm on Nikon using house as a hide
Film: Kodachrome 200

▼ **Subject:** Pallid ground squirrel (*Xerus rutilus*)
Location: Samburu Game Reserve, Kenya
Month: August
Time: Afternoon
Lighting: Dappled sunlight
Lens: 200 mm on Nikon
Film: Kodachrome 64

leave food on the ground overnight, however, since this may attract rats.

Once wild birds have begun to nest and there is plenty of natural food available, it is not necessary to continue feeding, although during a period of drought, feeding will help birds unable to extract earthworms from the parched ground.

Birds can also be persuaded to remain in the garden during the breeding season if nest boxes are erected during the previous winter, so that any unnatural smell is lost by weathering. Pictures can then be taken of birds carrying natural food to their young as they land on a perch outside the nest box.

Hedgehogs (p. 116), badgers and foxes can also be attracted to gardens by regular feeding, but either a very fast film or flash will be needed for photographing these essentially nocturnal visitors. Whilst staying with friends in Florida, we were able to use the house as a hide and take flash pictures of a racoon raiding a bird feeder at night.

In East Africa, ground squirrels are easily baited by day with bread or nuts and, once tamed, can be photographed without any cover using a 135 mm lens. These small mammals look especially appealing when they sit up on their back legs to feed, but make sure the picture is not spoilt with outsized bait. In many African gardens, careful searching will often reveal a chameleon exceedingly well camouflaged among bushes, fallen leaves, or on bark.

birds feeding is to pack suet into a pine cone or place nuts or fat in holes bored into the side of a 30-cm (1-foot) long branch. Hang the cone or branch vertically and birds will peck at the food. If you are really crafty, bore holes on one side of the branch only and hang this facing the window. Other foods which attract birds include portions of fresh coconut, cheese, apples (in winter these will attract fieldfares) and meal worms (robins love them), as well as natural berries, seeds and fruits.

When wild birds are feeding, they constantly look up to check that there are no predators lurking nearby. This makes for hurried, jerky movements, so either a fast shutter speed or flash must be used for photography. Direct light – whether from the sun or a flash – will add a sparkle to a dark eye as well as bringing out the subtle colours on a starling's plumage.

As birds feed, particularly from hanging wire feeders, some scraps fall to the ground where they are eagerly feasted upon by ground-feeding birds such as song thrushes and hedge sparrows. A friend of mine, whose garden backs on to woodland, has a cock and several hen pheasants which come to be fed daily at dawn. It is not advisable to

BAITING AND LURING

When wild animals prove wary of a close approach by stalking (p. 52), they can be lured towards the camera by a variety of techniques. Baiting is the most frequently used, for wild animals will soon learn to home in on a regular free meal. Car parks where visitors often picnic are easy places to photograph a variety of wild birds by baiting them with food. I have even noticed opportunist pigeons parading outside a local supermarket waiting for broken biscuits to be accidentally dropped from trolleys!

Remember that birds' bills and mammals' teeth are specially adapted to cope with a distinct diet, so it is important to select the appropriate bait for the particular species you want to photograph: for example, grain for seed-eating birds, nuts for squirrels, and animal corpses for carrion-eaters.

Repeated baiting of wild birds or mammals considerably increases the odds of getting a photograph. As with nesting birds, you have a known fixed point at which the animals will appear. The camera can then be set up on a tripod, pre-focused on the bait and triggered either from within a hide, or remotely by a long air release or an infrared trigger. If the available light is poor, it can be boosted by using fill-in flash (p. 44).

Before baiting an area, check the camera angles and particularly the background to make sure that the best site for photography has been chosen. Once the bait has been laid and a remote camera is in position or you are in the hide, it will not be possible to change the viewpoint.

Baiting is more rewarding in cold weather when natural foods are unobtainable or frozen. Timid birds may then become relatively tame, like the hungry robin I photographed in the snow without a hide (p. 19).

All the points covered for garden birds (p. 74) are also applicable here, but animals living out in the wild will tend to be even more wary of humans than wild animals which visit gardens, and a longer lens may be necessary. If fed regularly, however, some wildfowl – notably mute swans and various duck – will tolerate an extremely close approach without any need for cover. This not only means that anyone with a basic camera and fixed lens can take a reasonable picture, but also that a wide-angle can be used on a single-lens reflex camera for showing birds in their environment. The skill lies in making sure that the bait is not too obvious in the picture.

Fairburn Ings in Yorkshire is a wetland nature reserve formed as a result of mining subsidence and later flooding. Where the road runs adjacent to the water, there is a pull-off and it is here that people bring bags of sliced bread for feeding the wildfowl. To feed any bird solely on white bread is not to be recommended, but at Fairburn the wildfowl's diet is supplemented by natural food.

Throughout the summer, the Wildfowl Trust at Slimbridge in Gloucestershire nurtures the grassy swards adjacent to the Severn estuary so that up to 4000 white-fronted geese are attracted to feed there in winter. Covered walkways lead to hides where these wild birds can be observed and photographed.

In winter, the diet of wild birds at all the Wildfowl Trust reserves is supplemented by grain, always given at a regular time by the same person. At Welney in Cambridgeshire several hundred wild Bewick swans and several thousand duck (mainly wigeon) gather at feeding time in front of the hides overlooking the flood plain of the Ouse Washes; here there is endless scope for photography p. 113).

At the coast, gulls are easily lured to fish and it is a common sight to see herring gulls lined up on the quayside waiting for the fishing boats to return and the fish guts to be thrown overboard. The mêlée of birds in mid-air and swooping down into the water makes for a good action picture with a fast shutter speed.

Quite by chance when walking on a beach in California, I came across a gull feeding on a dismembered fish. The exposed red gills gave the sole area of colour to an otherwise virtually monochromatic picture.

Also in North America, but this time in Big Bend National Park, Texas, I came across turkey vultures feeding on a corpse by the side of the road. My husband backed the car on to the roadside verge at an angle so I could shoot through my open window. I managed to expose only a few frames of the birds homing in on the carcase before someone in another car saw what I was doing,

bait, which should be confined to a localized area. Then if a small aperture is used and the subject fills only part of the frame, red torch light (p. 116) is all that is needed to check that the subject is in the field of view.

Within an enclosure adjacent to the lodge at Samburu in Kenya, carnivorous Nile monitor lizards and crocodiles are baited daily. In the afternoon monitors take it in turns to climb up a tree to feed on their bait, while the crocodiles haul themselves out to feed by night.

Another way of drawing animals towards the camera is by means of acoustic lures. A technique which has been successfully used by only a few nature photographers is that of playing back recorded bird song in the field, and multiple bird songs are now available on a pre-recorded cassette tape. To attract a particular species, however, its song needs to be repeatedly dubbed. As with any kind of wildlife photography, the play-back technique should be used with caution and stopped immediately the birds show any signs of stress; for example, if a male bird hears another male, he may think his territory is being threatened and desert the nest. Play-back should preferably be done with someone who has experience of this specialized technique, as indeed should the use of decoy whistles, to prevent unnecessary distress to the birds.

◄**Subject:** Nile monitors (*Varanus niloticus*) attracted to bait
Location: Samburu Game Reserve, Kenya
Month: August
Time: Late afternoon
Lighting: Dappled sunlight
Lens: 200 mm on Nikon from fenced off enclosure
Film: Kodachrome 64

▼**Subject:** Turkey vultures (*Cathartes aura*) feeding on animal corpse at roadside
Location: Big Bend National Park, Texas, US
Month: April
Time: Late afternoon
Lighting: Direct sun
Lens: 300 mm on Nikon using car as hide
Film: Kodachrome 64

pulled up level with the vultures and hopped out of the car with an Instamatic! That was the end of my photography. This was an opportunist shot, but carrion-feeding birds can easily be baited by transferring animal road casualties to a remote track, where there is less likelihood of disturbance by passing traffic (and perhaps passing photographers, too!).

Small rodents can be baited with grain and if this is mixed with soil on the ground or inserted in cracks in a weathered tree stump, it will not be obvious in a photograph. Some sort of cover — either a camouflage net strung up between poles or a hide — will be necessary for photographing most wild rodents. For nocturnal species, the camera needs to be pre-focused on the

◄**Subject:** Herring gulls (*Larus argentatus*) feeding on waste thrown from fishing boat
Location: Shetland, Scotland
Month: August
Time: Late afternoon
Lighting: Light cloud
Lens: 200 mm on Nikon
Film: Kodachrome 64

At water

Water, as well as food, can be used to attract wild animals within photographic range. All the magical qualities associated with water, such as the reflections, highlights and ripples mentioned on p. 22, can also be brought into play here. Even a bird bath in a garden provides opportunities for taking birds drinking. The inside of the bath should have a rough finish to prevent the birds from slipping. Add a few stones in the centre so the birds can perch here as well as around the edge of the bath.

Most garden birds sip water and then throw back their head to swallow, and a sequence of pictures can be taken with a motor drive; doves and pigeons, on the other hand, swallow as they continue to drink and adopt a head-down posture.

Bathing helps to keep feathers clean, and dramatic action pictures can be taken of birds in a bird bath or in the shallows of a pond if they are backlit so that every drop of water is highlighted. On a hot day, birds are also attracted to spray from a hose or dripping water from a container hanging on a branch, and can be seen drinking water drops on plants.

The number of birds and the frequency of their visits to a pool can be increased if nearby pools are covered, so that the birds are not presented with any choice in the vicinity of the photographic site.

During periods of drought and in frozen weather when many natural sources dry up or freeze over, a water supply in the garden becomes even more attractive to animals in general. In severe cold weather, a portable shallow bird bath can be raised off the ground on to a brick base with a central hole, where a night-light candle can be lit to prevent the water from freezing. Water in permanently fixed bird baths can be kept warm by a thermostatically controlled photographic immersion heater (as used for printing in cold darkrooms), providing it is connected to a cable specifically designed for outside use. A conventional glass aquarium heater would work equally well, except that it would need to be protected against accidental damage. If ice does form on a bird bath, it can, of course, be melted simply by pouring hot water on to it.

Even garden birds at water will tend to fly off when suddenly approached with a camera, so either a portable hide or a house window overlooking a bird bath or pond will be needed for more than a lucky grab shot. From within a hide or house, however, it will be possible to photograph a succession of birds at water.

If more naturalistic surroundings are required, erect a hide either near a natural pool in a woodland clearing or, with the landowner's permission, create a pond in a natural depression. From the hide, pictures can be taken of birds not only drinking and bathing, but also resting on adjacent perches. As with perches beside a bird table

▲ **Subject:** Butterflies *Phoebis sennae* drinking on moist ground
Location: Urvina Bay, Isabela, Galápagos
Month: March
Time: Morning
Lighting: Sunlight
Lens: 80 mm on Hasselblad + extension
Film: Ektachrome 3 (ISO 64/19°)

◄ **Subject:** Warthog (*Phacochoerus aethiopicus*) in mud
Location: Waterhole at Mkuze, South Africa
Month: September
Time: Morning
Lighting: Direct sun
Lens: 400 mm on Nikon
Film: Kodachrome X (ISO 64/19°)

(p. 74), these need to be changed fairly frequently, or it will be too obvious that a series of pictures was taken at the same place.

Water – both moving and still – with muddy margins will attract house martins and swallows in early summer, when they need a constant supply of mud with which to build their nests. Muddy banks also attract butterflies in temperate summers, when they come to drink the moisture. Damp patches in woodlands serve a similar function by attracting woodland butterflies to an open spot down on the ground. In a dry summer, butterflies are readily attracted to water poured on to dried-up muddy patches where they are accustomed to drinking regularly. When photographing butterflies drinking, try to avoid any hurried move-ments, because the insects are much more likely to be disturbed than when feeding on a rich nectar source. A slow continuous approach works best and, even if the butterflies are disturbed, if you keep still they will soon return.

Any keen lepidopterist will know that urine is a most effective liquid bait for attracting butterflies to dry ground. I learnt this while working in a Peruvian tropical rain forest, when an eminent lepidopterist disappeared behind a bush and re-appeared with an old sardine can filled with the liquid bait. He carefully chose a suitable site in a clearing beside a river bank and, almost immediately, butterflies came down to drink at the damp patch.

The sudden appearance of temporary pools in deserts and arid regions attracts and concentrates wildlife – for example, the giant tortoises in the Galápagos (p. 115).

Towards the end of the tropical dry season, when water is in short supply, any source acts as a powerful magnet to animals in general. At this time, game tends to concentrate close to permanent water holes or rivers. In early morning and late evening in particular, a succession of game will visit a water hole. This situation is a photographer's paradise and anyone who experiences this spectacle for the first time invariably exceeds his normal daily film quota. The most memorable time I have ever spent working a water hole was at Mkuze in Natal, South Africa, a few days before the rains came. From within the elevated hide built beside the water hole we saw, among other animals, impala, kudu, nyala, wart hog, zebra, wildebeest, baboons, crocodiles, grey herons, yellow-billed egrets and helmeted guinea fowl. There are many advantages to working in a large hide, not least ample room to spread out lenses for quick changing. But perhaps most important of all, it allows for a variety of camera angles and, by using different focal length lenses, variations on the background compositions too.

For general shots of several animals drinking I used a 135 mm and occasionally a standard 50 mm lens, while for portraits I used 200 mm, 300 mm or 400 mm lenses on a Nikon. The zebra tended to be very nervous of any noise – including a camera shutter going off. We found the wart hogs easily the best value for, as well as drinking, they often lingered to wallow in the mud at the edge of the water hole. In certain lights the reflections of surrounding trees tended to dominate any composition which included a lot of water. At these times we concentrated on the game walking over land down towards the water.

For two days we focused our cameras on this ever-changing spectacle. On the third day the rains came and by the time the skies had cleared we drove out to our hide to see for ourselves what everyone had forecast – not a single animal in sight.

◄ Subject: Chapman's zebra (*Equus burchelli antiquorum*) with heron
Location: Waterhole at Mkuze, South Africa
Month: September
Time: Morning
Lighting: Direct sun
Lens: 200 mm
Film: Kodachrome X (ISO 64/19)

Water is essential to all life, although animals adapted to live in arid places can survive with minimal amounts. Animals are readily attracted to water and can be photographed drinking at large waterholes, small puddles or even damp ground.

RUBBISH AND WASTE

Rubbish accumulates the world over, and as the human population increases, so the problem of disposing of man's waste is exacerbated. Birds with an omnivorous diet are never slow to take advantage of potential food dumped on a tip. Indeed, flocks of gulls (chiefly herring gulls) weaving their way among the bulldozers on a corporation tip are a common sight throughout Britain, not just along the coast.

A low camera viewpoint works well when the sky is blue, or when it is dark and stormy but the sun is shining, for these coloured backdrops make a good contrast with the pale birds. When there is a colourless sky, search for a high viewpoint so the gulls can be contrasted against the (usually) darker tones of the tip itself.

If you are prepared to make a regular surveillance of a local tip you may be rewarded with the occasional rarity, such as a Ross's gull. Alternatively, joining a local birdwatching group can pay dividends in the form of early warnings of unusual sightings.

Walking around any rubbish tip is fraught with hazards and may even require special permission. The most evil-smelling dump I have ever experienced was one I came across years ago in Ireland, where starlings were squabbling over putrefying butcher's offal and rats were scurrying underfoot. Before I stepped out of the car I remember taking the precaution of changing my sandals for gum boots! The fading evening light and Kodachrome 64 could not produce a fast enough shutter speed to freeze the motion of the fighting starlings, but since several of the birds are sharp the blurring of the two frenetic bodies serves to emphasize and highlight the action in the centre of the frame.

With increasingly stringent legislation concerning health and safety standards in many countries, tips may not now be accessible outside normal working hours. In the late 1970s I noticed herring gulls feeding daily on a tip near the Devonshire coast. When I returned at dusk they were still there and, because I predicted that they would be conditioned to a vehicle approaching the tip, I decided to use the car as a hide. I opted for a 400 mm lens so that there was less chance of the birds lifting off before the fiery sun appeared from beneath the layer of cloud. The result was a dramatic picture of gulls silhouetted at sunset — albeit on a rubbish tip! The profile is not obviously that of a tip, and this is one of those instances where a picture has greater appeal if the true identity of the habitat is not revealed. For instance, if an advertising agency is looking for birds at sunset, it will be more inclined to look favourably at the shot if it is ignorant of the location.

In medieval times, semi-wild pigs were encouraged to scavenge on the food scraps, excreta and dead dogs which littered London's streets. But as the population grew and the pigs learnt to invade the kitchens, they had to be culled. By the end of the thirteenth century, when all of these pigs had been killed, red kites and ravens had taken over as scavengers and were protected by law. What scope there would have been for some dramatic photography of kites swooping down to scavenge among crowds in medieval London! Alas, this drama was enacted centuries prior to the invention of photography. By the eighteenth century the kites were no longer protected, and were rarely seen in London; by the late 1880s none bred in England. These attractive raptors are now endangered and once again completely protected. The scavenging instinct still persists at a place in mid-Wales where several kites feed regularly on a tip during the winter.

Gulls and starlings, assisted by crows, rooks and magpies, are the twentieth-

◀ **Subject:** Comma butterfly on tip
Location: Jinghong, Yunnan, China
Month: March
Time: Mid-day
Lighting: Dappled sunlight
Lens: 105 mm micro-Nikkor on Nikon
Film: Kodachrome 64

Rubbish tips attract a variety of wildlife — including insects, birds and mammals. Permission may have to be sought to gain access to a tip and care needs to be taken when walking among broken glass and sharp metallic objects.

heat and so they may attract house crickets, which can be heard chirping at dusk. Given suitable conditions, crickets will soon multiply and provide food for bats, which visit some tips by night. Mice and rats, sheltering in tips by day, also emerge at night to feed amongst the waste matter.

Butterflies are lured down to tips to drink moisture, to sip the juice of over-ripe fruit or to feed on flowers growing on more permanent tips. Since moving over any tip will be slow and ungainly, you will need to stalk a butterfly with either a 200 mm macro lens or a fixed 200 mm lens with a small extension tube.

Burying or sexton beetles can be attracted by baiting with rotten fish, or a dead mouse or small bird. Cover the bait with a piece of wood raised on stones to prevent its removal by larger scavengers. The beetles have an acute sense of smell, so if they are in the area they quickly home in on the carrion. Once they have located the carcase, they bury it by removing the soil beneath it. If flash is used to photograph these beetles, it should preferably be bounced to avoid a distracting highlight reflected off the shiny wing cases.

Many birds are attracted to sewage farms: swallows and swifts feast on the abundant midge swarms, waders are also frequent visitors, and birds in general assemble to roost. Bats take over from swallows as the night-shift consumers of midges, and where water shrews and rabbits occur, foxes are attracted to feed on them. These man-made habitats can therefore provide a rewarding place to take pictures of birds and mammals in an urban environment.

century scavengers of human waste in Britain; although human excrement is now flushed away, there are still places along the coast where outfall pipes are discharged on to the lower shore. As the tide rises, these areas are easily pinpointed by the frenzied activity of feeding gulls.

While visiting New Zealand I came across another kind of bird which was scavenging on a tip near Arthur's Pass on the South Island. Here keas fulfil the same function as red kites in Wales and black kites in mainland Europe, but unlike the kites, keas belong to the parrot family.

Birds are by no means the only animals that invade tips. Inedible and non-biodegradable items, such as tins, bottles and polystyrene cups, provide shelter for beetles, bugs, flies and spiders, as well as butterflies, moths, toads, lizards and rodents. Once plants begin to colonize a tip, they in turn provide food and shelter for a whole host of invertebrates. Tips, like garden compost heaps, generate considerable

▲ **Subject:** Herring gulls (*Larus argentatus*)
Location: Rubbish tip, Devon, England
Month: August
Time: Sunset
Lighting: Backlit from light of setting sun
Lens: 400 mm on Nikon
Film: Kodachrome X (ISO 64/19)

► **Subject:** Starlings (*Sturnus vulgaris*) squabbling over offal
Location: A tip in Ireland
Month: June
Time: Early evening
Lighting: Low-angled sun
Lens: 200 mm on Nikon
Film: Kodachrome 64

Subject: Encrusting lichens on sandstone rock
Location: Navajo National Monument, Arizona, US
Month: March
Time: Late afternoon
Lighting: Overcast
Lens: 55mm micro-Nikkor on Nikon
Film: Kodachrome 25

CHAPTER SIX

NATURE IN CLOSE-UP

In a similar way to a magnifying glass, a close-up photograph concentrates attention on detail – whether it is a tiny subject or a small part of a larger one. Indeed, when subjects are reproduced at magnifications greater than life size on the film, it is possible to reveal features normally passed over by a casual glance with the naked eye. The natural world offers endless scope for working at close range, encompassing still life subjects, and patterns and designs, as well as action shots. Appropriate lighting is of paramount importance in helping to highlight the form or emphasize the texture of close-ups.

GETTING IN CLOSE

Photographing nature in close-up opens up a completely new world by concentrating on small subjects or on portions of larger ones and often emphasizing colour or pattern. An imaginatively lit and sharply focused close-up immediately arrests attention and it may even reveal structures not visible to the naked eye. The range of close-up photography begins at a magnification of one-tenth (×0.1) up to life size on film. Pictures taken at greater than life size are usually erroneously referred to as macro-photographs (strictly, the term refers to the making of extra-large photographs, such as photo murals, and 'photomacrographs' would be more correct here). This range of magnifications, from life size upwards, is possible using a basic camera and lens with close-up accessories or a macro lens. If a microscope (even a low-power stereo-microscope) is used, the pictures are known as photomicrographs.

Taking nature close-ups can be both exhilarating and frustrating. If everything works – the subject appears correctly exposed, in focus, without blurred movement and clearly separated from the back-ground – there is a great sense of thrill and achievement. Often close-ups lack definition, though, due to camera shake, sloppy focusing, subject movement or a combination of all three factors. Some people might argue that it is one of the most difficult aspects of nature photography to master, yet simple close-ups can be taken using a prime (usually standard 50 mm) lens and a close-up or supplementary lens fitted to the front in the same way as a glass filter.

The advantages of using a close-up lens are that it does not reduce the amount of light passing to the film and being light-weight it can easily be carried in the pocket. Although close-up lenses are available in different strengths (expressed in terms of dioptres – a +2 dioptre lens magnifying twice as much as a +1 dioptre lens) and are relatively inexpensive, they each have a limited focusing range. A zoom close-up lens covers a bigger range of magnifications but the definition is not as good as with a close-up lens of a fixed focal length.

If you have a high-quality prime lens, resist the temptation to buy a cheap, inferior-quality close-up lens. Although it is possible to use two close-up lenses together it is preferable to use a more powerful single lens, extension tubes or bellows to gain a higher magnification.

None of the close-up lenses allows particularly high magnifications and by far the most popular accessory for the close-up enthusiast is a set of extension tubes or rings. These are inserted between the camera body and lens and can be used individually or in any combination together. Make sure you buy automatic tubes which will couple the lens diaphragm to the camera body, thereby automatically stopping down the lens iris diaphragm fractionally before the shutter is released. Fixed-length extension tubes suffer from the same disadvantage as a close-up lens in that each has a limited focusing range. The variable focusing extension tubes available for Olympus (55–116 mm) and Hasselblad (64–85 mm) systems are much more convenient.

Continuous variable extension, as well as increased magnifications, is provided by a bellows extension also inserted between the camera body and the lens. With a 50 mm standard lens and bellows extension, magnifications range from ×1 to ×3 with the lens used in the normal position. When the lens is mounted in the reverse position on the front of the bellows by using a reversing ring, the magnification range is increased and the quality of the image is improved. Once a lens has been reversed, the meter no longer couples with the camera and the automatic diaphragm ceases to function. A Z-ring attached to the rear end of the lens allows a double cable release to be connected here and to the shutter release, so the lens iris diaphragm is closed just before the picture is taken. A short extension tube fitted to what would normally be the back of the lens can function, if necessary, as a makeshift lens hood.

Bellows are more suitable for studio than field work, since bellows fabric is not as robust as metal extension tubes. Also an absolutely rigid camera support is essential for magnifications several times greater than life size when the depth of field is so minimal.

Extension tubes or bellows can be used with a wide-angle lens (such as 35 mm) and medium long focus lenses (135 mm), as well as a standard lens. The amount of magnification will vary with the focal length, a wide-angle lens giving a greater magnification for a given amount of extension than a standard lens and the latter giving more magnification than a long lens.

Anyone who plans to take more than a casual close-up would be well advised to invest in a focusing macro lens. The focal

◄Subject: Swallowtail butterfly wing (*Papilio machaon*)
Location: Studio bred specimen
Month: April
Lighting: Flash
Lens: 50 mm + bellows on Nikon
Film: Kodachrome 25

Three different ways of taking close-ups are illustrated on this spread; using a close-up lens, a macro lens and a macro lens with bellows extension.

The versatility of a zoom lens with a macro mode makes it appear more attractive than buying separate zoom and macro lenses, but it is a lot heavier than a single macro lens and not as quick to use, since it usually requires a button to be depressed to get into the macro mode. Highly specialist (and expensive) non-focusing 'true' macro lenses resembling microscope objectives have to be used with a bellows extension. They give excellent definition at magnifications many times life size.

Whatever the choice of close-up equipment, it is also essential to use a rigid camera support when working with available light so the maximum depth of field is gained. As the image size increases, so the depth of field decreases, therefore knowing where to focus a camera is much more critical when taking a close-up than for a wide-angle shot. When the aperture is fully open, a lens can be focused only on a single plane, but as the lens is stopped down the amount in focus (depth of field) extends behind and in front of the focal plane. This can be visually appreciated with most modern SLR cameras by depressing the depth of field preview button.

Although in general photography the depth of field extends twice as far behind the focal plane as in front, it is virtually equal on each side of the plane of focus in close-up photography. For most close-ups the aim will be to focus slightly behind the plane nearest to the camera so that when it is stopped down the maximum depth of field will be gained. Occasionally it may be preferable to open up a stop or two, narrowing the depth of field so as to ensure the subject stands out more clearly from an unfocused background.

length of the most popular macro lens is 50 mm or 55 mm, suitable for close-range static subjects, whereas the 105 mm or 200 mm macro lenses provide a larger working distance for taking active insects. Macro lenses have the extension built into the lens, allowing it to be focused continuously from infinity to a distance which gives a half life-size image, although the best definition will be gained when it is used at close range. A macro lens can also be used with extension tubes or bellows for still greater magnifications.

When using either extension tubes or bellows, the lens is automatically moved further away from the film plane, so the light has to travel further to reach the film. This means that the exposure must be increased. With TTL metering there is no longer any need for calculations, although when using bellows it may be necessary to revert to stop-down metering.

▲ **Subject:** 5-spot burnet moths (*Zygaena trifolii*)
Location: Disused railway line, Lancashire, England
Month: July
Time: Afternoon
Lighting: Overcast
Lens: 105 mm micro-Nikkor
Film: Kodachrome 25

▶ **Subject:** King protea (*Protea cynaroides*)
Location: Cape, S. Africa
Month: September
Time: Afternoon
Lighting: Direct sun
Lens: 80 mm + close-up lens, Hasselblad
Film: Ektachrome 64

STATIC SUBJECTS

When starting to take close-ups, it is best to concentrate on static subjects. You can then take plenty of time to assess the magnification and framing required, as well as the optimum lighting (p. 88). Flowers are by far the most popular of close-up subjects, probably because they are colourful and easily accessible, yet many flower portraits are disappointing.

Most of the faults arise from not using a firm camera support. Without a tripod (or ground spike for low-level subjects in some locations), static subjects are likely to suffer from one or any combination of the following: camera shake, lack of depth of field and imprecise focusing and framing. A tripod not only eliminates any chance of camera shake, but also allows for precise focusing so the maximum depth of field is gained (p. 85). The best-quality close-ups will only result from using slow-speed film (ISO 25/15° or 64/19°), stopping down the lens and using a fairly slow shutter speed. People who decry tripods and prefer to opt for high-speed film and fast shutter speeds instead immediately lose fine definition because of the obvious grain of the film.

Understanding depth of field is a fundamental factor in the success or failure of close-up photography. Since it decreases so markedly with increasing magnification, it is essential that the photographer maximizes the potential. A tripod allows slow speeds to be used, as well as time to check that the film plane is parallel to the subject so the maximum depth of field can be gained. For example, when photographing a series of small flowers arranged vertically on a spike, it is no good adopting a casually hand-held stance with the camera angled down on to

the spike, since very little will be in focus. A 35 mm format needs to be orientated vertically and parallel to the spike. On the other hand, flowers and leaves growing in a horizontal plane need to be photographed with the camera looking down from above so the film plane is again parallel to the subject.

Not all low subjects present their best profile uppermost; most tree seedlings, for instance, need to be viewed from the side to show the stalk, cotyledons and first leaves. There is a huge discrepancy in size between a seedling and the tree which produced the seed. This can be graphically shown by taking a worm's eye view looking across the leaf litter, with the trunks of the seedling's ancestor as an out-of-focus backcloth. Beached seashells are also immediately put in context when photographed from a low camera angle (a sandhopper's eye view) with the sea breaking behind.

But maximum depth of field is not always preferable for taking every close-up. Sometimes more impact may be gained by selectively focusing on part of the subject, such as the eyes of a dragonfly, thereby throwing the rest of the body out of focus. Taking a dragonfly side-on with the film plane at an angle of 45° to the body, however, will fall between two stools, since it can be neither a creative composition nor an authentic record of the subject. Differential focus can also be used to isolate a subject from a distracting background by selecting an aperture that throws the background (but not the subject) out of focus.

For taking encrusting lichens or mosses growing on vertical but angled rocks or tree trunks, a tripod which can have the length of all three legs adjusted independently of

each other is essential. Because small plants frequent such a wide range of sites, from ground level (alpine flowers, mosses, lichens and fungi) to eye level and above (flowers of trees and shrubs), it is worth investing in a versatile tripod. The uniquely designed Benbo allows the camera to be supported at any level on any kind of terrain. I have used one for almost twenty years and no habitat — whether it be a rocky shore, a forest, a cave, a river bed or a glacier — has ever defeated it. When climbing up mountains weight should always be kept as low as possible, but it is quite feasible to carry the 1.8-kg (4-lb) Baby Benbo strapped to a rucksack.

◄ **Subject:** Peony (*Paeonia* sp.) flower
Location: The Imperial Palace Garden, Forbidden City, Beijing, China
Month: May
Time: Morning
Lighting: Overcast
Lens: 55 mm micro-Nikkor on Nikon
Film: Kodachrome 25

The camera angle has been carefully chosen for these pictures; an overhead view into the peony flower and a side view, with the camera supported close to the ground, for the other two.

◀**Subject:** Still-life study — plants and beached wood
Location: Drift-line on sandy beach at Brandon Bay, Ireland
Month: June
Time: Afternoon
Lighting: Overcast
Lens: 55 mm micro-Nikkor
Film: Kodachrome 25

◀When I saw the beached wood and green nylon rope my first instinct was to remove the rope; but I decided to leave everything exactly as it had been created by the incoming tide.

▼**Subject:** Fungi (*Stropharia hornemannii*)
Location: Pine wood, New Forest, Hampshire, England
Month: November
Time: Afternoon
Lighting: Overcast
Lens: 55 mm micro-Nikkor
Film: Kodachrome 64

on the spot. Does the flower separate clearly from the background? Is there a brightly coloured flower (or any object out of focus in the background) which competes for attention with the subject? Are there conflicting objects cutting in front of or behind the subject? All this may sound rather complicated, but with practice it will become second nature and completely automatic.

Once the camera is attached to its support, look through the viewfinder to check if any conflicting objects still remain. If so, they can be judiciously 'gardened' away either by tying back larger branches with tape or removing dead bracken or bramble stems. For 'gardening' to be successful, it should not be apparent to anyone else, since all it is doing is providing a clear and unobstructed view of the subject. Cutting grass or branches with shears or secateurs is not to be recommended. The way in which a plant is 'gardened' very much depends on personal choice; I never like anyone else volunteering to do it for me. I shall never forget the day I set off to find a large rare plant growing on chalk grassland. An area of flattened grass caught my attention; in its centre was a perfect specimen looking completely unnatural, since everything had been removed down to ground level in a foot radius around the plant! Objects such as leaves of common trees, pine cones or acorns should be left since they provide useful natural scale as well as conveying the type of habitat.

The ground spike is an even smaller camera support which can be slipped into a pocket. It has a more limited use than a tripod since it cannot be used in rocky or very wet terrain. Ideally, the ground needs to be firm, and not too soft. Ground spikes can be made with a 10-cm (4-inch) metal tent peg as the spike. Horizontal arms need to be welded to the top to prevent the camera pulling the spike over to one side. The camera is attached to a small ball and socket head.

For low-level work in any habitat, but especially in a damp woodland or on a wet beach, a waterproof ground sheet is useful not only for putting down gear, but also for kneeling on. On hard ground, gardener's kneelers will make this more bearable. You will not have to stoop quite so low if you substitute the standard viewfinder on an SLR camera with a right-angle one.

Before releasing the shutter, look through the camera and check the flower is a good specimen undamaged by slugs or birds. A few seconds spent at this stage can save wasted frames later. With practice, you will learn to run through a quick checklist posing questions which you can only answer

LIGHTING STATIC SUBJECTS

The commonest faults with close-ups are incorrect focusing and lack of thought about selecting the light to suit the subject. As with larger-scale subjects, close-ups can be lit by direct light from the front, side or behind, with available light or flash, and with or without reflectors, while diffused light is preferable for some subjects. Assessing the light before taking close-ups is every bit as important as light on the landscape (p. 12), yet more often than not close-ups are unimaginatively lit.

Available light is generally preferable for *in situ* plant close-ups, but it may prove inadequate in a situation such as a dark forest. The direction of extensive shadows needs to be carefully appraised, for a large shadow can completely dominate a small close-up. Direct lighting should preferably be positioned (or when using sunlight, the camera viewpoint changed) so that the ground shadow is cast to one side of the subject, rather than cast forward where it will create a dark unlit area in the foreground. Conspicuous shadows cast by direct sunlight can be softened and filled in by using a reflector.

White flowers – especially in sunlight – present similar exposure problems to snow (p. 33). A metered reading will produce an under-exposed (grey) flower with the green foliage rendered almost black. The solution is either to meter off the flower and open up by 1 to 1½ stops, or to meter off the green leaves. A soft diffuse light, either from an overcast day or from a diffuser (p. 38), will ease the problem. A reflector (or a mirror) can also be used to angle light on to a subject in shadow. A mirror should be used with caution, for the light reflected from it may be too bright for some flowers. Professional circular reflectors, which collapse into a small pouch, come in a range of finishes – white, silver or gold. White, although not such an efficient reflector as the metallic finishes, can usefully double up as a diffuser. A silver reflector is not as warm as a gold one, so it is better to use it early or late in the day when the natural light appears much warmer. A silver-sided survival blanket can also be used as a reflector, although it may flap around in a strong breeze.

If distracting highlights appear from available light on wet seaweeds, shiny leaves or fruits, they can be reduced either by using a polarizing filter (p. 42) or by blotting out direct sunlight with a black umbrella or a dark coat.

Often when working in the field, a close-up subject will be found at a time when the available lighting is not suitable, bright sunlight on a white flower for instance, or an overcast day when direct sun is required to backlight grasses, a spiny cactus pad or

autumnal leaves. Changing bright sun to a localized area of soft diffused light is quite easy with a diffuser, but waiting for the sun to shine on a day with complete cloud cover may be a fruitless exercise. You will have to decide whether it will be more economical on time to return to photograph a plant on another day or to set up a direct flash to simulate sun.

When working with slow-speed film and using smaller apertures, it is rare to be faced with the problem of an excess of light. If a slower shutter speed is required, however, then a neutral density filter can be used to reduce the light level entering the camera.

With an animal – however static it may appear when you first see it – there is no guarantee it will stay put for any length of time, so it should always be taken when it is first found. The coiled chameleon tail was a lucky opportunist shot taken in a garden in Zambia, because moments later the chameleon descended to the ground and walked off into a shrub border.

Available lights and long exposures can

be used for all resting animals, particularly night-flying moths by day. But even some conventionally active insects, such as grasshoppers and crickets, have periods of inactivity: a sudden rain shower will force dragonflies and butterflies to alight on plants, for instance. During the time they have to spend drying out their wings before they can fly again, it is possible to approach at close range.

Grass flowers make especially challenging outdoor close-ups, for their long stalks wave in the slightest breeze, as do the ripe anthers hanging down from small and rather unspectacular flowers. By using a low camera angle, the larger grass heads can be profiled against the bright sky. This approach is not suitable for delicate grasses, however, which preferably should be viewed spotlit (by sun or flash) against a background in shadow.

Dewdrops on a spider's web are also shown to advantage against a dark background. If this is not naturally apparent, it can be created by holding the flash out to

◄**Subject:** Coiled chameleon tail
Location: Garden at Ndola, Zambia
Month: September
Time: Morning
Lighting: Overcast
Lens: 55 mm micro-Nikkor
Film: Kodachrome 25

◄On dull days, it is possible to use a long exposure to photograph normally active animals when they are at rest – though they may spoil your plans by deciding to move off suddenly in the middle of the exposure.

◄**Subject:** Young thorns of *Rosa sericea pteracantha*
Location: Author's garden, Surrey, England
Month: May
Time: Early morning
Lighting: Back
Lens: 55 mm micro Nikkor
Film: Kodachrome 25

◄This rose – a native of China – was planted in a south-facing aspect of our garden so we can see the glowing red thorns whenever the sun shines.

electronic flash set-up which is remote from the camera (p. 44).

When photographing plants there is plenty of time to set up a flash on a small lighting stand or on top of a wooden stake with a ball and socket head topped with a flash shoe instead of a tripod screw. I find stakes invaluable when backlighting a hairy or spiny subject with flash. If I want to check the precise angle of the flash to avoid flare on the lens, I tape a small torch to the side of the flash head and, of course, I use a lens hood on the lens. By using a Polaroid back on the Hasselblad, I can check the angle of the flash lighting before exposing any transparency film.

Flash does not need to be used as a direct light source. It can be bounced off a white umbrella or white card or a piece of diffuser trace taped across the flash window. Several medium-weight flashguns having an optional bounced light attachment.

The nature of the surface, as well as the tone of a plant or animal, affects the amount of light it reflects. For example, a pale-coloured shiny fruit or shell reflects a great deal of light, whereas dark, highly textured bark or soil reflects very little. Any textured surface, especially when viewed in close-up, can be exaggerated by using an extreme form of side lighting which literally grazes across the surface, illuminating the bumps and casting shadows in the depressions. This technique is invaluable for revealing the slightest texture on a leaf, a fruit or a shell. Direct sunlight can be used to provide grazed lighting in the field, but it is easier to control by using flash. Depending on the magnification and the tone of the subject, you may find it will help to have a foil reflector or mirror opposite the flash to reduce very contrasty shadows. Textured surfaces photographed in close-up often appear as abstract patterns and they therefore make good puzzle pictures.

Flat encrusting lichens growing flush with trees, rocks or even gravestones are good examples of textured plants which can be found in a range of colours. Encrusting lichens are particularly good subjects to take in winter, since they will not move in the wind and rain enriches their colours.

one side of the web and shining it across the surface in such a way that it fails to light the background. The catchlight from a direct flash also adds a distinct sparkle to each individual dewdrop.

Flowers generally look more natural, however, if they are not photographed with flash from in front so that a distant background is so under-exposed it appears like a nocturnal picture. If flash is required, try to balance it with sunlight so the background is correctly exposed (p. 45) making the entire

composition appear much more natural.

A single flash – either incorporated in the camera itself, or connected via a hot-shoe on the top of the camera – produces flat frontal lighting which causes distracting highlights on shiny leaves and fruits. One of the few instances when frontal flash is essential to ensure the subject is adequately illuminated is for deep-throated flowers: here the specialist ring flash (p. 139) comes into its own. For all other subjects, it is important to make sure you have the means of using an

SEQUENCES

The way in which a plant responds to light, a flower opens, a wind-dispersed seed falls or a small animal moves, can be conveyed by two or more still close-up images either on consecutive frames or on a single frame. Time-lapse photography is used to record long-term movement over a period of several hours or even days. A camera can be set up to expose automatically at pre-determined, equal intervals, but this is not always the best way of recording the sequence of a flower bud opening. For this, I prefer to sketch the flower after each exposure using a chinagraph pencil on a 6×6 cm ($2\frac{1}{2} \times 2\frac{1}{2}$ inch) viewfinder, so I can ensure that each stage is sufficiently different from the last one.

Movement by living plants may be induced by changes in temperature, by light intensity, or by tactile or chemical stimuli. Flowers which open their petals in response to a rise in temperature include bulbs, such as crocuses, brought into a warm room. Plants that open their flowers by day respond to increasing light levels, whereas nocturnal flowers are stimulated by decreasing light levels. Water-lily and cacti flowers both open in response to the sun. Water will be lost by evaporation from desert cacti flowers, so they open for only a few hours a day, coinciding with the time their pollinators are most active. Some cacti flowers, as well as gentians, are so sensitive to a change in light intensity that they close in response to a cloud passing over the sun.

The easiest way of recording the movement of plant petals is with a pair of pictures, one showing the flower closed and the other open. Remember to keep the image fairly small in the frame when taking the closed flower, allowing plenty of room for the petals to open out without being cropped at the edges of the frame. If sufficient space is not allowed, it may be necessary to decrease the magnification, and this nullifies a true comparison. The viewpoint also needs to be carefully thought about for, if the petals open out as a flat radial flower, they should be viewed from overhead; whereas if the bud hangs down before opening, it is best seen laterally. Once the viewpoint has been selected and the first frame taken, the camera must be kept on the tripod in this position for exposure of the second frame. In case the weather suddenly deteriorates, a heavy-duty plastic bag over the camera, tied below the tripod head, will keep the camera dry.

There may be a noticeable shift in the colour balance between an early morning shot of the flower in bud and one later in the day when the sun is shining. It is possible to 'warm up' slightly the colours of an available-light, early-morning shot by using

Subject: Cape stock rose (*Sparmannia africana*) stamen filaments before (left) and after touching
Location: Royal Botanic Gardens, Kew, Surrey, England
Month: September
Time: Afternoon
Lighting: Overcast
Lens: 55 mm micro-Nikkor + 25 mm extension on Nikon
Film: Kodachrome 25

an 81A or 81B filter, but even then one picture may have shadows, the other none. Taking both frames using direct flashlight by shading the subject from the sun with a coat can provide identical lighting, but it will be a false record of the natural light.

Insectivorous plants, such as sundew and the Venus flytrap, respond to touch. As a hapless insect alights on a sundew leaf, the sticky tentacles bend over to trap it. The tropical sensitive plant, *Mimosa pudica*, is often sold as a pot plant in temperate countries. The leaf rapidly responds to heavy rainfall or the touch of a hand by suddenly falling and the leaflets close tightly together. Some cacti and other plants have excitable stamens in their flowers; the tight cluster reacts to an insect visitor by moving outwards to dust the insect with pollen.

A series of multiple time-lapse images on a single frame can be taken only if the camera has some means of double exposing without advancing the film. On cameras with interchangeable backs, such as Hasselblad and Bronica, as well as the 35 mm Rollei SL 3003, the film magazine is removed before the shutter is re-cocked. On many 35 mm SLR cameras the photographer can prevent the film advancing simply by depressing a button. A special dial on the Canon T90 can be set to expose from two to nine exposures on a single frame, while the multiple exposure unit available for the Rollei 6000 series allows up to 10 exposures to be made on a single frame.

Multiple time-lapse images look most effective when their overlap is minimal and when they are photographed against a contrasting background. This may mean carefully observing the way a flower opens or doing a dummy run on Polaroid film. Large solid flowers, such as a protea or a dahlia, do not work well, since as the bud opens the increasingly larger images of the flower tend to obscure the outline of the previous exposures. The daffodil is an example of a flower with a slender bud that adjusts its position relative to the stalk as it grows and opens, thereby providing a series of quite distinct multiple images.

Since the tripod with camera must not be moved and the lighting needs to remain constant once the first exposure has been made, time-lapse photography is impractical in variable field conditions. Within a studio (or a glasshouse), however, the background and lighting can be controlled.

Analysis of faster movements, such as the way in which a wind-dispersed seed falls, requires either a fast, repetitive stroboscopic light source to fire several times while the shutter remains open. I use a Polaroid film back on the Hasselblad to determine the optimum repetition rate of the stroboscopic flash for each particular seed. Stroboscopic flash is widely used in industry to analyse moving machinery. You can estimate the repetition rate of the

stroboscopic light or the firing rate of the camera shutter required for photographing a winged seed by dropping it from a reasonable height (3 metres/10 feet or so) and timing how long it takes to reach the ground. Once this has been established, the camera is set up with a plain (preferably black) background so that the field of view is of sufficient depth to include several images of the falling seed; the camera is pre-focused on a piece of string tied along the expected path of the falling seed. The smallest possible aperture should be selected to allow maximum depth of field for the spinning seed. The camera shutter is either operated manually so that it remains open throughout the time the seed falls through the field of view, or alternatively an electronic camera is triggered as the seed breaks a light beam trigger aligned just above the top of the field of view. If the shutter is open for a second, the strobe needs to fire at least four or five times a second to ensure three or four separate and complete images on the frame.

▼**Subject:** *Anisoptera megistocarpa* seed from Malaysian rain forest showing spiralling falling movement
Location: Author's studio, Surrey, England
Lighting: Nikon SB6 strobe at 5 flashes/sec
Lens: 80 mm on Hasselblad
Film: Ektachrome 100

Subject: Sensitive plant (*Mimosa pudica*) leaves before (above) and after touching
Location: Mauritius
Month: May
Time: Afternoon
Lighting: Overcast
Lens: 55 mm micro-Nikkor on Nikon
Film: Kodachrome 64

ACTION CLOSE-UPS

When illustrating a small active close-up, better-quality pictures will be gained by using flash to freeze the movement in preference to a fast shutter speed with high-speed film. By boosting the light level, flash can also be used to increase the depth of field in dark locations. I have used flash for stopping the action of snakes flicking out their tongues, for taking active insects and a variety of nocturnal invertebrates, as well as frogs, toads and reptiles.

All the points covered in the general pages on flash (pp. 44–5) are equally applicable here, but the limitations of the smaller electronic flash do not apply when taking close-ups. The limited camera-to-subject distance required when working with a 55 mm macro lens means that the light source can be positioned close to the subject so lack of power is not a problem.

The position of the flash head(s) relative to the subject and the type of flash (direct, diffuse or bounce) need to be carefully considered in each case. A direct flash should be positioned so the shadow it casts falls to one side or behind the subject. For this reason, I prefer to have a completely mobile flash held in the hand, rather than fixed to a right-angle bracket, when photographing an animal which is changing the position of its head. The flash can then be quickly moved from one side to the other.

Top-of-the-range, medium-sized electronic flashguns have a built-in manual variable power ratio dial for varying the flash duration from 1/500 to 1/10,000 of a second. This converts a relatively slow-speed flash into quite a fast one – although the decrease in light output at the extreme end of the scale may require more than one head to provide enough light for taking the close-up. Professional guns with interchangeable heads offer still greater flexibility of lighting, including an infra-red head from which infra-red wavelengths are emitted for use with infra-red film.

When stalking insects feeding at flowers, however, I find the macro flash brackets, designed for using two or even three flash heads as part of an integral single unit, especially useful. The Hasselblad macro flash bracket is attached to the front of the lens using a lens mounting ring. Both the variable power output on this unit and the Hasselblad variable extension tube allow considerable flexibility when stalking insects feeding on flowers. Each flash head also has a diffuser which can be used to control the quality of light. The problem of adequately illuminating the background behind the subject is solved with a (third) background flash support designed to be used with a Kennett macro flash which is supplied with hot-shoe sync-cords.

It may seem extravagant to expose an entire colour film as a test run, but in the long term it will save many wasted frames. Several frames of each subject should be taken, carefully noting the film speed, the focal length of the lens and magnification, the distance of each flash head from the subject, the power output of each flash and the aperture used. I use a proforma sheet (p. 139) which is quick to complete and reminds me if I have forgotten one parameter. Keeping all the other variables constant, I then bracket the exposure one stop on either side of the original exposure by changing only the aperture.

This is standard practice whenever I get a

◄**Subject:** Ants (*Iridomyrex* sp.) attending membracid bugs
Location: Tollgate Is., Bateman's Bay, Australia
Month: January
Time: Afternoon
Lighting: Twin flash
Lens: 105 mm micro-Nikkor on Nikon
Film: Kodachrome 25

◄With constant movement of the ants up and down the eucalyptus stem it was impossible to compose the picture precisely. It was taken using a pair of small flash guns mounted with the camera on a boomerang bracket made by an Australian photographer.

◀ **Subject:** Grass snake (*Natrix natrix*) flicking out tongue
Location: Frensham, Surrey, England
Month: May
Time: Late afternoon
Lighting: Flash
Lens: 150 mm + extension on Hasselblad
Film: Ektachrome 64

▶ **Subject:** Painted lady (*Vanessa cardui*) on ice plant (*Sedum spectabile*)
Location: Author's garden, Surrey, England
Month: September
Time: Afternoon
Lighting: Hasselblad twin macro-flash
Lens: 150 mm + extension on Hasselblad
Film: Ektachrome 64

new flash set-up. After processing, I lay out the entire film on a large light box so I can compare one frame with another. I write the exposure on each frame and throw away any which are obviously under- or over-exposed. I then transfer the details of correctly exposed frames to a master notebook and also my current field notebook. If the flash output proved too great for a pale-toned subject even when using the smallest possible aperture, I use either a neutral density filter on the camera lens or a diffuser on the flash window(s), bounce the flash off a special umbrella, or reduce the power of the flash with a variable power control.

Bounced or indirect flash is also preferable for illuminating shiny subjects such as fruits, insects and shells. The large flash umbrellas used for studio and portrait work are far too cumbersome to use in the field, but the Lastolite Mini Apollo light modifier (p. 138) has been designed specifically for close-up work. The umbrella opens to form a silver reflector with a 41 cm (16 inch) square base. Attached to the base is a square of optical white nylon material, for providing an optional diffuser. The nylon can quickly be detached on three sides by pulling the Velcro strip fastener apart. (This should be done *before* a wary animal is stalked.) A flash – with a head that can be tilted up into the top of the umbrella – is attached to the central handle via an extendable camera mounting bracket. Even when the diffuser is being used, adjustments can be made via a zipped opening on one side of the umbrella. On its own, the mini

umbrella weighs only 240 g (8½ oz), but even with the extendable bracket flash it can easily be used as a hand-held unit complete with a 35 mm camera in the field. The light loss varies with the flash used, but it is about 1 stop when bounced off the reflective surface and 1.3 stops when diffused through the nylon.

If a narrow flash beam is required for lighting very small static subjects which are being moved around by the wind, a light-weight portable fibre optic unit (p. 139) is available. A Fresnel lens fits over the window of the electronic flash complete with fibre optic unit and focusing lens. Since the angle of the beam is so critical, it is essential to use this attachment with a portable flash that has a built-in modelling light, such as the Olympus OM system macro flash units.

The ring flash is a specialized unit used chiefly for medical and dental photography. The circular flash surrounds the lens to give completely shadowless lighting. It is useful for illuminating subjects with concave areas, such as deep-throated flowers and bromeliads – although any rain water trapped in the central leaves of a bromeliad will reflect the flash back into the lens. A ring flash is not suitable for insects with a shiny thorax or wing cases, since it produces a circular reflection which, if centrally positioned, can be mistaken for a diagnostic pattern. Modifications can be made to the complete circle of light if necessary by masking off portions with black tape or by covering parts with diffuser trace.

▲ **Subject:** Bumblebees foraging for pollen in poppy flowers
Location: Author's garden, Surrey, England
Month: June
Time: Early morning
Lighting: Hasselblad twin macro-flash
Lens: 80 mm + extension on Hasselblad
Film: Ektachrome 64

▲ We grow poppies in our garden specifically to attract bumble-bees. They begin to forage at first light as new flowers unfold their petals to reveal the rich pollen load. By mid-morning, when the bees have gathered all the pollen from the copious stamens, the flowers begin to fade.

PATTERNS AND DESIGNS

Patterns exist on different scales throughout the natural world but are particularly evident in close-ups which can be taken both in the field and in the studio. The shapes of natural objects can be divided into four basic forms – the circle, the spiral, the polygon and the mirror image.

Designs based on a circle exhibit radial symmetry and within the animal kingdom are widespread among the sea anemones, coral polyps and jellyfish, as well as the echinoderms. The pentaradial symmetry within the echinoderms is most obviously displayed by starfish and brittle stars.

Plants from the daisy family, such as sunflowers, asters, dahlias, gerberas and zinnias, are cultivated throughout the world for their ornamental radial flowers. The so-called flower of these plants is, in fact, a mass of small flowers. What looks like a petal is a complete flower called a floret. Other flowers which are radially symmetrical include anemones, roses and water-lilies. Although the design of radially symmetrical flowers may look almost identical, the floral parts may be arranged in different ways to achieve this symmetry. The petals of cherry and rose flowers, for example, are arranged in whorls, whereas the parts of magnolia and buttercup flowers are arranged in spirals.

Attractive radial designs also exist as leaf rosettes of flowering plants and include foxglove, stork's bill, saxifrages, many succulents and cacti, as well as the giant African lobelias. The full beauty of tiny flower-like rosettes produced by mosses in spring and autumn can be appreciated by viewing with a magnifying lens or with a bellows extension on a camera. In the centre of the whorls of bracts, female and male reproductive organs develop, but they are not true flowers as erroneously thought by early botanists. The advantage of this design is that each leaf overlaps its neighbours to the same extent so all the leaves receive the same amount of light.

Radially symmetrical flowers tend to pro- duce similar-shaped fruits. A transverse cut through many of the most popular cultivated fruits – apples, pears, oranges and quinces – shows seeds arranged in sectors around the centre of the fruit.

These kinds of fruit and flower, like sea anemones, starfish and leaf rosettes, are best photographed from directly overhead with the film plane parallel to the plant or animal. Soft diffused light (p. 00) works well for static subjects such as plants and leaves, but flash will have to be used to arrest the movement of sea anemone tentacles. The colour of the gills beneath the cap of radially symmetrical fungi with a central stalk or stipe can be seen only from beneath – either by picking a fungus or by holding a small mirror beneath the cap.

Once you have an eye for pattern and design examples appear in every kind of habitat. Sometimes the subject itself is not radially symmetrical, but it displays a radial pattern within. For example, gnarled old trees are worth looking at for circular

▲ Subject: Leaf rosette of *Lobelia deckenii* subsp. *bequaertii*
Location: Bog at 3500 m on Mt Ruwenzori, Uganda
Month: September
Time: Early morning
Lens: 55 mm micro-Nikkor
Film: Kodachrome 64

▲ This lobelia is one of several tree-like forms which are confined to Mount Ruwenzori (also known as the Mountains of the Moon). Other species occur on Mounts Kenya and Elgon.

◀ Compare these small repetitive spiral forms from the Jurassic era with the living chameleon tail on page 88 – a transitory shape.

◀ **Subject:** Ammonites (*Promicroceras marstonense*)
Location: Studio
Geological period: Jurassic
Lighting: Tungsten-halogen spot
Lens: 55 mm micro-Nikkor
Film: Kodachrome 25

spawn of nudibranchs or sea slugs, and the shell of some marine tube worms.

The most economical way of packing many similar-sized objects together is for each one to have a regular polygonal form – honey-bee comb is a perfect example. The repetitive pattern of the waxy hexagonal cells is best shown before they become filled with honey or pollen. Viewed from above, the polygonal basalt columns such as occur on the Giant's Causeway in Northern Ireland make exciting repetitive patterns. Ripe maize seeds also adopt a neat packing pattern, while the pores on the underside of boletus fungi make exciting close-ups. The intricate arrangement of scales on butterfly and moth wings is appreciated when seen at magnifications greater than life size; only then can they be seen to overlap each other like tiles on a roof.

Other repetitive close-up patterns occur on the outer coating of many animals. The scales of snake and lizard skin make beautiful patterns, as do the larger scales of fish, tortoise-shell plates, bird feathers and mammalian fur. The bark of some trees forms regular repetitive patterns (alligator juniper) or irregular patterns (the flaking bark of plane trees). Fungi which produce tight clusters of toadstools instead of solitary ones make striking repetitive patterns when tightly cropped. On the seashore, encrustations on seaweeds of minute regular-shaped boxes (discernible with a hand lens) formed by sea mats need to be taken several times larger than life size, whereas the ripple pattern on a sandy beach is on a much larger scale. When salt pans, or any wet, muddy area dry out and the mud begins to crack, the stress patterns produce an intriguing polygonal design.

Many of these subjects have an obvious texture as a result of this repetitive pattern, and this is greatly enhanced by using grazed lighting (p. 89). On the other hand, the arrangement of leaves or fruits on a tree may create a more convincing design if silhouetted (p. 37).

Bilaterally symmetrical forms are also widespread in nature and include huge groups of animals such as insects and vertebrates – in fact, anything which is a mirror image of one half of its body.

Patterns in nature do not exist simply to delight the photographer's or artist's eye – in many cases they function as an attractive mechanism. Shapes and patterns of flowers attract pollinating insects, while colourful fruits attract foraging mammals that then disperse the seeds. Sudden flashing of false eye spots on the underwings of a butterfly or moth deters a potential predator, while eye spots on fish serve to confuse predators as to where to make their attack.

callous patterns over the stump of a lost branch. If they are too high up for taking with a standard lens and close-up accessories, try using a longer lens with an extension tube.

On a smaller scale, animal eyes and their surrounding patterns are well worth a detailed photographic study. Several lepidoptera have attractive false eye spots on their wings, notably the owl and peacock butterflies, the eyed hawk-moth and several hawk-moth caterpillars. Many tropical fish, particularly the marine butterfly fish, also sport attractive eye spots and when the peacock erects and fans out his tail feathers to attract a mate, a glorious array of irridescent eye spots is displayed.

All circular forms fit most naturally into a square, so radially symmetrical plants and animals look better if they are taken on a square 6 × 6 cm rather than a 35 mm format. If a rectangular format is used, either the margins of the circle have to be cropped or, if the complete circle is included, then some background must also be visible.

Spiral forms are fun to photograph for they can be taken so they spiral horizontally, vertically or diagonally across the frame. Spirals in nature include young fern fronds, the arrangement of seeds in a sunflower head, tendrils of plants such as cucumbers, pumpkins and sweet peas, the arrangement of leaves on a twig and scales on a cone; but perhaps most spectacular of all is a coiling snail or ammonite shell. A longitudinal section of a shell reveals the way the chambered shell is attached to the central axis. Other natural spiral forms include a transverse section of cabbage, the

STUDIO LIGHTING

Certain close-up subjects can be photographed more successfully if lighting and background are carefully selected in a studio: for example, small aquatic organisms (both marine and freshwater), small mammals, seeds, fossils and shell sections. Time-lapse studies (p. 90) of flowers opening and winged seeds falling are also easier to take within the confines of a studio.

The main advantage of close-up work is that the studio does not have to be anywhere near as spacious as conventional studios like those used for photographing fashion models. Part of a room will do; indeed, when working abroad I often have to make do with a small table. If natural light is required for still-life studies of flowers or fruits, a sunroom or conservatory can be used, providing the glass is clean and does not throw an unnatural colour cast.

In my own studio, which measures 4×5 metres ($13 \times 16\frac{1}{2}$ feet) I have 16 power sockets, fixed benches along two walls and backgrounds on rolls; flash and tungsten lights are suspended from the ceiling on a Bowens Hi-glide light track, to which extendible arms are attached enabling them to be raised or lowered at will.

I also use fibre optics for precise lighting of small areas, various light tents for creating a diffused source for highly polished shells and seeds, and a light table. An optical bench allows me to mount the camera at one end and the specimen at another so that I can move either a fraction of a millimetre at a time to ensure the optimum depth of field when using bellows extension.

The first nature picture I ever took was of a sea anemone in an aquarium. Since then, I have photographed many aquatic organisms in specially designed aquaria, as mass-produced rectangular aquaria have the wrong proportions for working on a square 6×6 cm format. Glass is preferable to Perspex which easily scratches. Small aquaria are easy to make using special glass adhesive. I use shallow glass dishes for containing flatworms that creep over the bottom, whereas narrow upright containers are better for taking massed planktonic organisms moving up and down the water column. Tanks 30×30 cm (12×12 inches) square are suitable for photographing frogs and newts. Since these animals are amphibious, they can be photographed either in water or in a vivarium with stones, mosses and maybe a shallow pool.

If photography is done through the glass front, it must be kept completely clean and free of algal growths. A matt black mask, as described for photographing fish in large public aquaria (p. 68), also needs to be used for smaller aquaria. Electronic flash provides the best lighting for aquatic life, since

▲ Subject: Pickerel frog (*Rana palustris*)
Location: Aquarium in author's studio, Surrey, England
Lighting: Electronic flash
Lens: 80mm + extension on Hasselblad
Film: Ektachrome 64

▶ Subject: Shark's tooth ($\times$ 3 magnification)
Location: Author's studio, Surrey, England
Lighting: Oblique backlighting from two fibre optics
Lens: 80mm + bellows extension on Hasselblad
Film: Ektachrome 64

it freezes all movement and gives off negligible heat. It can be directed from above to simulate sunlight, or through the side glass walls. Lighting through the front glass is not to be recommended unless photographing an animal, such as a leech or a limpet, clinging to it. The flash should then be used off the camera, angled in at about 45° to the glass. Backgrounds in tanks can be authentic weeds and stones or an artificial plain-toned waterproof board. The latter makes no pretence to simulate the natural habitat, but it can be useful for highlighting the subject's structure.

For non-aquatic subjects, black velvet makes the best non-reflective black background. It can be used on a roll suspended from the ceiling or fixed to free-standing boards with triangular supports behind. Fibre optics illuminated by a tungsten halogen light source provide a most effective cold light for spotlighting a small subject or a small area of a larger subject with a narrow angled beam. I used two to backlight the serrated edge of a shark's tooth, checking the correct exposure with Polaroid film on the Hasselblad. The clamp stands produced by biological laboratory suppliers are ideal for precisely clamping the fibre optic arm in position. Fibre optics are particularly effective at creating the extreme form of side lighting known as grazed lighting (p. 89) in the studio. Highly textured subjects, such as fossils, lichens and the reproductive sori produced on the backs of fern fronds, are emphasized by this lighting. If they are connected to an electronic flash (pp. 136–7), fibre optics can also be used for lighting moving subjects in the studio and in the field.

Translucent subjects, such as leaves (especially autumnal ones), insects in amber, and flowers, can be lit from below using a light table. This consists of a curved sheet of rigid white translucent material on which the subject is laid and the light directed up from below. A convenient alternative is a light-box for viewing transparencies lit by daylight colour-corrected tubes.

Generally, tungsten lighting is unsuitable for photographing delicate living material, since it gives off too much heat. It also requires either artificial light colour film which is balanced for working with a colour

▶ **Subject:** Insect trapped in amber
Location: Author's studio
Lighting: Trans-illuminated on light table
Lens: 80mm + bellows extension on Hasselblad (× 1.5 magnification on slide, × 3 here)
Film: Ektachrome 64

▼ **Subject:** Wood mouse (*Apodemus sylvaticus*)
Location: Vivarium in author's studio
Month: September
Time: Evening
Lighting: Twin electronic flash triggered by two crossed light beams
Lens: 80mm + extension
Film: Ektachrome 64

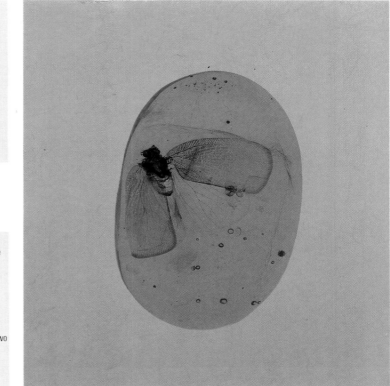

temperature of 3200K or a pale blue 80A or 80B filter to correct daylight colour film which is balanced for a colour temperature of 5500 K (p. 112).

Dark-field illumination involves lighting fairly flat, translucent or obviously textured subjects from below so that they appear brilliantly lit against a black background. The light source can be either tungsten lights (for static subjects) or electronic flash (for moving subjects). I have built a special dark field illumination table 15 cm (6 inches) high to use with the camera mounted above on a copying stand. Small lights (or flashes) are angled up outside the field of view through a central hole cut out of the table top. Dry subjects such as seeds or leaves can be laid directly on to a sheet of glass placed on the table, while small aquatic organisms are placed in a glass petri dish. Although setting up this lighting can be tricky, if correctly done it provides a particularly dramatic studio light source.

Active animals, such as small mammals and insects, can be photographed in the studio by containing them in a vivarium and setting up a pair of crossed light beams with suitable foliage. The camera is pre-focused near a point where the two beam triggers cross. The exact point will depend on how fast the animal moves and in which direction it breaks the beams. The wood mouse took its own picture at night by breaking a pair of beams connected to a motorized Hasselblad and two electronic flashes.

Subject: Vultures
feeding on zebra
carcase
Location: Masai Mara
National Reserve,
Kenya
Month: August
Time: Morning
Lighting: Direct sun
Lens: 150mm on
Hasselbad using jeep
as hide
Film: Ektachrome 64

CHAPTER SEVEN

NATURE IN ACTION

Capturing in a still picture a brief moment in time which depicts an interesting facet of animal behaviour can be one of the most exciting yet frustrating aspects of nature photography. With practice, much can be achieved with quick reactions and a fast shutter speed. But with specialized accessories, such as high-speed flash and automatic camera triggers, photographs can record fleeting moments which the human eye is incapable of perceiving. Relatively slow movement in a predictable plane can be recorded with a slow shutter speed so as to give a blurred impression of motion.

FAST SHUTTER SPEEDS

There are various approaches to freezing the movement of nature in action. The most obvious way to stop the activities of larger and more distant subjects is by using a fast shutter speed. Clouds racing across the sky or trees blowing a gale can often be taken with a standard or a wide-angle lens. Since short-focus lenses tend to have wider maximum apertures than long-focus lenses, fast shutter speeds present few problems even when the camera is hand-held.

When working with timid mammals or flying birds (p. 54), however, a long lens will be essential; in low light this will mean working with fairly large apertures, so the focus has to be spot-on. A uniform ground-glass screen is much easier for focusing quickly than a split-image viewfinder. Other methods of freezing action (or conveying movement) are covered on subsequent pages in this chapter.

Aquatic animals which congregate by day to spawn in shallow water are best photographed using a fast shutter speed, since a flash will invariably disturb them too much. Mention has already been made of how to stalk frogs and toads spawning (p. 53); they may require a fast shutter speed only when large numbers of males are constantly moving around at random in search of a mate.

As salmon return up river to spawn, they ascend weirs and falls. A fast shutter speed – coupled with a fast reaction – is essential for capturing a salmon leaping clean out of the water. Even so, shots may well be missed unless the camera is pre-focused on the area where the salmon are seen to leap most frequently. It will be less tiring to use a long lens if the camera is set up pre-focused on a tripod. If objects such as boulders are noted to mark the extremities of the field of view, the picture can be taken by looking at the falls and triggering the camera with a cable release once the subject appears in the right position. This is an example of how using fast shutter speeds does not always involve fast action by the photographer. It may be a question of patiently waiting and observing the scene so that when the action is about to take place it can be pre-empted and so not missed.

Arboreal monkeys or lemurs leap from one tree to another with such great agility that it is virtually impossible to frame and focus on one animal before it disappears again behind branches. Sometimes members of a troupe will follow one another along the same route. It is then possible to pre-focus the camera at a point where the first animal crossed a gap between the branches.

When the light is constantly changing, the easiest way to record action is by using a camera set on shutter priority mode; in that way a fast shutter speed is pre-selected and the camera then sets the appropriate aperture depending on the film speed used and the amount of light present. Exciting action shots can be taken of deer during the rutting season when male stags or bucks repeatedly clash antlers to gain supremacy.

With experience and careful observation lions intent on a hunting foray can be spotted long before a kill takes place. In this way, a vehicle can be manoeuvred into a strategic position beforehand. Taking pictures through open windows when travelling over uneven ground is not to be recommended though, for a sudden jolt can result in a camera banging against the face. When travelling overland on level surfaces by coach, however, pictures of the changing landscape can be taken quite successfully through an open window using a shutter speed of 1/500 second.

If an extra-fast shutter speed is needed, many slide films (but *not* Kodachrome) can be double-rated (p. 41). The picture of the Indian elephant charging in Sri Lanka was taken in this way. We had stopped our jeep to listen to the bird song. Suddenly, a bull elephant came out of the forest on to the track towards us with his ears outstretched and trunk upturned. The only accessible camera had a 200 mm lens on it, but the fast-approaching elephant still filled most of the frame. When I realized we could not make a hasty retreat and the light was fast fading at the end of the day, I made a snap decision to double-rate the film in the middle of the roll – thereby wasting the normally-rated first half of the film – so I could use 1/250 second. Only two of the half-dozen frames I took show the charging elephant with rising dust, as it fortunately lost interest in us suddenly and veered off the track back into the forest, but duplicate transparencies of the two frames have been reproduced dozens of times.

A fast shutter speed is also obligatory for gaining a clear image of the individual primary feathers of a large bird's wings as they fan out prior to landing. When working in the Masai Mara in Kenya, I used the pre-

focus technique on several occasions to take vultures coming in to land on and beside a zebra or wildebeest corpse.

It was during the last century that a whaling captain – Charles Scammon – discovered grey whales calving in sheltered lagoons along Mexico's Baja California coastline. Each year, the whales migrate south from Arctic waters where they spend the summer feeding on bottom-living amphipods. February is the peak month for viewing the whales at close quarters blowing, raising their front portion vertically from the water (spy-hopping), and leaping right out of the water before crashing down again (breaching). As the calves accompany their mother, they sometimes hitch a short ride on her back.

When the water is completely calm, whales can be spotted easily, but even then fast reactions are needed to frame the shot, focus and shoot before the whale submerges again. Choppy waves and vibrations from an outboard motor necessitate a shutter speed of 1/500 second. In this situation, an auto-

▶ **Subject:** Indian elephant (*Elephas maximus*)
Location: Wilpattu Park, Sri Lanka
Month: May
Time: Early evening
Lighting: Overcast
Lens: 200 mm on Nikon
Film: Ektachrome 200 rated at ISO 400/27

Both these pictures could be achieved only by fast reflexes reacting to the sudden appearance of the animal on to the scene, combined with a fast shutter speed. For this reason, it is wise to keep one camera body loaded at the ready with a fast film and set on a fast shutter speed.

◀ **Subject:** Grey whale calf (*Eschrichtius gibbosus*) spy-hopping
Location: Magdalena Bay, Baja California, Mexico
Month: February
Time: Morning
Lighting: Overcast
Lens: 200 mm on Nikon
Film: Kodachrome 200

focus lens is no help, for the lens continues to track back and forth on the sea long after the whale has disappeared. A zoom lens, such as 100–300 mm, is useful for quickly framing whales at varying distances. When used with a motor drive, it will enable many frames to be taken of rapid and unpredictable action such as breaching and spy-hopping. Occasionally, an inquisitive grey whale will swim towards and even beneath a small skiff close enough for the occupants to touch it. At such close range, a long lens is an embarrassment, but a second camera with a wide-angle lens and polarizing filter will reveal details of the parasitic barnacles and whale lice attached to the whale's skin both out of and in the water.

Slow shutter speeds

Instead of using a fast shutter speed or fast flash to freeze movement, a completely different and sometimes more creative approach is to use a slow shutter speed to produce deliberate blurred motion. This representation of movement can be most effective, although it does not work for all subjects. The final effect of movement blur depends on the camera angle, the shutter speed used and the size of the image. The slower the speed used and the larger the image, the greater will be the blurred effect.

Large single-coloured flowers, such as red poppies or yellow sunflowers blowing to and fro in a field, resemble the paintings of the French Impressionists. Moving grasses backlit against an area in shadow also work well using this approach.

Slow-speed films are essential for using slow shutter speeds without over-exposure by day, and in brightly lit locations a neutral density filter on a camera lens may be the only way of achieving the desired effect. Even then, the lens may still need to be well stopped down, so a macro lens with a minimum aperture of f32 will be more suitable than a fast lens with a minimum aperture of only f16. In dull weather or in places where shadows are cast by rocks or overhanging trees, there will be more flexibility in selecting the most appropriate speed for the subject.

Long lenses used in this way have to be just as well supported to avoid camera shake as when aiming for a pin-sharp image, since camera movement will confuse and reduce the impact of the flowing lines which run in the same direction as the subject itself.

Mention has already been made of taking moving water with a slow shutter speed (p. 21). A stream, river or waterfall makes an excellent subject for experiments with slow shutter speeds. Once the camera is set up on a tripod, comparative pictures can be taken using fast and slow shutter speeds to see the different effects. Where there is a lot of turbulent white water, a long exposure will tend to be over-exposed if the water is metred as it appears to the naked eye. By metering with a shutter-priority mode, however, a more accurate exposure will be gained of the misty moving water.

Adopting a flexible – and optimistic – approach to nature photography means that something will always be gained from the most unpromising of situations. I can recall a visit I made to the island of Islay off the west coast of Scotland specifically to photograph barnacle geese for a book. After two days of solid rain, my cameras were still packed in the rucksack and I was due to return on the ferry later that day. A chance stroll up a hill – still in the rain – led to a peaty stream in full flood. With an umbrella to shield the

camera from rain as well as a towel draped over it for extra protection, I chose a low camera angle and a 1 second exposure to emphasize the brown water streaked with white turbulence. This produced a picture which was used in place of the geese and has been reproduced lots of times since then; it appears on p. 41.

Moving animals are more difficult to take with a slow shutter speed unless they remain in the same plane of focus. Colourful fish, such as goldfish or koi carp, swimming just below the surface of the water appear as soft swirls of colour during a 1 second exposure with no two identical frames. As it is impossible to predict what the picture will look like, many frames need to be taken in the hope that all the possible variations will combine to produce an exciting composition.

When sun shines on slightly turbulent water, tiny highlights are reproduced on film during a long exposure as irregular white lines. This can be seen in the picture of the red maple leaves (opposite) taken in a stream during the fall. I noticed that the colourful leaves were dropping from overhanging trees into the water and quickly being carried downstream. When I found a leaf that had become wedged between stones, I decided to set up the camera on a tripod in the stream with this leaf at one

◀Subject: Ornamental koi carp
Location: Garden pool, Kyoto, Japan
Month: May
Time: Afternoon
Lighting: Overcast (1 second exposure)
Lens: 105 mm micro-Nikkor on Nikon
Film: Kodachrome 25

◀There was no way of knowing what the composition would look like at the end of a one second exposure, with a mêlée of different coloured carp swimming around at random. Several pictures were spoilt by all the fish being bunched up in a small part of the frame. Notice how the bright highlights appear as irregular white lines.

side of the picture adjacent to a section of the stream. I did not have to wait too long before another leaf appeared in the frame. The 1 second exposure resulted in an impression of the second leaf beneath the traces of the erratic surface highlights. By including the static leaf in the picture, this not only helps to convey what the blurred image represents, but it also gives more detail of the story of this natural seasonal occurrence.

When falling water – in the form of large raindrops or snowflakes – is photographed using a slow shutter speed, it appears as long streaks. This effect is most apparent when viewed against a dark background. Repetitive water drops which follow the same path appear as a continuous line when photographed using a 1 second exposure.

A flock of birds caught at the moment of lift-off all in much the same plane but with their wings in different positions can, like the fish, be taken using a slow shutter speed to blur just the wings or the whole bird. The

effect works best when the background colour shows a marked difference to the wing colour. In contrast to taking birds in flight using a fast shutter speed (p. 54), a shoulder pod may not be rigid enough to prevent all trace of camera movement and so it is best to play safe by using a tripod.

The apparent movement of stars in the night sky resulting from the rotation of the earth can be recorded on film by keeping the shutter open for many minutes rather than seconds. A slow-speed film such as Kodachrome 25 is essential and a clear moonlit night works best. The ambient light given off by street lights in a city or town will spoil the effect, so a remote site well away from habitation needs to be chosen. An exposure time of 30–60 minutes will register the movement of the stars as light trails forming part of the arc of a circle against a dark blue sky. A tripod is essential for such long exposures made by using either a B or T shutter setting, as explained on p. 40.

▲ **Subject:** Red maple leaves in stream
Location: Acadia National Park, Maine, US
Month: October
Time: Afternoon
Lighting: Overcast (1 second exposure)
Lens: 55 mm micro-Nikkor on Nikon
Film: Kodachrome 64

▲ As leaves fall in autumn, drab streams are enlivened with patches of colour. If leaves get trapped the colour persists, but more often than not, it is transitory as a leaf is carried downstream by the tumbling water.

Calm windless conditions will also be an advantage, for there will be no chance of camera shake; if trees are included as silhouettes to frame the picture, they will not appear blurred as they would if blown by the wind during the long exposure.

Panning (p. 106) is another way of creating blur; in this case, the background is blurred instead of the subject and the moving subject stands out more clearly from a confused background.

Motor drives and auto-winders

It is impossible to re-cock the shutter and advance the film manually on a hand-held camera without slightly moving the camera and taking the eye – albeit briefly – off the subject. This means that a moving subject has to be re-located and the lens re-focused.

Auto-winders and motor-driven cameras automatically advance the film immediately after an exposure, allowing the eye to be kept focused through the viewfinder of a hand-held camera. They also enable more frames to be shot of fast action (pp. 90–109) than is possible by winding on the film by hand. When auto-winders were first introduced, they were an optional extra to the basic SLR camera; nowadays more and more cameras have a built-in auto-winder. Motor drives tend to have a larger battery compartment and are heavier than auto-winders, but they do have a much faster exposure rate – up to five frames per second (fps), while the Nikon F2H and the Canon FI high-speed models expose at nine and fourteen fps respectively.

My own philosophy about motor drives and auto-winders is that they are a helpful tool for fast action and behavioural nature photographs such as birds in flight (p. 54) or mammals running. They are also useful to scientists for recording time-lapse studies of plant movement and for analysing the interaction of birds in a densely packed seabird colony. Motor drives are certainly not essential for static subjects. Indeed, when climbing up a mountain, the additional weight can be the straw that breaks the camel's back.

Since motor drives and auto-winders are much noisier than a basic SLR camera, they may disturb some wildlife. The noise may, however, sometimes be used to advantage if it makes a mammal look more alert by pricking up its ears. It is impossible to know how a particular animal will react to a motor drive or an auto-winder until you have tried it out. The solution is either to carry both a motor drive and a manual camera, or to use a camera which can be re-wound either automatically or manually.

Motor drives have the option of either a continuous mode in which successive frames continue to be exposed as long as the shutter release button is depressed, or a single-frame mode which winds on the film after each exposure is made but does not expose another frame until the shutter is released again. Even though the continuous mode allows the film to be exposed so much more quickly than is possible using a manual camera, it is still possible to miss the peak action in between the exposures. For example, when using the continuous mode with a shutter speed of 1/250 second at a rate of five frames per second, the action in five frames will be recorded during a total of only 5/250 second. It will *not* be recorded for 245/250 second or, putting it another way, only 2 per cent of the action is recorded, 98 per cent is not.

When used continuously at the fastest rate, the standard motor drive has to have the mirror locked up, so the image cannot be seen in the viewfinder. Even when the mirror is not locked up, it is impossible to check the focus between consecutive frames in a fast sequence. Some photographers therefore prefer to use the single-frame mode so they can quickly check the focus before getting one perfect action shot.

Exposing a whole 36-exposure film in a matter of seconds also means you end up spending more time re-loading film than exposing it. Therefore, for both high-speed action and time-lapse photography (p. 90) over long periods it is advisable to substitute the standard camera back with the bulk film back available for some 35 mm SLR cameras – giving up to 250 or 750 exposures per roll. A bulk film magazine is also available for some of the medium-format roll-film cameras such as the Hasselblad and Rollei 6000 series.

Motor drives and auto-winders are a big drain on batteries, so it is important to re-load with fresh batteries at the beginning of each day. In the long run, rechargeable batteries will be much more economical than disposable batteries. Nearly all cameras have a battery check button, but this will only tell you whether the batteries are sufficiently charged to be used. A separate battery tester is a worthwhile investment for seeing the amount of charge left in disposable or rechargeable batteries.

Some motor drives have the facility for pre-setting a frame counter to expose a specific number of frames during a single sequence. The motor drive will then automatically stop when this number of frames

▶ Once a multi-exposure sequence is set in motion the interval between the separate exposures cannot be varied, so if the bird suddenly stops swimming, the images completely overlap. Also, if the sun goes behind a cloud, the exposure changes.

▶ **Subject:** Black-necked swan (*Cygnus melanocoryphus*)
Location: Wildfowl Trust, Arundel, England
Month: June
Time of day: Morning
Lighting: Bright
Lens: 150 mm on Rollei 6006 + multi-exposure unit
Film: Ektachrome 1000

has been exposed. This can be most frustrating if the action should continue after the pre-selected number of frames, but if the camera does not automatically stop at the end of the film, setting the frame counter can prevent the sprocket holes from being torn. This problem will not, of course, arise on models which automatically re-wind as soon as the last full frame has been exposed. At temperatures around freezing point or below, however, film becomes very brittle and easily breaks, so motor drives and auto-winders are *not* recommended for use in cold weather.

For some very wary animals, the only way of getting a picture at bait or a nest may be to set up a motor drive on a tripod and to fire it remotely. Nesting birds, for example, will accept a camera on a tripod much more readily than a hide which will take several days to move gradually into position for nest photography. Remotely controlled cameras can be triggered by the animal breaking a light beam (visible or infra-red) or making contact with a pressure pad; alternatively, the photographer can fire the camera using an electronic or a radio release. The motor drive will then advance the film automatically, avoiding the need for the subject to be unnecessarily disturbed by someone having to return to the camera to re-cock the shutter. To fire the shutter by radio control requires a receiver on the remote camera and a matching transmitter unit held in the hand.

As when stalking (p. 52), all shiny parts of the camera or tripod should be covered with matt black tape. The noise of the shutter and the motor drive can be reduced by soundproofing the camera with a ready-made blimp (soundproof cover). Alternatively, a padded tea cosy can be modified, provided openings are left for the lens and the electronic or radio trigger.

The main problem with any remote triggering is that you cannot see the composition through the viewfinder, so that it is a matter of luck as to whether the animal has its head turned towards the camera as the shutter is released and whether the peak of activity is caught on film.

▶ This pair of pictures is part of a sequence taken using the motor drive set on single frame mode, so that I could select the moment to expose each successive frame. I wanted to show how the relative positions of the heads and necks change as flamingos feed.

▶ **Subject:** Flamingos (*Phoenicopterus chilensis*)
Location: Wildfowl Trust, Slimbridge, Gloucestershire, England
Month: June
Time of day: Morning
Lighting: Direct sun
Lens: 200 mm on Nikon MD2
Film: Kodachrome 200

PANNING

When a bird is flying or a mammal is moving in a straight line in front of a camera, it can be photographed by following the movement in the viewfinder. Once the bird or mammal is located, the camera is moved in the same direction in which the subject is travelling, using a steady continuous motion up to, during, and after the shutter has been released. Known as panning, this technique can give a much better impression of speed than the use of a fast shutter speed, as it keeps the subject stationary relative to the film. When this is correctly done, it results in a blurring of the whole background, yet maintains a sharp subject image.

Sports photographers often follow a racing car with their camera so as to blur the spectators, for even if the background is out of focus, a kaleidoscope of colour patches can be very distracting. In the natural world, panning is particularly effective when used for taking large birds in flight or a mammal running flat out.

The basic principles behind panning can perhaps best be explained by using the analogy of a merry-go-round. The photographer stands in the static centre while the subject moves around the perimeter. When the subject is photographed using a static camera, it moves in relation to both the camera and the background. A fast enough shutter speed (p.100) will freeze a

moment in time so that neither the animal nor the background is blurred by camera shake, although the background may lack sharpness due to being out of focus. The relationship between the subject, the camera and the background changes when the camera is panned by the photographer, moving it in the direction in which the subject is travelling. The background then moves in relation to both the subject and the camera.

A slower shutter speed can be used when the camera is panned than for a static camera in an identical position. This can be a great advantage when the light is poor and the camera is loaded with a slow-speed film. With practice, shutter speeds as slow as 1/30 or 1/15 second can be utilized; because the effects cannot be predicted, it is sensible to vary the shutter speed. Successful panning will never be achieved without using a pentaprism on a single lens reflex camera and it is useless to attempt it with the lateral reversed image seen in the waist-level viewfinder of a medium-format camera.

To practise the panning stance, place your feet apart so the body can be swung from the hips without moving the feet, and brace the camera and long lens. Once the stance and swing have been mastered, the next step is to visit a park or a wildfowl reserve where wild birds continually fly in and out.

Practise without film, supporting the camera either by bracing your arms tight against your body or by using a shoulder pod (p.137), and check that the bird remains in focus as the camera is panned in a continuous smooth action.

Select a lens which allows space all round the bird when viewed in the horizontal frame, for not only is it very difficult to pan a tightly cropped subject, but also the image is lost in an SLR viewfinder as soon as the mirror rises. In addition, the blurred background invariably makes an attractive abstract design. Use as small an aperture as possible to gain the maximum depth of field. When film is loaded into the camera, try to take plenty of shots and critically appraise the results on a light box to see how well you have fared.

You will know when your panning technique is correct for the bird will remain in the centre of the viewfinder; if you have either to slow down the pan or speed it up to maintain the bird's position, you are obviously not panning at the same speed as the bird in flight (or the mammal running on the ground).

Mammals tend to be more difficult than birds to pan successfully unless they are moving over flat ground without any trees or rocks to impede a continuous line of clear vision. A leopard or cheetah running flat out

Birds flying, or mammals running, make good subjects for panning the camera so the background appears blurred. They need to be moving parallel to the camera so that the focus will not change as the subject is kept in the viewfinder.

◄ **Subject:** Himalayan griffon vulture (*Gyps himalayensis*) panned in flight against a rock scree
Location: Kashmir, India
Month: July
Time of day: Afternoon
Lighting: Side
Lens: 300 mm on Nikon
Film: Kodachrome 64

after its prey is an impressive subject to take in this way, but such opportunities will rarely arise on a fortnight's package tour to a game park. A tiger running through grass is also most effective when it is panned with a camera – even though the legs may be hidden in the grass.

The longer the focal length of the lens, the greater the working distance; this means that you will not have to move so fast as when working at a closer distance with a shorter lens, but overall subject blur from a jerky camera movement is more likely. The extent to which the background is blurred depends on the shutter speed; the longer the exposure you use, the greater will be the background blur and therefore the impression of speed. Slow shutter speeds will also tend to produce some blurring of the animal's extremities which are moving in a different plane to the animal itself. Thus the wing tips of a bird will often appear blurred, as will the feet of a mammal. As with a blurred background, this may not be

too distracting and it also adds to the impression of speed. If, however, an overall crisp image is required, then a fast shutter speed will need to be selected.

Raptor collections, such as the British Hawk Conservancy, which stage free-flying displays offer opportunities for practising panning techniques. Once perfected, panning the camera will be found to be less tiring on the arm and wrist muscles than rigidly bracing the camera for long periods.

Slower-moving animals which repeat a circular path and come back to a point at a fixed distance from the camera – such as fish or turtles in large public aquaria – can also be panned. If there are not too many people around, it will be possible to mount the camera on a tripod. You will need to use a tripod head which has the facility of panning through 360° without altering the height of the camera. The locking screw is gently loosened so the head plus camera can be swung smoothly but not too quickly. If the light level is low a fast film will be needed,

▲ **Subject:** Heerman's gull (*Larus heermanni*) coming in to feed
Location: Ocean World, San Diego, California, US
Month: January
Time of day: Evening
Lighting: Low-angled
Lens: 200 mm on Nikon
Film: Kodachrome 200

▲ Wild birds quickly learn to take advantage of a free meal. This was one of several gulls swooping in to an enclosure to scavenge on scraps of food. The spotlit gull stands out well against the unlit background of the enclosure.

even when using a slow shutter speed. Special precautions associated with photography through glass are covered on p. 68. The movements of dolphins and whales which are trained to leap out of the water can also be followed by panning the camera.

Even though landscapes could never be considered as action subjects, panning the camera back and forth across a landscape is an excellent way of quickly appraising the best viewpoint.

HIGH-SPEED FLASH

To freeze rapid movement and to record motion which takes place faster than the eye can perceive is a particularly exciting and challenging aspect of nature photography. Accurate focusing is even more critical when using high-speed flash than with any other kind of action nature photography; when recording fast movement, the subject may have moved out of focus or even out of shot by the time the shutter opens.

An ordinary flash gun is too slow to prevent a blurred image of rapid movement. High-speed flash will freeze it, but this is only one step towards achieving a pin-sharp action shot, for it is no good arresting the movement with a fast flash if the subject is out of focus. Some means of reducing the reaction time between the subject appearing in the field of view and the flash firing is therefore also essential.

An automatic triggering device will help to reduce this time. A beam of either visible or infra-red light can be set up so that the camera is automatically tripped when any object breaks the beam somewhere between the light source and a photo detector. I used this method to record the relatively slow movement of a frog leaping in mid air in my studio. The trip consisted of two metallic boxes powered by a 12-volt battery. A visible light beam was directed forwards diagonally from one box across a table and down on to the photo detector, housed in the second box attached to another lighting stand next to the camera. I used two Vivitar 275 electronic flashes with a vario-power module, set on the minimum power to ensure a short flash duration. The light trigger was connected to a motorized Hasselblad and before taking each shot, I locked up the mirror on the camera to reduce the reaction time. The two frames reproduced here are among a series I took of a pickerel frog leaping from my assistant's hand through the light beam. With the effective flash speed set at approximately 1/20,000 second, the frog was caught in a slightly different position in each frame.

With the frog we were able to control the direction of the leap. Also, since it was a fairly large subject, the magnification was smaller and hence the depth of field greater than when taking a smaller and more active subject, such as an insect in mid flight. This presents much greater problems in terms of achieving high definition pictures.

Insects can be frozen in flight in the studio by enclosing them in a glass terrarium with some judiciously positioned plants. A higher proportion of successful shots will be gained by setting up a pair of crossed beams and pre-focusing the camera near to the point where the two beams intersect. The precise point of focus can be calculated only when the delay time of the set-up and the speed off the insect's flight are both known (this can be estimated by trial and error with the aid of a series of Polaroids). Wastage of film can be further reduced by setting the trigger to respond only when the light beams are broken by an insect flying in one direction, but not in the other. Then if the automatic trigger is linked to a motorized camera and flashes, the insect will continue to fire the camera and flashes (even when the camera is unattended) every time it breaks the intersection.

The short-duration flash, which can now be achieved using the variable power control on the more sophisticated thyristor-type electronic flash guns, simply will not produce enough power to take a flying insect on a slow speed film with life size magnification and the lens fully stopped down. A special high-speed flash unit will need to be used to gain both a short flash duration *and* the necessary high level of illumination. A variety of triggering systems for use both in the studio (mains powered) and in the field (battery powered) are produced in Britain by Triggertec. Lightec triggers are available with visible or infra-red beams while the Soundec trigger is sound-activated. The delay between the sound going off and the trigger firing depends on the distance the sound has to travel to reach the microphone, so by varying the distance between the latter and the subject, the delay time can be altered. As sound travels at 340 m (1115 feet) per second, moving it 30 cm (1 foot) away gives a delay of approximately 1/1000 second. When using a sound trigger, a delay time needs to be built into the mechanism to ensure that the sound of the camera shutter does not repeatedly fire the trigger and thereby waste a whole roll of film. Triggertec units have been designed not to do this on the newer built-in motor driven cameras. Both triggers are housed in a small casing measuring 110 × 60 × 30 mm (4 × 2½ × 1¼ inches) which has an optional sound/light-activated switch that directly triggers electronic flash units. The unit is powered by an alkaline 9-volt battery which will last for approximately 5000 triggerings.

▶At first glance, this is a very simple image, but a closer look at the water drops shows how each is functioning as a miniature fish-eye lens, for an image of the *Maranta* leaf appears (upside down) in each one. Notice also the drop falling from the leaf.

▶ **Subject:** Water drops falling on leaf, frozen in mid-flight
Location: Author's studio, Surrey, England
Lighting: Triple high-speed flash triggered by drop breaking light beam
Lens: 80 mm + extension on Rollei 6006
Film: Ektachrome 100

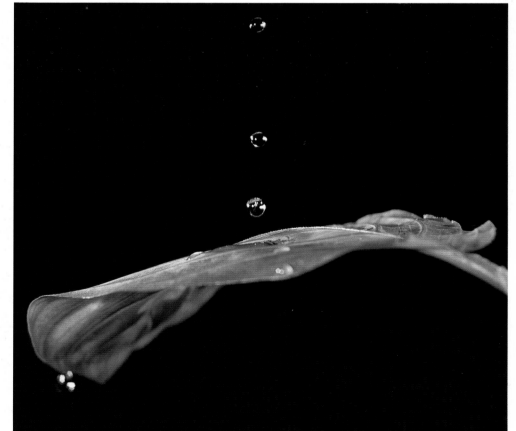

A third type of sensor activated by means of vibrations can be plugged into the casing. It is extremely sensitive to the slightest movement. I tried using it to take the picture of water drops landing on a leaf. The vibration sensor is a 2.5-cm (1-inch) diameter pad which I fixed to the underside of a leaf. The Triggertec was connected to a Rollei 6006 with a quick-release mechanism and the mirror was locked up before each exposure was made. 'Rain drops' were created by dropping water several drops at a time from a pipette held in a clamp stand out of shot. I used a pair of Vivitar 285 and one Sunpak auto 622 professional flash guns with the variable manual power ratio set on minimum power to give an effective speed of approximately 1/20,000 second.

The reaction time for the vibration trigger proved to be so fast I was getting the water drop as it hit the leaf instead of as it bounced back off it. The pot plant was too small to move the trigger further away to a more remote part of the plant so as to increase the length of the reaction time, so I decided to opt for the light trigger. This proved to be much more sensitive than the one I used some years previously for the frog, for the beam has only to be modified, not completely broken, for the trigger to be fired. I used Polaroid prints to determine the correct distance above the leaf to position the light beam. By placing the pot plant on a lab jack, I could raise or lower it a fraction of an inch at a time without upsetting the adjustment of the light trigger.

A motorized camera makes these kinds of pictures much easier to take, but they can be taken with any basic SLR camera with a 'B' shutter setting, by working in the dark using the open flash technique. Before the shutter is opened, the lens is covered with a lens cap (or a black card): the cap is then removed, the flash exposure made, the cap replaced and finally the shutter is closed again. Care must be taken not to move any part of the set-up inadvertently.

As the light beam and the trigger unit together weigh only 345 g (12 oz), they are easily portable for use in the field. The photo detector is not sensitive to sunlight.

High-speed flash offers exciting potential for taking fast action nature pictures. Both subjects illustrated here were photographed in a studio, but portable units now make it possible to use this specialized technique in the field.

▶ **Subject:** Consecutive frames of a pickerel frog (*Rana palustris*) leaping
Location: Author's studio, Surrey, England
Lighting: Twin high-speed flash, triggered by frog breaking light beam
Lens: 80 mm + extension on Hasselblad
Film: Ektachrome 64

Subject: Sea lion
(*Zalophus californianus
wollebaeki*)
Location: Seal Island,
Floreana, Galápagos
Month: December
Time: Dusk
Lighting: Reflected
afterglow
Lens: 135mm on Nikon
Film: Kodachrome 64

CHAPTER EIGHT

NATURE AT NIGHT

Working with nocturnal animals presents a special challenge for the photographer. Insects, amphibians and marine life can be located using a torch and photographed by hand-holding a camera and flash. A completely different approach is to take shots of nocturnal animals as they return to a fixed position, such as a nest site or bait. The camera is set up and pre-focused with the flashes in position before nightfall – downwind, since mammals have an acute sense of smell. Alternatively the camera can be remotely triggered by the subject as it breaks a beam or steps on to a pressure pad.

SUNRISE AND SUNDOWN

On some days, landscapes become transformed for a brief time by spectacular sunrises or sunsets. At these times of day the light changes rapidly, so it is important to find the optimum viewpoint and to select the best lenses well beforehand.

We tend to see a sunrise or sunset as a panorama, but this may not always make for the best picture and a narrower angle of view may provide more impact. Bold silhouettes or the reflection of a fiery orange sun in still water can help to provide foreground interest.

The most intense red skies appear when the weather is clear; dust or moisture in the atmosphere results in the red becoming diluted to an orange or yellow colour. At dawn the air is cooler than at dusk and when the humidity is high, mists will form. These aid the atmopshere of a dawn picture by producing soft muted colours instead of the harsher ones so often associated with sunsets when the air is warmer and drier.

Twilight is caused by the scattering and reflection of the sun's rays in the atmosphere. In the tropics twilight is shortlived, but during the summer in the polar regions it is prolonged and locations north of 49°N latitude experience midnight twilight.

Depending on the final effect required, various approaches can be used to meter a colourful sunscape. A camera – expecially with a long lens – should never be used to meter directly off the sun for three reasons. Most important of all, direct viewing can be harmful to the eyes. In addition, it will give a very high reading (thereby making everything else appear under-exposed) and it may cause flare. When featuring a silhouette, a reading is simply made directly from the sky. For a natural-looking sunrise or sunset, meter off a mid-tone part of the sky. This will ensure that a range of tones appears correctly exposed. As there is no single correct exposure for a sunset, it pays to bracket the metered exposure. Richer, more intense colours will be gained by deliberate under-exposure.

Colours can also be strengthened by using an orange or a red filter; although this technique is popular among pictorialists,

nature photographers in general prefer not to falsify the way they record natural light on the scene.

If the sun itself appears as a bright spot in the sky, it may be preferable to exclude it from the picture altogether; on the other hand dust or atmospheric haze can result in a dramatic orange ball looming out of a grey sky. The apparent size of the sun can, of course, be increased by using a long focus lens, but even with a 400 mm lens on a 35 mm format, it will have a diameter of only approximately 4 mm ($\frac{3}{16}$ inch). However, the size can be increased still further by de-focusing the image. This will happen automatically if a long lens is sharply focused on a plant, bird or mammal silhouetted in front of the sun.

As the shadows lengthen at the end of the day, the light level drops off sharply, so it becomes necessary to use increasingly slower shutter speeds until ultimately a tripod is essential to ensure crisply defined images. This is clearly impractical when photographing from a moving boat; a shutter speed of at least 1/250 or 1/125 second will need to be used and therefore a fairly fast film is required.

Colour film is balanced for a particular kind of light and a certain colour temperature measured in Kelvins (K). Daylight colour films are balanced for direct midday sunlight when the colour temperature is reckoned to be 5500 K.

When white light passes through a prism it becomes split into the spectral colours it comprises. This can be seen when sun shines on water drops to form a rainbow. Around midday, when the sun reaches its highest elevation relative to the earth, the proportion of blue and red wavelengths is roughly equal and daylight colour films – if correctly exposed – should give the most authentic colour reproductions.

Early and late in the day, however, when the sun is low in the sky, many of the short blue wavelengths in sunlight are filtered by the atmosphere, resulting in a high proportion of orange and red wavelengths producing a warmer light. The colour temperature at these times of day drops to around 4000K and thereby produces distinct colour casts on daylight colour film. This is most apparent on pale-toned areas such as a blanket of snow on the ground.

Some very dramatic pictures can be taken

Photographing at sunrise or sundown often means working fast, since dramatic skies and their reflections on water or ice only last a few moments. Even though no two days will produce identical lighting, it can pay to seek out vantage points beforehand.

▶ **Subject:** Grasses beside pond
Location: Shibdon Pond, Blaydon, Tyne and Wear, England
Month: July
Time: Sunrise
Lighting: Indirect
Lens: 250mm on Hasselblad
Film: Ektachrome 64

small proportion of the frame or is cropped out altogether.

Alternatively, with a sky suffused with a pink or orange glow, look for a viewpoint where the colour is reflected on water, ice or snow. Sometimes the best composition may be seen as a reflection in water rather than the twilight-coloured sky itself.

Getting up early in the morning before sunrise during the summer in temperate latitudes requires special dedication, and may prove to be completely abortive. When, however, a dramatic sunrise results in a magical few moments of spectacular lighting, the effort always seems to have been worth while.

◄**Subject:** Clouds lit by afterglow (taken from a boat)
Location: Magdalena Bay, Baja California, Mexico
Month: February
Time: Sundown
Lighting: Setting sun
Lens: 50mm on Nikon
Film: Kodachrome 200

▼**Subject:** Wildfowl on frozen flooded fields
Location: Welney Wildfowl Trust, Ouse Washes, Cambridgeshire, England
Month: February
Time: Sundown
Lighting: Afterglow
Lens: 85mm on Nikon
Film: Kodachrome 64

at twilight when the sun is invisible below the horizon, either as it paints a coloured base to a cloud formation above the horizon or casts a magical coloured after-glow across a clear sky. A similar effect can be seen before the sun rises above the horizon at dawn. These sorts of picture usually work best with a fairly large area of sky as seen by a standard, or even a wide-angle lens. A completely uniform colour cast will need a distinct silhouette to make it into a memorable picture, whereas a cloud pattern often works better if it is uncluttered by foreground objects and the horizon comprises a

DUSK AND DAWN

As well as providing opportunities for taking sunrises and sunsets, dusk and dawn are the only times of day when many mammals are active. In tropical locations, in particular, mammals cease to be active during the heat of the day and either seek the shade of trees and rocks or retreat into underground burrows. Photography of these crepuscular animals is fraught with problems not least because they tend to blend in with their surroundings; other points are outlined on the previous pages covering landscapes at sunrise and sundown, as well as in the section on low light photography (p. 40).

Unlike the use of flash for the photography of nocturnal animals (p. 116), when it is a prerequisite for any picture at all, I believe that flash destroys the magical natural lighting found early and late in the day. This means using either long exposures with static subjects or, more often than not, fast films.

Most of the African parks fortunately have lodges built inside their boundaries so that the minimum time is wasted getting in amongst the game at first light. Some of the most exciting moments I have experienced in Africa have been at dawn or dusk, often when the available light is very poor. The advantage of working in the morning is that the light level is constantly improving so that, providing the activity continues, faster shutter speeds or smaller apertures can be used as the light increases; at the end of the day, on the other hand, the light progressively declines.

Aquatic habitats with large sheets of water or ice that reflect the colour of the sky (p. 113) tend to make more striking pictures at these times of day than a dark location, such as a woodland. At the woodland edge or in an open glade, however, a shaft of sunlight falling on a deer or a hedgehog from behind can help to highlight it by natural rim-lighting. An early morning mist will create atmosphere in a picture of birds on water or deer in an open setting.

When a misty dawn shot is required, it is essential to get up early to be on location before the sun rises above the horizon, for when the mist is thin it rapidly evaporates in the warmth of the sun and the atmosphere is lost. The best possible solution is to sleep on site, either in a camper van or in a tent. In 1975 my husband and I spent several days camping inside Alcedo Crater in the Galápagos. At dawn each morning we awoke to the curious sounds of mating giant tortoises. As we looked outside our tent, we saw a primeval scene of giant tortoises emerging from temporary pools in an early morning mist. Within half an hour the mist had cleared and the sun cast long shadows across the floor of the caldera.

If sleeping on site is impractical, try to visit a location the day before to check the best camera viewpoint for working at first light. Failing that, either refer to a map or talk to a local naturalist for, even if not a photographer, he or she will know the direction of the rising sun, as well as the places most often frequented by birds or mammals as dawn breaks.

Several years ago I stayed at the Station Biologique de la Tour de Valat in the Camargue in southern France to get pictures of flamingos. Although small groups of birds can be seen from the public roads, I was lucky enough to be driven along the tracks bordering the salty lagoons in an area where these birds breed. Fortunately, the dawn turned out to be spectacular, the sun rising like an orange ball reflected as a ribbon of gold in the water. I continued to take pictures long after the sun rose, until the sky was tinged with a subtle pale pink hue.

Wetland sites known to be frequented by dragonflies are worth visiting at dawn in summer, for dew-spangled dragonflies are easily approached at close range when their bodies are torpid after a cold night.

In Britain, wild mammals — unlike birds, most of which are active by day — tend to be rather secretive, appearing either at twilight or during darkness. The best time to see rabbits is at dawn and dusk when they are most active around their warrens, although heavy rain or strong winds at these times will discourage them from feeding. Like mammals in general, rabbits have a good sense of hearing and smell so they need to be stalked into the wind. When disturbed, rabbits — like wary ghost crabs (p. 52) — will bolt down their burrows. On farmland where rabbits are used to vehicles, I have used my four-wheel-drive estate as a mobile hide.

In habitats where access on foot is practical, it pays to do some homework during daylight hours. Look for field clues of crep-

◄ **Subject:** Flamingos (*Phoenicopterus ruber*) in shallow lagoon
Location: The Camargue, France
Month: August
Time: Dawn
Lighting: First light
Lens: 300mm on Nikon using car as hide
Film: Kodachrome 25

The ethereal lighting and atmosphere which sometimes prevails at dusk and dawn can be quite magical. I can well recall the moments when all these three pictures were taken, although they span a period of more than a decade.

uscular mammals, such as food remains, frayed bark or hairs caught on the lower strand of barbed wire fences. If a fox's earth can be located, you may be rewarded on warm spring mornings by cubs coming outside to play. An elevated platform in a tree, or an overlooking slope across a ravine, can make a good vantage point from which to photograph foxes.

Some birds gather together at dusk before flying to their night-time roosts. A commonplace occurrence throughout Britain – most often seen in cities – are the noisy flocks of starlings which congregate in trees, on buildings or on telegraph wires at dusk. Suddenly the air is quiet as they cease chattering. This is the cue for them to lift off in unison, a myriad of silhouettes against the twilight sky *en route* to their roost.

When bats emerge from their daytime roosts in caves, they too appear silhouetted against a dusk sky. The effect will not look very impressive, however, if they trickle out a few at a time.

Some animals, such as whales surfacing in the sea, are not especially active early and late in the day, but photographs taken then will have greater atmosphere and more

▲ **Subject:** Giant tortoises (*Geochelone elephantopus vandenburghi*)
Location: Alcedo crater, Isabela, Galápagos
Month: March
Time: Dawn
Lighting: Misty
Lens: 35mm on Nikon
Film: Kodachrome 25

▶ **Subject:** Male common waterbuck (*Kobus ellipsiprymnus*)
Location: Samburu Reserve, Kenya
Month: August
Time: Dawn
Lighting: Low-angled oblique
Lens: 200mm using jeep as hide
Film: Kodachrome 64

interesting lighting than pictures taken well after the sun has risen or well before it sets.

While some twilight pictures of animals may be achieved completely fortuitously by being in the right place at the right time, most will be gained only after hours of patient field work.

Plants need not be neglected at these times of day, for there are some which open only at dusk in readiness for their nocturnal pollinators. In the fading light, evening primrose sepals spring back, allowing the large yellow petals suddenly to unfurl, providing scope for a flash-lit photo sequence.

NOCTURNAL LIFE

Owls and badgers are well-known nocturnal animals, but there are also some insects, amphibians and reptiles which emerge only at night. Many marine animals congregate on the shore at night as they synchronize their spawning to coincide with a particular phase of the moon. Since our own biological clock is naturally a diurnal one, working at night for extended stretches necessitates a complete change to our sleep pattern.

True nocturnal mammals react mainly to the blue and green wavelengths of the visible spectrum and they are much less active when a full moon is shining. They can, however, be observed with a red light. A cheap way of producing such a light is by covering a torch or a car headlamp with red cellophane. It is worth spending time observing the behaviour pattern of nocturnal animals before attempting to photograph them. Mammals have an acute sense of smell and so need to be observed either from downwind or on a platform raised from the ground. Nocturnal birds can be photographed at their nest site by using a hide erected during the day. When working out in the open at night wear dark, non-reflective clothing and cover shiny parts of the camera and tripod with black tape.

Night photography can be as simple as stalking a spring hare in East Africa, which is busily occupied stuffing its cheek pouches with grass: a camera is held in one hand and a flash in the other, while an assistant keeps a torch on the subject. Alternatively, it can involve setting up a camera to be triggered either remotely or by the animal itself, using trigger-beams or pressure pads.

Hedgehogs can be difficult to photograph since they are very sensitive to sounds and ground vibrations. I have exposed an entire 36-exposure film of a hedgehog only to find that every frame showed the head tucked in towards the body – the animal had reacted to the noise of the mirror going up fractionally before the flash was fired. Hedgehogs are, however, easily baited with bread and milk diluted with water and can become quite tame in gardens.

Many frogs and toads call only at night and I have found that they are more easily approached on windy nights when there is a continuous rustling of waterside plants. A torch is needed for quickly locating and focusing on a calling frog, for a continuous beam of light may induce frogs to stop calling. As always when working with water, the flash should be used off the camera, but a computerized flash will give a correct exposure – providing all the settings have been carefully checked beforehand in daylight. With a long lens, it is preferable to use a flash with a zoom head set on the tele setting, so that the light is concentrated into a narrow beam.

Nocturnal animals can also be photographed by setting up the camera on a tripod and pre-focusing it in visible light at an entrance to a nest site or a bait. Preferably select a lens with a focal length that will ensure the animal fills only part of the frame. Then if the lens is stopped down beyond the maximum aperture, it is possible to operate the camera using a remote release without needing to look through the viewfinder. Position the flash away from the camera axis so as to avoid the problem of 'red eye' (p. 44). I prefer either to strap a flash to a tree trunk or to use additional Benbo tripods, instead of flimsy lighting stands which can easily be knocked over.

Another approach to photographing nocturnal mammals is to set up a mechanical trip, pressure pad or light beam at a nest hole, at bait or in front of a gap in a hedge on a regular path, so that the animal takes its own picture. It is obviously impractical to leave a camera unattended unless working on private land or in a remote location.

All equipment – especially flash connections – needs to be well insulated against rain. I cover each piece with a black plastic bag and seal down the edges with waterproof tape. From bitter experience, I known it is all too easy to forget some vital

► **Subject:** Orb web spider
Location: The Dordogne, France
Month: September
Time: Night
Lighting: Flash
Lens: 55mm micro-Nikkor on Nikon
Film: Kodachrome 25

◄**Subject:** Natterjack toad (*Bufo calamita*)
Location: Dune slack pool, Ainsdale Dunes, Lancashire, England
Month: June
Time: Night
Lighting: Flash
Lens: 105mm micro-Nikkor on Nikon
Film: Kodachrome 25

Grunion are fish that live off the southern Californian coast, but from March to August they come ashore at night when an exceptionally high tide coincides with a full or new moon. Just after the tide has turned the grunion are washed up on to beaches where the female uses her tail to dig into the sand. As she lays her eggs, the male curves around her to fertilize them. As the female lays her eggs in the dark this behaviour has to be photographed using flash. The eggs remain in the sand for two weeks until a high tide flushes them out of the sand and then the young fish can hatch.

Female turtles also emerge from the sea at dusk to lay their eggs on shore. After hauling themselves to the top of a sandy beach, they laboriously excavate a hole and lay their eggs. A flash is essential for photographing this nocturnal behaviour and, since a direct light will produce conspicuous highlights on the glistening white eggs, it should ideally be bounced from a portable flash umbrella.

Close-ups of nocturnal insects are most easily taken in the field by using a macro flash with a built-in modelling light, since this will ensure fast focusing in the dark. Flowers such as honeysuckle, which bloom at night, are pollinated by night-flying insects, while other insects emerge to feed on lichens or algal growths on tree trunks.

After the sun has sunk below the horizon and the moon has risen on a clear windless night, trees and larger stationary mammals can be photographed so they appear silhouetted against the sky. A cloudscape can be backlit by the light of the full moon at night, similar to the way in which it is lit by sun during the day.

piece of equipment or procedural step, so now I always run through an equipment check-list before leaving base and then adopt a step-by-step approach to setting up the equipment and camera. It is also most important to insert fresh batteries in both the camera and flash.

Nocturnal animals which become conditioned to a continuous light source, such as geckos that emerge from crevices in houses to crawl over pale coloured walls, can be photographed using a fast film instead of flash. Badgers will also gradually become accustomed to continuous lighting, but they should never be suddenly subjected to bright photofloods. They can be photographed for a brief time by available light as they emerge from their set at dusk, by using a very high speed film such as Ektachrome P800/1600 (p. 41) or, once it is darker, with flash. Since a set often has several entrances, it pays to examine each one by day to detect which shows most use.

These pictures illustrate different approaches to nocturnal photography. Two are close-ups using electronic flash: the badgers were taken with extremely fast film in very dim light.

Subject: Badger cubs (*Meles meles*) playing
Location: Oak wood, New Forest, Hampshire, England
Month: June
Time: 9.15 pm
Lighting: Available
Lens: 85mm on Nikon
Film: Ektachrome P800/1600 rated at ISO 1600/33°

LIVING LIGHT

It is a magical experience to swim or row a boat through calm sea water on a summer's night and see the disturbed water sparkling with myriad flashing lights. Various microscopic planktonic organisms produce these phosphorescent displays; in British waters they are caused by a dinoflagellate called *Noctiluca*, whereas in the Caribbean copepods are responsible. Like the better-known terrestrial glow-worm, they produce their own light by means of a chemical reaction. Bioluminescence creates a completely cold light, which is also produced by tropical fireflies and some deep-sea fish.

Any bioluminescent animal presents a distinct challenge to the photographer, who has to utilize the faint natural light given off by the animals themselves to expose a recognisable image on the film emulsion.

The glow-worm is, in fact, a beetle and it is the wingless female which produces a conspicuous blue-green light. As dusk sets in on a warm summer's night, she climbs up a grass stem so the light-emitting organs on the underside of the last three segments of her abdomen are prominently displayed. Light is produced by the substance luciferin which is broken down in the presence of oxygen and water.

Adult glow-worms feed very little, but the larvae prey on snails and slugs, and so they tend to be confined to limestone and chalk grassland areas in southern Britain. Glow-worms can be photographed by their own light, although the obligatory long exposures may result in blurred images if the bodies move; the final effect may be a series of isolated blue-green lights looming from an inky blackness. Adding a touch of light either by using a torch or a flash helps not only to reduce the length of exposure (and the chance of subject blur), but also to define the overall shape of the glow-worm without overriding the bioluminescence. If torchlight is used with daylight colour film, a warm glow will result which can simulate orange rays of the setting sun.

▶ Although the fungus has not moved during the exposure, the image is not so crisply defined as the one taken by available light, because the bioluminescing area changed during the lengthy exposure.

The honey fungus (*Armillaria mellea*) lives parasitically on shrubs and trees, spreading from one plant to another by sending out black bootlace-like underground rhizomorphs. Wood infected by this fungus luminesces from the bacteria which live on it. The autumn 1987 hurricane in south-east England resulted in a rare phenomenon in a private Surrey garden. As boughs were torn from an oak tree, an anxious owner went outside to investigate and, much to his surprise, noticed a faint greenish light on the ground. It was a root, torn up from the ground, infested with luminescing honey fungus. The white threads which grow on the wood beneath the bark are not normally visible.

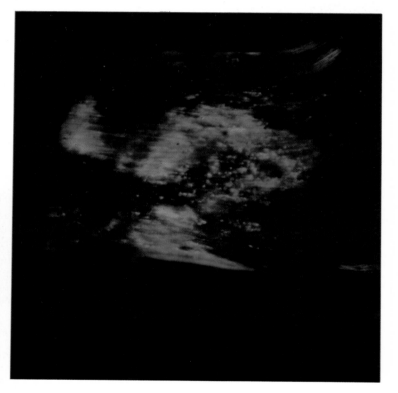

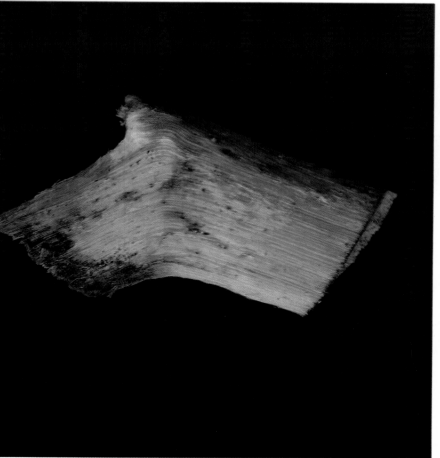

Subject: Honey fungus (*Armillaria mellea*) mycelium on wood
Location: Author's studio, Surrey, England
Month: October
Time: Night (above) and day (left)
Lighting: Bioluminescence, 8-hour exposure (above), available light (left)
Lens: 80mm + extension on Hasselblad
Film: Ektachrome 64

During the day, I brought a piece of the infected wood into my darkroom to see the luminescence for myself. When I failed to get any image on a Polaroid print even after several minutes exposure, I decided to keep the shutter on a Hasselblad camera open overnight. The picture reproduced here is the one I obtained on ISO 64/19° transparency film after an eight-*hour* exposure! This is by far the longest exposure I have ever made and part of the reason for it's length can be apportioned to the phenomenon of reciprocity failure (p.40).

Image intensifiers are used by police and military as a surveillance tool linked to a video camera. They would appear to be an invaluable (albeit expensive) accessory for observing and photographing nature at

served a practical purpose by allowing Japanese soldiers to read their dispatches undetected at night. The soldiers carried dried specimens which were activated by wetting when a localized light was required.

In recent years, marine ostracods have been discovered in the Caribbean which produce luminescent clouds during late twilight as they swim among the coral reefs. The bright clouds deter predators by temporarily blinding them. After twilight, the males produce short flashes of light to attract the deep-living females, resulting in a slowly moving lighting spectacular which spreads across the reef.

Living in the sea at a depth of 1000–2000 metres (3250–6500 feet) is an angler fish with a luminous lure. This flashing lure serves two purposes: it attracts prey towards the female angler and it also attracts the smaller male towards his mate. These fish have no swim bladders so that if they are kept cool when they are brought to the surface they are quite lively, despite the great pressure difference. Scientists have been able to take photographs of these and other deep-sea fish, as they continue to luminesce when brought to the surface and placed in an aquarium.

night. The first wave of image intensifiers produced a poor still image with obvious grain. The second-generation multipliers are more feasible for photographers working at night in situations where flash is impractical and a picture cannot be obtained by any other method. The principle of the intensifier is that each photon is split into a shower of electrons and so the quality of the still image is not comparable with fine-grain film lit by conventional means.

The Maclennan Marine IM101N and IM151 intensifiers can be used either as hand-held units or on Canon or Nikon cameras. They are capable of boosting the existing light level 50,000 times and can be used for photographing subjects on a moonlit night, or even by indirect moonlight when it is momentarily masked by a passing cloud, by using ISO 400/27° film and a lens having a maximum aperture of at least f2.8. If a slower lens is used there is a loss in quality of the circular image which is given a greenish cast. Such a cast would be quite acceptable for recording bioluminescence, since the colour of most luminescent organisms is blue-green.

Cypridina is a small but abundant marine crustacean which luminesces. Each animal has a bivalve shell and measures 2 mm (0.079 inch) long. These ostracods occur in the Indian and Pacific Oceans and can be concentrated by baiting with fish heads. During the Second World War *Cypridina*

Subject: Yellow flags
(*Iris pseudacorus*)
overshadowed by
gasometers
Location: Camley Street
Natural Park, London,
managed by the London
Wildlife Trust
Month: May
Time: Morning
Lighting: Direct sun
Lens: 60mm on
Hasselblad
Film: Ektachrome 64

CHAPTER NINE

MAN AND HIS ENVIRONMENT

There are now few locations left on earth where man has not altered the natural environment in some way. The changes wrought on the landscape may be dramatic and sudden – when tropical rain forest is felled, for example, or ancient chalk grassland ploughed up – or they may be gradual and almost imperceptible, like the initial effects of aerial pollution. However, as the knock-on effects are now all too apparent, man is attempting to redress the balance. The camera is an invaluable tool in making young and old alike aware of the need to conserve the dwindling natural resources of planet earth.

IMPACT ON THE ENVIRONMENT

As the human population has increased by leaps and bounds and the speed of transport has accelerated during the second half of this century, so man's impact on the natural environment has intensified.

The destruction of British woodlands began as far back as the Neolithic period, but since the Second World War many other habitats have also been destroyed: hedgerows have been grubbed up to enlarge fields, wetlands have been drained and uplands planted with exotic conifers.

The story is repeated the world over, but perhaps the most tragic loss of all is the clearance of tropical forests. Although these forests cover only 7 per cent of the earth's surface, over half of the species on our planet live there. Over 40 per cent of all topical forests have been destroyed to date. The knock-on effects are considerable: rainfall is affected, and erosion is no longer controlled so that landslides occur and flooding takes place during the monsoons. Even coral reefs can be affected by the destruction of tropical forests, for when silt-laden rivers flow into the sea they can smother and kill off the coral.

Man's activities have also been responsible for various forms of pollution which degrade the environment. Foaming rivers,

once a commonplace sight in industrial cities, are fortunately now rarely seen. Following the *Torrey Canyon* (1967) and *Amoco Cadiz* (1978) disasters, the fines now imposed for oil spillages into the sea have dramatically reduced the instances of oil pollution. However, in recent years Europe and Canada have been subjected to a new and extremely serious pollution problem. Acid rain has been responsible for the destruction of huge areas of forest on hard acidic rocks and soil. The trees are killed not simply by the acid rain itself, but by the action of the acidic water causing aluminium to be released from the rocks. Over extensive areas of Scandinavia, lakes are now sterile because all plants and fish have been killed by acid rain.

The picture showing the effect of acid rain on a Bavarian spruce forest was taken after a dusting of snow had fallen in April 1985. It exemplifies how a photograph – even an essentially monochromatic one – can convey a message with greater impact than any words. Since the death of a forest by acid rain is such a gradual and irreversible process, there is no great urgency to get pictures; this is not the case with oil pollution when, immediately after a spillage, efforts are begun to counteract the problem.

Invariably by the time an oil spillage appears as a news item, opportunities for taking the most dramatic pictures have passed. But on one occasion when I was visiting a botanist at York University he received a telephone call about an extensive creosote spillage into an ornamental lake on university property and I was on the spot within minutes.

When an oil (or creosote) spillage occurs in still, enclosed water, floating booms can confine the damage to a localized area; in the sea, on the other hand, the oil is treated by dispersal, either by water jets or by spraying with detergent. A thick layer of oil will kill marine organisms on the shore by smothering them, but in the 1960s many

▼ **Subject:** Spruce forest killed by the action of acid rain, with a light dusting of snow
Location: Fichtelberg, Bavaria, West Germany
Month: April
Time: Afternoon
Lighting: Overcast
Lens: 35mm on Nikon
Film: Kodachrome 64

Pictures illustrating man's impact on the environment may often be discovered purely by chance, although a news item can be invaluable for providing a lead to a potential location.

depict the aftermath of man's interference with the environment and as such can be used to communicate a conservation message. Compared with conventional nature photography, a totally different approach needs to be adopted for this kind of work; for the image to arrest attention it must be a powerful one. This may mean using a wide-angle lens to exaggerate the foreground, dramatic lighting or a novel camera angle. It is probably difficult for any nature photographer suddenly to adopt such a photojournalistic approach.

Sometimes, though, man's activities bring about a beneficial spin-off for wildlife, which quickly adapts to making use of man-made structures. For example, telegraph wires are often utilized by raptors as high vantage points for spotting their prey running along the ground. I have seen ospreys nesting on top of telegraph poles in Baja California and outsized *Nephila* spiders sitting in webs spun between telegraph wires in the Seychelles.

If a ship is wrecked in shallow tropical waters it provides an artificial reef which fish and other marine life can colonize. Pieces of debris floating out in the open ocean increase the sites where the larvae of stalked goose barnacles can settle.

more animals died as a result of detergents being used in the clean-up operation. Often, extensive mussel beds along the shoreline could be found to contain gaping shells or mounds of rotting limpets. Divers reported finding crabs underwater with many legs missing. In recent years, research into the toxicity of detergents has resulted in the development of new products with the toxicity reduced by some 90 per cent.

A match or cigarette end carelessly discarded during a prolonged dry summer can cause widespread damage to both heathlands and coniferous forests, destroying not only many plants, insects and reptiles, but also nesting sites for birds and cover for mammals. With time, burnt ground will regenerate, but initially it is the most vigorous species such as bracken which invade after a fire, although rosebay willow herb flowers bring a welcome splash of colour.

One approach to photographing pollution and destruction of a habitat is to take a long-term sequence showing the devastation and the gradual regeneration and invasion of the affected area.

As well as destroying habitats, man has also been responsible for exterminating animals though over-exploitation. Persistent slaughtering of the Biscayan right whale by the Basques working from open boats in the eighteenth and nineteenth centuries resulted in it ultimately being wiped out. As the numbers of other whales became drastically reduced, catch quotas were set up by the International Whaling Commission, but some countries are still finding ways to bypass these quotas by so-called 'scientific study'. The three most endangered species are now the bowhead, the humpback and the right whale. Although the magnificent blue whale has been fully protected for 20 years, there is still cause for concern. The sight of seabirds gorging themselves on a whale carcass being hauled ashore at an Icelandic whaling station illustrates how the fate of one animal may provide beneficial opportunities for another.

Although none of the pictures reproduced on this spread is attractive, they all

CONSERVATION

The adverse effects of man's impact on the environment have resulted in the realization that we now need to conserve our dwindling natural habitats. There are various approaches to this aspect of nature photography; one is simply to take portrait photographs of rare or endangered plants or animals for conveying the conservation message. Good-quality photographs of endangered animals – whether taken in the wild or in captivity – are a powerful way of educating the public at large.

Quite a large number of plants and animals are now protected by law in Britain under the 1981 Wildlife and Countryside Act and some require a special permit for photography (p.142). Some endangered mammals are especially appealing, however photographed, perhaps none more so than China's giant panda (photographed on p.64), which has been adopted by the World Wide Fund for Nature (formerly the World Wildlife Fund) as its symbol.

However, it is not good enough to preserve a species in isolation; the habitat as a whole must also be conserved. Biologists therefore need to have as much information as possible about a particular habitat and preferably should be able to construct a food pyramid. To do this, they need to know the answers to queries such as: What species are dominant? Which animals are herbivores and which are carnivores? Are any species susceptible to extreme climatic conditions? If so, what is the knock-on effect?

As biologists learn more about the lifestyles of rarer animals in remote locations, so those animals' specific requirements can be more clearly understood. The camera serves as an invaluable tool to the biologist or naturalist in many ways. For example, it can aid a census of an animal population. Aerial photographs were used in the 1960s to estimate the population of wildebeest in the Serengeti in Tanzania. The herds were systematically photographed by dividing the ground into a grid. A large black and white print was made of each square so that individual wildebeest could be laboriously counted by sticking a pin through each body on the print. Since these photographs were never intended for public display, the quality of the images only had to be good enough for the biologist to be able to distinguish one wildebeest from another.

Likewise, the composition of still photographs and the framing of video sequences used by a handful of scientists to analyse animal behaviour or to record inaccessible habitats, such as the depths of the ocean, do not need to reach such a high standard as photographs and films used to educate the general public about conservation issues. If a message needs to be conveyed to a large

number of people, then the images do need to arrest attention and preferably should be immediately comprehensible without having to read a caption.

For a long time I have argued that because scientific photographs must be truthful, it does not mean that they have to be uninteresting. A subject which is carefully composed in the viewfinder and features striking lighting will be a much more powerful image than a tiny, out-of-focus, blurred one.

Either good-quality still photographs or cine film of a threatened species is essential for gaining public sympathy and financial backing for a conservation appeal. With such a magnificent animal as the tiger this was not difficult, although it was saved from extinction very much at the eleventh hour.

▲ **Subject:** Storm damage to ancient beech (*Fagus sylvatica*)
Location: New Forest, Hampshire, England
Date: 18 October 1987
Time: Morning
Lighting: Overcast
Lens: 80mm on Hasselblad
Film: Ektachrome 64

Nature photography can be a most effective way of putting over a conservation message, and in today's visual world nature photographs are reproduced not only in magazines and books, but also on a wide range of consumer goods.

Excessive hunting by Indian maharajahs and the British under the Raj, as well as the destruction of the forests which the tigers inhabited, led to a 100,000-strong population being reduced to a mere 5000 animals in a span of only four decades.

It was the naturalist Guy Mountfort who set the ball rolling by a speech he made in 1972 during a fund-raising tour on behalf of the World Wildlife Fund. Operation Tiger was launched a few months later and £800,000 was raised in 18 months. As reserves were set up in India, so the tigers began to multiply and additional reserves were formed in Indonesia, Malaysia and Thailand. Operation Tiger is the notable wildlife conservation success of this century.

The initial reaction to the hurricane which swept across south-east Britain in October 1987 was shock and horror. It is, however, important to keep the disaster in perspective; it was, after all, a completely natural event. The loss of 15 million trees has meant that many beloved and familiar landscapes have been changed out of all recognition, but natural clearings will encourage impressive floral carpets of primroses and bluebells in successive years. The food plants of many woodland butterflies also grow in open, well-lit parts, so the clearings will tend to encourage an increase in these kinds of butterflies.

Among the thousands of trees lost in the New Forest, Hampshire, were conifers in young plantations and aged pollarded beeches in the Ancient and Ornamental Woodlands. Not all of these old beeches were uprooted; since they were already weakened by parasitic fungi, huge boughs tended to be ripped from the trunk at a level where the tree was pollarded.

Since the early 1970s, the Nature Conservancy Council – the statutory advisor to the British government on policy likely to affect nature conservation – has stipulated that 20–100 per cent of windblown timber must be left on the ground in ancient New Forest woodlands which are of significant entomological and botanical importance. Over the next few years, saprophytic fungi (which grow on rotting wood), mosses and beetle larvae will all benefit from the aftermath of the storm.

In woodlands which suffered severe windblow damage, access on foot was impossible and so aerial photographic surveys were commissioned to estimate the extent of the damage.

There is no doubt that the dramatic press pictures and television coverage of the storm brought home the fact that trees do not last forever and made people appreciate the need constantly to plant trees for the enjoyment of future generations – proof once again that well-executed photography can be a powerful communicator.

▲**Subject:** Tuatara (*Sphenodon punctatus*)
Location: Stephens Island, New Zealand
Month: January
Time: Afternoon
Lighting: Oblique direct
Lens: 60mm on Hasselblad
Film: Ektachrome 64

▲The tuatara is a primitive and rare reptile confined to 30 off-shore islands in New Zealand. The population was drastically reduced by introduced rats eating the eggs, but it is now stable on rat-free islands.

◄**Subject:** Siberian tiger (*Panthera tigris*)
Location: Longleat Safari Park, England
Month: April
Time: Afternoon
Lighting: Back
Lens: 200mm on Nikon from inside car
Film: Kodachrome 200

URBAN WILDLIFE

As city boundaries have grown and expanded into rural areas, wildlife has learnt to adapt to city life. Throughout Britain there are many examples of wildlife invading urban habitats. For example, there are several instances where seabirds which traditionally nest on sheer cliff faces, utilize high-rise buildings as nesting sites. In 1980, I photographed a family of herring gull chicks walking around the parapet of a multi-storey building in Aberdeen, with a constant stream of traffic passing below. In order to show the gulls obviously in their city setting, I had to use a wide-angle lens which, because it was impossible to get very close to the birds, meant they appeared fairly small in the frame.

When aiming to depict any animal or plant in a town or city environment, it is important to select a camera viewpoint which includes an obvious urban background in the frame. There is no point in taking a flower filling the frame or a flock of birds against a clear sky, for there will be nothing to link them with a city or town. Selecting the best camera viewpoint is much easier for urban flowers than for birds or mammals, which often have to be taken immediately they are first seen before they fly or run away. Birds and mammals frequenting parks will often tolerate a much closer approach than when they live in wild habitats where humans are rarely seen. Even so, it will pay dividends to be out in the park early before dogs are exercised. A low camera angle may be needed so as to include high-rise buildings in the frame. Even if a gasometer, factory or dockyard is out of focus, it still conveys the urban setting.

Birmingham lies in the heart of the industrial British Midlands, at a considerable distance from the coast, yet in 1987 a pair of lesser black-backed gulls bred in a factory in the city centre. Throughout the week, the parents ignored office workers passing on the street below, but at weekends they attacked passers-by whom they regarded as a threat to their nestlings. In 1988, several pairs chose Birmingham as their nest site. In cities such as London and Birmingham, where starlings use window ledges on high-rise buildings as their night-time roosts, flash is needed to take the birds huddled together, since they lift off at first light.

The kestrel, which is now the most widespread and numerous raptor not only in Britain but also in the western Palaearctic, will utilize church towers for its nest site. Being diurnal, it is becoming a familiar sight in urban environments all over Europe. These birds can often be seen perching on telegraph wires — elevated vantage points for keeping an eye on passing prey such as short-tailed voles.

On the other hand, foxes, being normally nocturnal, are sighted much less frequently, but now that they are invading urban habitats, many sightings have been recorded in gardens during the day. During 1978 and 1979, BBC cameramen recorded the activities of a pair of city foxes living in a derelict Victorian house in Bristol. Infra-red lights together with special electronic cameras were installed in the cellar and a series of fascinating live television 'Foxwatch' programmes was broadcast late in the evening, showing the growth and development of four cubs raised by the vixen.

Certain wild plants quickly invade waste ground and derelict buildings. Plants such as rosebay willow-herb produce copious seeds, each with a miniature parachute that aids wind dispersal in the slightest breeze. Wartime bomb sites in London which caught fire were transformed by rosy swards of this plant — known also as fireweed, because it colonizes burnt ground. The coming of the railways was responsible for the spread of the yellow-flowered

◀ **Subject:** Raven (*Corvus corax*), watching guardsmen on parade
Location: Tower of London
Month: June
Time: Afternoon
Lighting: Dappled sunlight
Lens: 85mm on Nikon
Film: Kodachrome 64

The most interesting urban wildlife pictures are ones where the animal or plant is positioned in the frame so that its urban environment is clearly apparent. In many cases these photographs will be opportunist shots.

Oxford ragwort, introduced to Britain in 1699 at the Oxford Botanic Gardens. British urban landscapes would appear to be a far cry from the native home of this plant – the volcanic deposits of Mount Etna in Sicily – but as the seeds were blown into open railway carriages and out again, the plant soon spread along the railway, flourishing on the clinker ballast.

Even more substantial in size is the woody buddleia which can often be seen growing on waste ground and high up on derelict buildings, such as those found in London's dockland. The flowering spikes produced in late summer are eagerly sought after as a source of nectar by butterflies.

Providing urban ponds and rivers are unpolluted, fish and wildfowl will thrive. The quality of water in London's River Thames has seen several changes. Centuries ago, trout and salmon were so abundant that they were caught and eaten by the poor. As the Thames had more and more waste – including untreated sewage – dumped into the water, its quality deteriorated. In the middle of the last century, sheets soaked in disinfectant were hung outside the Houses of Parliament in an attempt to counteract the potent stench of the water flowing past at Westminster.

But it was not until 1959 that an anti-pollution campaign was launched and efforts were begun to clean up the River Thames. Within a few years, fish and birds began to

▲ **Subject:** Fox (*Vulpes vulpes*) cub with remains of old boat on foreshore
Location: Syon Reach, river Thames, London
Month: June
Time: Early morning
Lighting: Low-angled
Lens: 300mm on Nikon from boat
Film: Kodachrome 64

▶ **Subject:** Oxford ragwort (*Senecio squalidus*)
Location: Disused platform, Guildford railway station, Surrey, England
Month: May
Time: Afternoon
Lighting: Overcast
Lens: 60mm on Hasselblad
Film: Ektachrome 64

return, so that now the river harbours a rich assortment of wildlife, although in recent years a new threat to swans has been discovered. Lead shot used by anglers for weighting their lines has resulted in the death of many swans. Throughout the year, herons can be seen along Syon Reach up river from Kew Gardens. While it is possible to photograph them from the towpath on one side, looking across to the other, more detailed pictures can be taken from a boat in the middle of the river. An early morning walk along a towpath or a trip on a boat will invariably be rewarded with interesting sightings; or one occasion I was out photographing herons, and I spotted a young fox running down to the foreshore from the grounds of Syon House.

WILDLIFE GARDENS

The current trend of many magazines and broadcasts covering gardening matters, to advocate using pesticides and herbicides as the best way to fight pests and weeds, is abhorrent to any naturalist. While a clump of stinging nettles may not look very attractive, it may tempt small tortoiseshell and peacock butterflies to lay their eggs, as this is a food plant for their caterpillars.

As natural habitats in Britain continue to be lost to the plough or through drainage, private gardens become increasingly important wildlife refuges, although immaculate weed-free lawns surrounded by beds and borders filled with cultivated flowers will not appeal nearly so much as a garden providing a varity of habitats. Insects, amphibians, reptiles, birds and mammals soon invade gardens which offer the conditions they require for cover, to feed or to breed. In Britain alone, it has been estimated that private gardens total around 3800 square kilometres (1500 square miles) and those which have a variety of habitats – water, a log pile, a stone wall, a compost heap, hedges, shrubs and trees, flowers which secrete copious nectar and shrubs which produce attractive fruits – will be veritable wildlife havens.

A pond introduces a new dimension to any garden and it is surprising how quickly aquatic life homes in to a new patch of water. After we built a series of pools in our garden, we soon found pond skaters dashing around on the surface film; in the summer damselflies and dragonflies flew in to drop their eggs into the water, and in the following spring frogs and toads came to breed.

The advantage of having a pond in your own garden is that you can keep a daily check on the number of amphibians and take a series of pictures showing the successive stages in their breeding. This can include heads of lone males (they always arrive first) bobbing above the surface, a pair in amplexus, several individuals with spawn, tadpoles and finally tiny frogs or toads emerging from the water. After breeding is over, the odd frog or toad may re-appear, providing opportunities for portrait studies. We have seen a frog sitting on a lily pad on more than one occasion (p. 72).

Emergent plants should be grown to allow dragonfly nymphs to crawl up out of the water when the adults are ready to appear. If the pond is designed with a shallow shelf that can be filled with soil, marginal aquatic plants can be grown, including wild plants such as water forget-me-not, yellow flag and water plantain. These should always be bought from garden centres in preference to digging up plants growing in the wild. In any case, no wild plant can be dug up in Britain without gaining permission from the owner or occupier of the land and some very rare plants are completely protected by law.

Wildflower gardens are becoming increasingly popular. A wildflower meadow can be made by sowing seed or by planting pot-grown specimens. The gardener at Hanbury Hall – a National Trust property in Hereford and Worcester – told me how he had encouraged the spread of cowslips (from an initial single plant) along the bank above the ha-ha, by collecting the seed each year and scattering it by hand. The deep ditch of the ha-ha prevents sheep in the adjacent field from browsing on the wild flowers. Maintaining a mown path which winds through an extensive wildflower meadow will make an attractive contrast between the long and short grass as well as a convenient walkway for photographing the wild flowers and the butterflies and other insects that visit them.

Among the cultivated plants grown in gardens, butterflies are attracted to the older cottage garden flowers more readily than the highly bred modern cultivars. Buddleia (known as the butterfly bush), ice plant (*Sedum spectabile*) and Michaelmas daisies are well-known butterfly plants for late summer. Bugle is a woodland plant that produces attractive spikes of blue flowers in May. It is often grown in gardens as ground cover among taller plants.

Early in May 1988 I noticed four painted lady butterflies in our garden, whose appearance coincided with the announcement of a fallout of Sahara dust in Britain. As one butterfly fed avidly on bugle, I was able to expose all 36 frames before it stopped feeding and basked in the sun on a brick path. You can never be sure how long a butterfly will continue feeding, so I decided to use a camera already loaded with Kodachrome 200 on a tripod without any flash. This makes an interesting comparison with the technique used to photograph the same kind of butterfly taken feeding on an ice plant in August and reproduced on p. 93. Notice that the May butterfly has damaged wings, which is not surprising since it is a migrant that has flown to Britain from Morocco; the butterfly photographed in August, however, is in perfect condition, for it has recently hatched from the summer brood laid in Britain.

The dictionary definition of a pest is a 'troublesome or destructive animal' but, speaking as an enthusiastic nature photographer, I find bright orange lily beetles and iridescent green mint beetles well worth

◀Subject: Painted lady (*Vanessa cardui*) feeding on bugle (*Ajuga reptans*)
Location: Author's garden, Surrey, England
Month: May
Time: Morning
Lighting: Bright
Lens: 105 mm micro-Nikkor on Nikon
Film: Kodachrome 200

The wings on this painted lady are damaged because it is a migrant butterfly that has flown to Britain from Morocco early in the summer. Offspring produced by migrant adults provide better specimens for photography later in the season.

encouraging — even if our lilies and mint suffer. Unfortunately, my husband does not agree!

By creating a congenial environment, you will be surprised what wildlife will sooner or later find its way into a modest-sized patch. Animals which appear sporadically in our garden include common lizards and slow worms (in fact legless lizards), as well as countless birds which come to drink and bathe in our pools and bird bath. The photography of birds in gardens, especially at bird tables, is covered separately (see pp. 74–75). For a spell we had a fox which walked through our garden each night, and after finding deer droppings we knew that roe deer had come right up to the back of our house to browse on the plants growing in our rock garden.

Photographing completely wild and free animals in gardens need not be despised as being easy; if anything, the problem of distracting backgrounds is exacerbated. However, garden photography provides many opportunities for interesting behavioural pictures and it is an excellent way to test out a new lens.

▲ **Subject:** Giant toads (*Bufo marinus*) with water lily
Location: Pond in Andromeda Gardens, Barbados
Month: February
Time: Afternoon
Lighting: Overcast
Lens: 105 mm micro-Nikkor on Nikon
Film: Kodachrome 64

◀ **Subject:** Cowslips (*Primula veris*)
Location: Hanbury Hall, Hereford & Worcester, England
Month: May
Time: Morning
Lighting: Bright with light cloud cover
Lens: 60 mm on Hasselblad
Film: Ektachrome 64

Subject: White form of red-footed booby (*Sula sula*)
Location: Tower Island, Galápagos
Month: March
Time of day: Evening
Lighting: Low angled
Lens: 250 mm on Hasselblad
Film: Ektachrome 64

CHAPTER TEN

WORKING ON LOCATION

Working in the field, especially in remote locations which few other people have visited, can be one of the most rewarding aspects of nature photography. Foreseeing possible problems before departure, by careful preparation and planning, will greatly enhance the chance of success. It is most important to dress comfortably and sensibly for each kind of habitat, whether it is desert, tropical rain forest or Arctic tundra. There is now a wide range of specialized equipment available for carrying and using photographic gear on the roughest terrain, as well as in wet or very cold environments.

PLANNING A FIELD TRIP

Before embarking on any field trip – even one a few miles from my home – I make sure that I do my homework, so that I know precisely where the subject is most likely to be found; time spent driving or walking around at random can be better spent taking photographs. However, if I should happen to stumble accidentally across an unplanned, but photogenic, subject then I grasp the opportunity for capturing a striking image. Even if the main objective proves fruitless, it will not be an entirely wasted journey.

In the past, there have been occasions when I began to work on location only to find that I had forgotten some vital piece of equipment. From bitter experience, I have compiled a basic checklist for field work as well as subsidiary ones for working in extremely hot or cold locations.

The camera equipment varies depending on the objective of the field trip. Apart from action shots of birds and mammals, I regard a tripod as essential for achieving sharply defined pictures. A reflector and a diffuser are both invaluable for modifying natural light falling on static subjects. Deciding which flash, if any, to take into the field is always a problem; small, lightweight models produce only enough power for lighting close-up subjects, whereas large models are a great weight to lug over any distance on

the off chance that they may be used.

When working in an unfamiliar terrain for the first time, it is extremely difficult to foresee all the useful gadgets that might come in handy. Much of the time in Britain I use my four-wheel-drive estate as a base, in which I keep a fisherman's tackle-box fitted with individual compartments containing the emergency kit listed opposite.

When stalking mammals, in particular, care must be taken to approach them upwind. If there is any doubt about the wind direction, it can easily be checked by dropping sand out of the hand or holding up a blade of grass. Some deodorants and aftershave lotions have particularly strong scents so, like perfume, they should not be worn when stalking.

Aquatic and wetland life can be approached more closely in a boat. In calm water, the best way to work is to drift with the current towards the subject, with an occasional gentle paddle; drifting in choppy coastal lagoons, however, may take you off course. To maintain a good camera position in water with a fairly swift current, it may be necessary either to tie the boat up to an overhanging tree or to drop anchor.

Since sea water and even a fine salt spray are highly corrosive, great care must be taken of equipment at all times when working at the coast, but most especially on

stormy days. When not in use, keep all gear in a gadget bag or plastic bag. When using a camera on a tripod, cover it with a plastic bag in which a hole has been cut for the lens hood to project through. It is a wise precaution to use a haze filter to protect the lens coating, for a filter will be much less expensive to replace than a prime lens. If any equipment falls into sea water, it should be removed and immediately plunged firstly into fresh water, then into alcohol, before rushing it to a repair shop.

Sea water will also corrode metallic tripod legs if they are not anodized. On sandy beaches, or among wet seaweeds, the legs can be protected by standing each one in an empty yoghurt carton.

Sand can also cause problems to both cameras and film, at the coast or in deserts. A single grain inside a camera is enough to ruin an entire film, so it is well worth taping up every nook and cranny before setting off – notably hinges to the camera back and, if a flash is not needed, the flash sync socket – and avoiding film changes on windy days.

Additional problems arise when working in very hot or very cold climates. In high temperatures, film – both unexposed and exposed – needs to be kept as cool as possible. I use an insulated cooler-box which I pack out with refreezable cooler-packs. In highly humid conditions, silica gel

◄**Subject:** Flowering cacti with snow
Location: Outside Carlsbad Caverns, New Mexico, US
Month: April
Time: Afternoon
Lighting: Overcast and snowing
Lens: 85 mm on Nikon
Film: Kodachrome 25

◄This rare picture of a cactus covered with snow proves that you should always be prepared for the unexpected picture. After spending the day underground in the Caverns, we emerged to find it had been snowing for several hours.

(p. 25) will help to lower the humidity inside the box. Film should never be carried in cassettes on camera straps, for on a hot day the black plastic canisters act like miniature greenhouses.

In extreme cold, great care must be taken to ensure that bare skin does not come into contact with cold, bare metal. I usually wear a balaclava over my head and cover all bare metal on the camera with gaffer tape. Also, since film becomes very brittle when cold, great care must be taken that a small piece is not inadvertently left in the camera when films are changed.

Hands and body can be kept warm with a rechargeable thermogel pack, several kinds of which are sold in sporting and mountaineering shops. Once activated, the thermogel gives off heat as it begins to crystallize. It is recharged simply by boiling the sachet to convert the crystals back to a liquid state again. For prolonged work at sub-zero temperatures, cameras should be winterized. This involves replacing the normal lubricant with one which functions at low temperatures. Once treated in this way, the camera must either be kept for winter work or the process reversed if the camera is to be used in normal temperatures. Special cold-weather battery packs (p. 26) are available for some camera systems.

◄**Subject:** Grey heron (*Ardea cinerea*) in willow tree
Location: Syon Reach, River Thames, London
Month: June
Time: Early morning
Lighting: Overcast
Lens: 400 mm on Nikon, from a boat
Film: Ektachrome 200 rated at ISO 400/27°

Basic equipment checklist for a 35 mm SLR system

Camera(s) – preferably with optional manual/automatic exposure, time exposure and depth of field preview
Wide angle lens (28 mm or 35 mm) ⎫
Standard lens (50 mm) ⎬ or 35–85 mm zoom lens
Medium long lens (85 mm or 135 mm) ⎭
Llose-up lens, extension tubes or macro lens
Long lens (200 mm plus ×2 converter or 400 mm lens for small birds)
Films
Cable release
Filters (haze, polarizing, graduated)
Tripod (for landscapes, close-ups and slow-moving subjects)
Monopod or shoulder pod (for active birds and mammals)

Tri-bag or bean bag (for supporting long lens on window frame of car)
Reflector (cooking foil, handbag mirror or circular Lastolite reflector)
Diffuser
Self-adhesive labels (for numbering films)
Notebook and pencil (ballpoint pens do not write when cold)
Polythene bags (for protecting equipment during rain)
Plastic sheet (for kneeling on wet ground)
Spare batteries for camera and flash
Lens tissues and brush
Electronic flash (optional)
Camera case (preferably strapped to the body so both hands are free – see p. 134)

Emergency kit
Spare camera batteries
Watchmaker's screwdrivers
Spare tripod screw
Spare cable release
Plastic-coated wire
Black tape
Gaffer tape

Additional items for tropical climates
Silica gel crystals
Dustproof/waterproof bags
Cooler-packs

Additional items for cold conditions
Cold weather battery pack
Thermogel reusable packs
Gaffer tape
Snow shoes for using tripod in snow

CARRYING EQUIPMENT

Once a reasonable amount of money has been invested in equipment, it is false economy to skimp on a robust yet practical method of carrying it in the field. An aluminium camera case, although rigid, immediately indicates expensive camera equipment, whereas a rucksack may not. Also, any kind of case is impractical for carrying over rough terrain, since it leaves you with only one free hand.

Conventional gadget bags with a single broad strap simply make you adopt a lop-sided gait by weighing down one shoulder. It is much better to distribute the weight evenly by carrying the equipment in a shock-resistant bag, firmly strapped to the body and carried either on the back or around the waist. In this way, both hands are left free for holding a tripod or clambering over rocks.

An ordinary rucksack without padding

◀The CCS photographer's Workbench can be used as a wading bag when working in marine or freshwater habitats. It is tightly secured around the waist using the integral waistbelt with a quick-release buckle. This model hinges on the side opposite to the body.

▼When empty, the CCS photographer's waistcoat weighs only 1·25 kg (2¾ lb). It is made to special order in white, green or black Fryma fabric which is used for aircrew survival vests. The perforations prevent sweating in hot weather.

will not protect camera equipment from knocks. It is also very uncomfortable if you should accidentally fall against an unpadded bag with hard, angular equipment inside.

All the examples for carrying cameras illustrated on this spread are made by Camera Care Systems (CCS) in Bristol, England. Designed by expeditionary and adventure photographers, the bags are durable yet lightweight, weatherproof and shock-absorbent, and have been tried and tested on many international expeditions.

I never go out to work in the field without wearing a photographer's vest. Mine was made to special order and has a total of ten pockets on the front and side as well as two pockets inside and a large one on the back. The vest is made of a cellular material which prevents sweating in hot climates. Even when all the pockets are full, it is possible to run safely, for each outer pocket has a flap secured by a Velcro strip or a strap that tightens around the top. The only word of caution I would add is that when working inside a hide at close range to a timid animal, it is advisable to secure all the flaps of the film pockets back with a safety pin, to avoid disturbing the subject with the noise of Velcro being undone.

It is essential to be systematic about what items you place in each pocket of the vest, otherwise you can spend a lot of time searching for one item. Kodachrome films (removed from their packaging and film canisters so that four of them fit into an upright plastic Kodachrome slide box) go

into one bottom pocket, and Ektachrome roll films go into another on the opposite side. I also carry in the vest my notebook and pencil, various filters, close-up lenses, extension tubes, spare camera batteries, watchmaker's screwdrivers and sometimes a short focal length lens.

When I am wading into water, I tend to substitute the vest with a CCS Photographer's Work Bench – which I refer to as my wading bag – worn around the waist. With this bag there is no risk of accidentally pulling an item out of a pocket and dropping it into the water. The lid can be hinged on the side nearest to the body or on the opposite side. I have opted for the latter, so I simply unzip the lid and lift it up to see straight into the bag. When actually taking a photograph, I make sure the lid is fastened and, if necessary, I can push the wading bag round to one side.

A wading bag – like a skier's waist pouch – is also useful when working on snow-covered ground, where it would be equally impractical to rest any gadget bag on the ground.

The bulk of my camera equipment, however, is carried in a rucksack made to special order from the same materials as the wading bag. In the rucksack I carry a Hasselblad with 50 mm, 80 mm, 150 mm and 250 mm lenses, as well as a Nikon F3 body with 20 mm, 35 mm, 50 mm, 55 mm micro-Nikkor, 85 mm, 105 mm micro-Nikkor and 200 mm lenses. Most items are well protected inside individual holes cut into an

some small planes, I usually empty it and pack it flat inside my checked baggage and carry my cameras and lenses as hand baggage in a pilot's case. Now that checked baggage is X-rayed and some airports display warnings that these X-rays *will* harm films, I carry all my film as hand baggage. Although the latest machines are film safe up to ISO 1600/33° older models in some third-world countries can be suspect and films can become fogged by repeated exposure to X-rays. When I am making a lot of internal flights within a country it can mean as many as a dozen or more check-ins, so I always request a hand search. However, by checking in well before my flight time, I have rarely met with any opposition. It can be tiresome when security guards insist on opening every black film canister to check there is a film and not explosive inside, but it is also very reassuring.

It obviously helps to save time by carrying films in transparent canisters, as supplied with Agfa and Fuji films, or removing them from the canisters and carrying them in upright Kodachrome slide boxes (four at a time) with see-through lids, as I do now. When I have invested a lot of money, not to mention time, in organizing a trip I never let my exposed films out of my sight.

◀**Subject:** Banded agrion (*Agrion splendens*) on water crowfoot
Location: An Oxfordshire river, England
Month: July
Time: Morning
Lighting: Sunny
Lens: 200 mm micro-Nikkor on Nikon, by wading
Film: Ektachrome 200 rated at ISO 400/27°

▼After having waded out into the middle of a river, it is most frustrating to discover you need a filter or another lens stored in a gadget bag on the towpath. As shown here, the workbench provides a safe and convenient gadget bag for a limited amount of equipment.

ethafoam block, while others are carried in exterior pockets. Small, circular Lastolite reflectors are carried in an interior pocket in the lid. To help spread the load, the rucksack has a wide waist belt in addition to padded shoulder straps. The rucksack has to be removed and laid flat on the ground before it can be opened by undoing the robust zip fastener. This may sound somewhat tedious, but in reality it can be a very speedy operation. Even though my rucksack has had to weather several heavy storms and has been splashed with sea water, all equipment contained within the ethafoam block has always remained quite dry.

CCS also make padded 'elephant trunk' pouches worn on a waist belt. Each holds a camera complete with long lens.

As I have had problems carrying my rucksack as hand baggage when flying in

SUPPORTING THE CAMERA

The majority of photographs in this book were taken using a rigid camera support, simply because I need to ensure that my photographs are pin-sharp for reproduction purposes. Only when I take action shots, or use flash in the field, do I dispense with some means of supporting the camera.

Invariably I use a versatile Benbo (short for 'bent bolt') tripod. The standard model, which extends to 1.57 metres (5 feet 1 inch) high and weighs 3.4 kg (7½ lb), is adequate for nearly all subjects, although the model which extends to 2.46 metres (8 feet) does allow high-level close-ups to be taken, provided that I can use a stepladder to see through the camera viewfinder! If low-level plants – flowers, fungi, lichens, mosses or ferns – are likely to be the most abundant subjects, the Baby Benbo, which extends to 66 cm (26 inches), will be ideal. Also the weight is only 1.8 kg (4 lb) and is much less tiring to carry at altitude up a mountain.

All three models are based on a unique but extremely simple design, involving a bent bolt connecting the three legs, while the centre column is secured by a single locking handle. When this is unlocked all three legs can be moved up to, and beyond, the horizontal position. The angle of the centre column can also be varied while the legs are being positioned. Once the legs have been positioned so the camera plat-

◄ The Tri-bag is invaluable for supporting the camera on the base of a window frame, when using a long lens with the vehicle as a hide. The lightweight synthetic granular filling allows it to be moulded into any shape to fit the lens.

▲ The Cam support is ideal for long lens work in places where a tripod is impractical. One part hooks over the shoulder while a pivotable support rests against the chest. A quick-release strap secures the Cam support, leaving both hands free to clamber over rough ground.

form on the ball-and-socket mounting is in the required position for photography, they are locked into place by tightening the handle. While the legs are being adjusted, it is essential to hold on to the centre column – especially if the camera is attached – as it may otherwise suddenly lunge forward and crash on to the ground.

It is possible to use the tripod in a conventional position at one moment, with all three legs resting on flat ground for a landscape picture, and the next moment move the legs so that two are placed almost vertically against a wall or a tree while the third is on the ground.

After the tripod is firmly locked into position, the centre column can be adjusted by using a separate locking screw. Depending on the angle of the centre column this may simply be a question of raising or lowering it, but when in a horizontal position, it can be moved towards or away from the subject.

I never travel anywhere without a Benbo tripod and I have used it on the roughest and most uneven of terrains, including rocky shores as well as jagged lava fields in the Galápagos and Hawaii. The reversible centre column allows the camera to be supported beneath the pivoting part of the tripod, close to the ground for low-level shots. The centre column can then be used to focus the subject roughly by raising or lowering it at will. Another excellent design feature is the position of the outer telescopic tube on each leg, which is nearest to the ground – the reverse of conventional tripods. Since the ends are thus completely sealed, the Benbo can be safely used standing in mud or water.

A useful accessory for quickly supporting a long lens on a rigid base is the lightweight Tri-bag. This recent variation on the bean bag theme is filled with lightweight synthetic granules (which will not sprout when wetted, like peas and beans!) and weighs only 100 gm (3½ oz) – less than the weight of an average 50 mm lens. A Tri-bag can be positioned on the base of a car window frame when using a vehicle as a hide, on a tree stump or against a tree trunk. The bag is laid against the rigid support so the lens makes a natural depression, supported on either side by the bag. Provided the camera is pushed firmly against the bag, it makes an extremely quick and adaptable support as well as being surprisingly firm.

Velcro strips on each bag allow two or more Tri-bags to be joined together for supporting extra-long lenses. Even when not supporting a camera, a Tri-bag helps to act as a buffer to equipment in a camera bag, whether it is being carried around on foot or transported in a car.

The influx of video cameras on to the market in recent years has resulted in the production of some robust shoulder supports. One of these, known as the Cam support, is also ideal for taking action photographs using a stills camera fitted with a long focus lens.

The support hooks over the shoulder with a pivotable brace resting against the chest, and is held firm with a wide, quick-release strap fastened around the chest. The camera is mounted on a pivoting platform that can be adjusted so that the camera is in a comfortable position, and the viewfinder level with the eye. The whole support is firmly locked to the body, so that once the

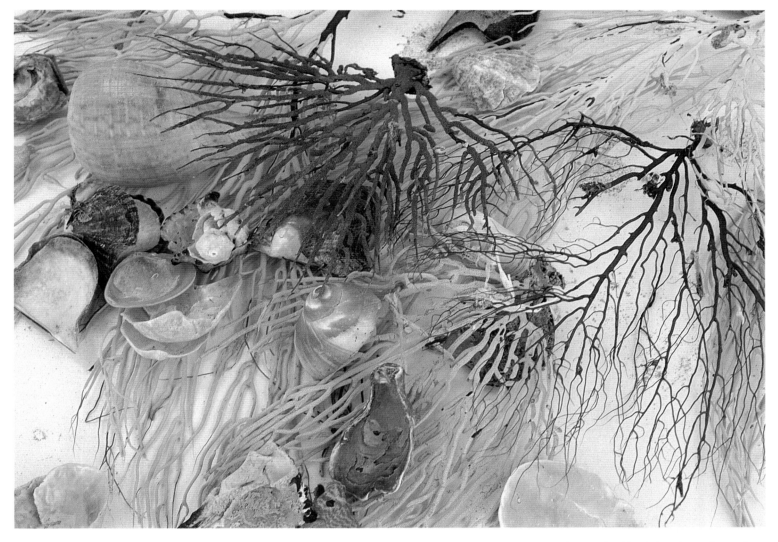

▲ **Subject:** Still life –
sea fans and shells
Location: Baja
California, Mexico
Month: February
Time: Morning
Lighting: Overcast
Lens: 55 mm micro-
Nikkor on Nikon
Film: Kodachrome 200

◄ A standard Benbo
tripod being used in a
near-vertical position to
photograph epiphytic
growths on a tree trunk.
The still-life close-up
picture above was also
taken using a Benbo, this
time to support the
camera in an overhead
position.

camera is attached both hands are free when
moving around.

Before I found the Cam support I used to
use a monopod for stalking and taking
action shots, but the leg length does have to
be adjusted to ensure the camera is at eye
level. One advantage of the monopod,
however, is that it is relatively cheap compared with a support designed for use with a
video camera. It is also lighter in weight
(some 700 gm/1½ lb compared with 900 gm/
2 lb of the Cam support), making it much
easier to carry with you when flying abroad
to an overseas location.

Other camera supports include a ground
spike (p. 87) for low level close-ups in
reasonably firm ground. Although this is
much lighter than a tripod, it has relatively
limited use.

The type of support that you choose will
very much depend on the kind of subjects
that you most enjoy photographing; a
tripod for landscapes and static subjects, a
monopod or a Cam support for more active
subjects, or a Tri-bag for places where you
can rest the camera on a solid surface.

SPECIAL LIGHTING FOR CLOSE-UPS

Throughout this book emphasis has been placed on the selection of lighting most appropriate to the subject. Until recently, there was relatively little scope for subtle modification of the available light falling on a close-up subject in the field. Most simply, shadows could be filled in by using a reflector, harsh direct sunlight modified with a diffuser, or dull light boosted with a flash. There are now a range of accessories modified from studio lighting set-ups and scaled down to assist in the production of creative close-ups in the field.

The additional light provided by electronic flash aids close-ups by allowing a greater depth of field with a slow film speed. It can also be used to arrest the movement of active subjects.

Various systems are available which support the camera and multiple electronic flash heads as a single unit. The Hasselblad macro flash bracket illustrated here is attached to the front of the lens, as is the Olympus T28 Macro Twin Flash. Both systems allow the heads to be angled in to the desired position. They can be fired together or singly and the power output can be varied. Unlike studio flash units which have built-in modelling lights, most macro flashes dispense with this extra facility, so that — unless a Polaroid back is used on a medium format camera — you can only guess the final result. The Olympus OM system Macro

◄The Lastolite Mini Apollo light modifier held in position in the field by using a clamp stand. This miniature flash umbrella provides subtle indirect lighting for close-up subjects. The white nylon cover is shown rolled back so the flash can be seen in position.

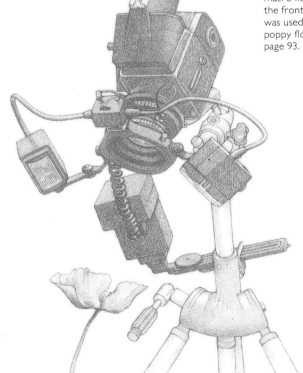

◄A Hasselblad twin macro flash, mounted on the front of the lens, was used to light the poppy flower on page 93. The flexible arm mounting and the angled basal brackets allow the position of the flash heads to be varied to suit each particular subject.

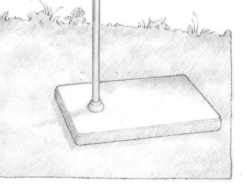

▼A flash can be mounted inside the Mini Apollo light modifier so that it either gives a diffuse light through the white nylon cover (below) or is bounced off the reflective interior of the brolly (below right).

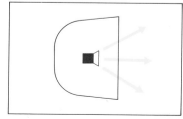
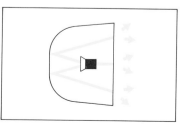

Flash units do, however, incorporate a modelling light.

Selective spot lighting of a small subject or a small part of a larger subject can be made using a fibre optic unit fitted over the window of an electronic flash (p. 93). Although the speed of the flash will be fast enough to arrest all movement of a plant blowing in the wind, it is advisable to clamp the fibre optic, either to a clamp stand or a wooden spike pushed into the ground, so that the narrow-angled beam can be precisely positioned. The diameter of the beam can be adjusted using a focusing lens on the end of the fibre optic arm. If the fibre optic unit is connected to a flash without a modelling light, however, the area of the beam cannot be seen (and modified if necessary) without making an instant Polaroid print.

When lighting pale-coloured flowers, or wet or shiny subjects such as shells and beetles, avoid using direct flash; instead use indirect bounced flash. The Lastolite Mini Apollo light modifier (p. 93) is a miniature version of a large studio flash umbrella and it can be used in the field, held either in the hand or in a clamp stand. A detachable square of optical white nylon functions as a diffuser over the base of the umbrella. The flash can either be positioned facing the reflective interior of the umbrella (with a light loss of 1 stop), or turned through 180°

so it diffuses through the white nylon (with a light loss of 1.3 stops). In either case, the soft indirect light makes a pleasant change from the conventional direct flash close-up.

To reduce the problem of direct reflections off wet or shiny surfaces when using a ring flash, Olympus have produced a cross-polarizing filter. The outer part, which fits over the flash ring, polarizes the light falling on the subject, while the inner part polarizes the light passing through the lens.

When I plan to use any portable electronic flash system in the field for an extended period, I prefer to power it from a rechargeable Quantum battery pack which can be hooked on to a waist band or hung from a lighting stand.

Whenever I use a new lighting set-up for taking a close-up – either in the field or the studio – I fill in a pro-forma data sheet with the film speed, magnification used, number of flash heads and their distance from the subject. In this way, I can refer back to the data sheet as a rough guideline for the correct exposure when using a similar set-up in the future.

◄**Subject:** Mexican wall daisy (*Erigeron mucronatus*)
Location: Author's garden, Surrey, England
Month: June
Time: Evening
Lighting: Single fibre optic flash
Lens: 80 mm + extension on Hasselblad
Film: Ektachrome 64

▼Fibre optic unit attached to electronic flash. The fibre optic cable is shown secured in a clamp stand so the narrow beam can be used to spotlight precisely a single daisy flower amongst a cluster of flowers.

DATA SHEET

Subject *Shark's Tooth*   Date *2/2/86*

CAMERA *Hasselblad 500 c/m*

   Lens .... *80 mm* .... (Reversed? yes/no)

   Close-up lens .... Magnification *× 1·75*

   Filter ....

   Extension tubes ....

   Bellows? .... *140 mm extension*

LIGHTING Daylight ☑ Tungsten ☐ Flash ☐

   Flash set up .... *Pair of fibre optics, oblique back lighting*

   Diffuser ☐ Reflector ☐

   Filter over light ....

DISTANCES Flash to subject: ....

   Lens to subject: ....

BACKGROUND *Black velvet*

FILM *Ektachrome 64*   Neg/Slide Number *HP HOT 54*

EXPOSURE DATA: 1 *f22* 2 *f22* 3 *f16/22* 4 *f16/22* 5 *(f16)* 6 *f16*
7 *f16/11* 8 *f16/11* 9 *f11* 10 *f11* 11 *f8/11* 12 *f8/11* 13   14
15   16   17   18   19   20   21   22
23   24   25   26   27   28   29   30
31   32   33   34   35   36

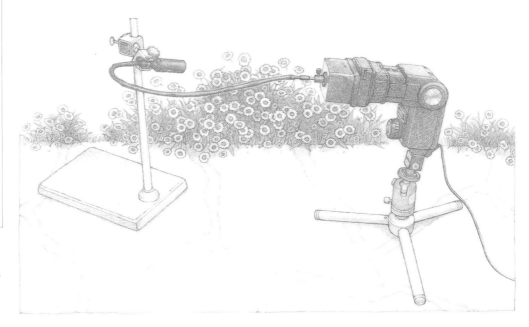

▲A completed data sheet for the studio photograph of a shark's tooth, reproduced on page 96. The shot required the use of a pair of fibre-optics to provide the dramatic backlighting. It is always worth recording all the details for a complex set-up like this.

HIDES

A wildlife photographer has a better chance of reducing the working distance between a wary subject and the camera either by using camouflage material to blend in with the natural surroundings or by working from inside a hide or blind.

I use a camouflage net in a variety of ways: to cover my body while lying prone on the ground or in a boat, to disguise a car as a hide or as a vertical screen. The holes in the mesh are large enough to poke the hood of a long lens through. The main problem with a camouflage net is that it easily gets snagged on twigs or stones when you are crawling over the ground.

This problem does not arise with the very fine mesh material used for the Lastohide – a variation of the circular Lastolite reflectors. A camouflage curtain hangs from the 69 cm (27-inch) diameter brim of the hat so as to conceal the body. This mobile hide weighs only 335 gm (12 oz), can be assembled in seconds and folds away into a 31 cm (12¼-inch) pouch. When in use, the lens is pushed out from the top of the front opening, while the flap is secured below by Velcro strips. The Lastohide can be used to camouflage the body while stalking on foot or when lying prone. A home-made version can be produced from a bee-keeper's hat and a piece of muslin, dyed green or brown and sewn on to the brim. Wind will cause the material to flap, so this kind of portable hide is practical for use only on calm days.

As explained on p. 58, photography of nesting birds requires a hide erected gradually on site. Ready-made portable hides are available in a limited size range, so a hide often has to be specially tailored to suit the particular location.

As kestrels normally nest high up in trees or buildings, a high pylon-hide is usually required; I have used one to photograph kestrels nesting in a dead elm tree. Years later, I was shown an extraordinary sight in a private woodland which was being cleared. A beech tree had been felled before the forester realised that kestrels were nesting in it some 8 metres (25 feet) off the

ground. After the woodland had been clear-felled, the forester found three young kestrel chicks which he put back in their nest in a 1-metre (3-foot) length of beech trunk propped up against a fallen tree. The adults did not return at all on the first day, but they began to feed the chicks on the second day and miraculously reared them successfully.

As the ground sloped away from the re-positioned nest, I had to use a high hide which I erected some distance away from the nest and gradually raised and moved forward. For the framework I used a builder's portable tower support. This is a very robust yet adaptable way of constructing a high level hide. Wooden boards formed the elevated floor of the hide and the whole structure was covered with hessian.

At first light in the morning the sun shone on to the low-level nest so it was possible to use available light for photography, but as the chicks grew and became more active I used two electronic flashes supported on stands. Flash extension leads are often the weak link in the chain, so I covered all the connections firstly with tape and then with plastic bags tightly secured with rubber bands. I always carry plenty of safety pins to secure any flapping parts of the hide.

There was no need to 'garden' any branches on this exposed nest, but if this should be necessary I use garden wire to tie back overhanging branches, rather than cutting them off with secateurs.

It is most important to check you have the correct focal length lens and all the other equipment in the hide before a companion sees you in and leaves the site. The adults birds will be alarmed by the sudden appearance of a photographer from the hide to collect some piece of forgotten equipment. I have my own checklist, but you may well like to modify it for your own needs. To make sure the exposure is correct I always use a Polaroid back on the Hasselblad before I expose any transparency film. A padded blimp may be needed to muffle the sound of the camera.

▲ The Lastohide is a lightweight portable hide worn on the head. A fine mesh hangs down from the rim of the hat as a circular curtain. fastening at the front. The lens is projected through a small window. The Lastohide can also be used in a prone position.

Checklist for hide photography
Camera with correct lenses (check)
Film
Tripod
Cable release
Flash(es)
Flash poles/stands
Flash extension leads, taped together and covered with plastic bags
Multiple flash connector
Polaroid back
Blimp for camera
Food/drink
Safety pins
Garden wire to tie back branches if necessary
Someone to see you into hide and get you out

▶ A camouflage net makes a useful portable hide for covering the body, when working in a location where there is no natural cover. In these circumstances, the only way to stalk is by inching forward in a prone position.

►**Subject:** Kestrel
chicks (*Falco tinnunculus*)
exercising in nest
Location: Private
woodland, Hampshire,
England
Month: June
Time: Early morning
Lighting: Flash
Lens: 350 mm on
Hasselblad using a hide
Film: Ektachrome 64

▼The drawing below
shows the set-up used
for photographing the
kestrel chicks (above).
They were reared on
their nest in the short
length of beech trunk
left after a woodland had
been cleared. The hide
was erected further
away from the trunk and
gradually moved
forward. Two flashes
were mounted on
lighting stands outside
the hide.

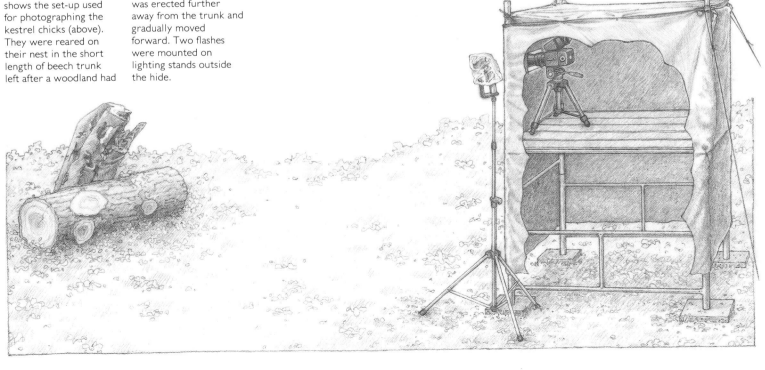

NATURE PHOTOGRAPHY AND THE LAW

Responsible nature photographers will always make sure they run no risk of endangering the subject as a result of their photography. For example, if wary animals are disturbed by stalking or erecting a hide, then the obvious thing to do is to retreat or move the hide further back. This may, of course, result in no picture being taken, but since any good field naturalist will be able to detect if an animal appears under stress in a photograph, there is no point in recording an anxious animal. 'Gardening' should be minimal so that it is barely detectable.

If you know of, or are shown, the site of a rare plant or animal which would suffer from repeated visits, this should not be disclosed in a lecture, article or book.

No self-respecting nature photographer today would consider taking a stuffed specimen, but I can recall some years ago being shown photographs of golden eagles on the nest. Although the background to each eerie varied, the bird was depicted in an identical pose in each one!

All nature photographers working in Britain would be well advised to read a free leaflet entitled *The Nature Photographers' Code of Practice*. This not only contains sound practical advice but also a resumé of the legal aspects now applicable when photographing plants and wildlife in Britain. The leaflet – which was produced by The Royal Photographic Society Nature Group in consultation with the Nature Conservancy Council (NCC) – is available from the NCC headquarters, Northminster House, Peterborough, PE1 IUA.

The Code of Practice provides a voluntary form of control to ensure that animals are not disturbed nor sensitive sites damaged as a result of ignorance. However, even if all nature photographers were to follow the Code to the letter, there are many rare and endangered species in Britain which require legal protection. This is provided under the Wildlife and Countryside Act 1981, which makes it illegal to collect or even move many rare animals without a permit from the NCC. The photography of nesting birds is regarded as a potential distrubance, so that specially protected wild birds listed under Schedule 1 of the Act may not be photographed at or near their nest without gaining written approval from the NCC Peterborough office by sending proof of your ability to work nests from hides to the Licensing Section.

The range of birds which breed on mainland Europe is much greater than in Britain, so that the list of bird species protected under a directive of The Council of the European Communities is larger than the British Schedule 1 list. It should be remembered though, that some species which are rare in Britain are much more abundant in Europe, so it is preferable to photograph them there. Alternatively, resist the urge to photograph birds while they are nesting and then stalk them away from the nest.

All British bats are specially protected and it is encouraging to see an increasing number of bat boxes being erected. Even wild flowers are afforded protection under the Act, for it is an offence to uproot any wild plant deliberately except on your own land or with the landowner's permission.

However, it is not good enough simply to preserve individual species, for none will survive in isolation. The complete habitat must be conserved and throughout the country especially important areas are designated as Sites of Special Scientific Interest (SSSI's). Owners and occupiers of these sites must notify the NCC in advance if they wish to make any major alteration to the site so that an alternative solution can hopefully be found.

All Australian native flora and fauna is protected and a permit is required to collect and/or keep native fauna for photography under controlled conditions. Many parts of the Australian National Parks have restricted vehicular access, and in some foot access is also restricted. The New Zealand Wildlife Act protects all native birds. Extremely rare species such as the takahe (Notornis) afford special protection since this bird lives in restricted areas which require an entry permit from the (New Zealand) Department of Conservation.

An excellent way of learning from experts and furthering your knowledge is to join one of the many Natural History Photographic Societies in Europe, Japan and North America. The Nature Group of The Royal Photographic Society (The Octagon, Milsom Street, Bath BA1 1DN, England), for example, produces a quarterly newsletter and arranges lectures and field outings.

Sadly, a few ruthless photographers who adopt a paparazzi approach to their wildlife photography – instead of putting the welfare of the subject first and foremost – can make it all the more difficult for *bona fide* workers to gain access to sensitive sites. Several years ago I wrote to the relevant New Zealand government scientific body for permission to photograph the unique tuatara (see p. 127). After many letters, telephone calls, and assistance from a respected New Zealand wildlife photographer, I was given the go ahead a year later! After I had landed on Stephens Island in the Cook Strait, I was told about an overseas professional photographer who, after being shown the sole site of an endemic species of frog, was found destroying the rock pile to unearth the frogs. If he had been a naturalist, he would have known that he should simply wait for the frogs to emerge at night.

WILDLIFE AND COUNTRYSIDE ACT 1981: Schedule 1

Part 1: Wild Birds Specially Protected At All Times

Avocet	Dartford warbler	Little gull	Serin
Barn owl	Divers (all species)	Little ringed plover	Shorelark
Bearded tit	Dotterel	Little tern	Short-toed
Bee-eater	Fieldfare	Long-tailed duck	treecreeper
Bewick's swan	Firecrest	Marsh warbler	Slavonian grebe
Bittern	Garganey	Mediterranean gull	Snow bunting
Black-necked grebe	Golden eagle	Merlin	Snowy owl
Black redstart	Golden oriole	Osprey	Spoonbill
Black-tailed godwit	Goshawk	Peregrine	Spotted crake
Black tern	Green sandpiper	Purple heron	Stone curlew
Black-winged stilt	Greenshank	Purple sandpiper	Temminck's stint
Bluethroat	Gyr falcon	Red-backed shrike	Velvet scoter
Brambling	Harriers (all species)	Red kite	Whimbrel
Cetti's warbler	Hobby	Red-necked	White-tailed eagle
Chough	Honey buzzard	phalarope	Whooper swan
Cirl bunting	Hoopoe	Redwing	Woodlark
Common quail	Kentish plover	Roseate tern	Wood sandpiper
Common scoter	Kingfisher	Ruff	Wryneck
Corncrake	Lapland bunting	Savi's warbler	
Crested tit	Leach's petrel	Scarlet rosefinch	
Crossbills (all species)	Little bittern	Scaup	

Part II: Wild Birds Specially Protected During the Close Season

Goldeneye
Greylag goose (in
    Outer Hebrides,
    Caithness,
    Sutherland and
    Wester Ross only)
Pintail

This list is periodically revised and additional species may be added from time to time, so you should check with the NCC Licensing Section when planning to photograph uncommon birds at the nest.

INDEX